KT-454-077

Critical Issues

George Eliot

Pauline Nestor

ʹ1783087

LIBRARY

ACC. No. 36021615	DEPT.
CLASS No.	

UNIVERSITY
OF CHESTER

palgrave

© Pauline Nestor 2002

All rights reserved. No reproduction, copy or transmission of
this publication may be made without written permission.

No paragraph of this publication may be reproduced, copied or
transmitted save with written permission or in accordance with
the provisions of the Copyright, Designs and Patents Act 1988,
or under the terms of any licence permitting limited copying
issued by the Copyright Licensing Agency, 90 Tottenham Court Road,
London W1T 4LP.

Any person who does any unauthorised act in relation to this
publication may be liable to criminal prosecution and civil
claims for damages.

The author has asserted her right to be identified as
the author of this work in accordance with the
Copyright, Designs and Patents Act 1988.

First published 2002 by
PALGRAVE
Houndmills, Basingstoke, Hampshire RG21 6XS and
175 Fifth Avenue, New York, NY 10010
Companies and representatives throughout the world

PALGRAVE is the new global academic imprint of
St. Martin's Press LLC Scholarly and Reference Division and
Palgrave Publishers Ltd (formerly Macmillan Press Ltd).

ISBN 0–333–72200–0 hardcover
ISBN 0–333–72201–9 paperback

This book is printed on paper suitable for recycling and
made from fully managed and sustained forest sources.

A catalogue record for this book is available
from the British Library.

Library of Congress Cataloging-in-Publication Data
Nestor, Pauline.
   George Eliot : critical issues / Pauline Nestor.
      p. cm.
   Includes bibliographical references and index.
   ISBN 0–333–72200–0 (cloth) — ISBN 0–333–72201–9 (pbk.)
   1. Eliot, George, 1819–1880—Criticism and interpretation.
   2. Psychoanalysis and literature—England—History—19th century.
   3. Women and literature—England—history—19th century.
   4. Psychological fiction, English—History and criticism. 5. Feminist
   fiction, English—History and criticism. 6. Difference (Psychology) in
   literature. I. Title.
PR4688 .N47 2002
823'.8—dc21   2001056369

10   9   8   7   6   5   4   3   2   1
11   10   09   08   07   06   05   04   03   02

Printed and bound in China

Contents

Acknowledgements

I would like to thank Martin Coyle and John Peck for their invitation to write this book, and for their exemplary good cheer and good sense as editors. I am most grateful to Monash University for assistance with the project in the form of study leave, travel grants and teaching relief. I have long been fortunate in my colleagues at Monash, who understand and value the work of scholarship, sometimes against the odds. In particular, my friend Barbara Caine has been generous in her encouragement, giving freely of her expert knowledge and her library. My family has always offered the double blessing of support and perspective, at once enthusiastic in their concern for my professional endeavours and assured in their conviction that there is more to life than books. With their radically different sense of priorities, my young nieces and nephews have been a regular and welcome distraction from the task at hand. My sister Jan has provided sustenance of all kinds, combining culinary and sisterly skills in equal measure. The stresses of writing have been assuaged by the warmth, humour and encouragement of many friends. In particular, my thanks go to Raju Pandey, Sanjay Seth, Bronte Adams, Joanne Finkelstein, Glenda Esposito, Margaret Harris, Karen Dynon, Hilary McPhee and Don Watson. Above all, I am indebted to Leela Gandhi for her whole-hearted support. It is in some small measure of thanks that I dedicate this book to her.

1

Introduction

I

On the last day of December 1872, George Eliot's publisher, John Blackwood, declared that the publication of *Middlemarch* would be 'one of the events by which 1872 will be remembered'.[1] If, from our vantage point, the claim now seems exaggerated, it is not difficult to forgive the hyperbole. His client and friend, George Eliot, was the greatest living writer of the time, and she had just delivered to him her finest novel. With its publication, her reputation was at its zenith and her influence extended far beyond literary circles. More than simply a novelist, she was a public intellectual whose contribution to the public debate was constantly sought across a wide range of topics. Campaigners for women's rights, for example, solicited testimonials in support of the extension of the franchise to women, the reform of laws relating to married women's property, increased educational and employment opportunities, and the admission of women as doctors. Followers of Auguste Comte entreated her to produce a work that would embody his Positivist vision for an ideal social state and to provide a liturgy for their Religion of Humanity. John Blackwood urged her to intervene in the debate surrounding the Second Reform Bill of 1867, and prevailed upon her to write an 'Address to Working Men, by Felix Holt', emphasising the 'new responsibilities' of the recently enfranchised (IV, 395). Her work was quoted in parliamentary debates and her 'wit and wisdom' were collected into a popular volume by Alexander Main.

The extent of Eliot's influence was testimony in part to the popularity of fiction in the period and to its potency as a form of social commentary. With the spread of literacy and the increasing availability of cheap books and newspapers, reading had become democratised as never before. The repeated connection in literary reviews between novels and public morality, the merging of fact and fiction in the industrial novels of the mid-century, and the reliance on didactic fiction even in Evangelical pamphlets, all attested to the profound relevance of fiction to public life and to its capacity not merely to reflect but to amplify and deepen public debate. Thus, Dinah Mulock described the contemporary novel as 'one of the most important moral agents of the community. The essayist may write for his hundreds, the preacher preach for his thousands; but the novelist counts his audience by millions. His power is three-fold – over heart, reason, and fancy.'[2]

This generic power of fiction was combined in Eliot's case with a formidable intellect and an unrivalled breadth of knowledge concerning the latest developments in contemporary social and scientific theory. Eliot was one of the nineteenth century's great polymaths, with an intellect and curiosity matched only by a prodigious application for learning. Her research for her novels was almost inconceivably thorough and painstaking. Whether it was for the broad sweep of Renaissance history and literature in *Romola*, the minutiae of legal procedure in *Felix Holt* or botanical detail in *The Mill on the Floss*, Eliot spared no effort at mastery. She travelled extensively and became fluent in seven languages – French, German, Italian, Greek, Latin, Spanish and Hebrew. Having had only a modest formal education, she never relented in her educational self-improvement. On her first trip to Europe, for example, her relief from translating Latin was to read Voltaire, play the piano and 'take a dose of mathematics every day to prevent my brain from becoming quite soft' (I, 321). In addition, she attended a course on experimental physics by 'M. le professeur de la Rive, the inventor amongst other things of the electro-plating' (I, 325). Taking stock of life at forty-seven, she felt no diminution of either her faculties or thirst for learning, only frustration at opportunities missed and time running out:

> I enjoy all subjects – all study, more than I ever did in my life before. But that very fact makes me more in need of resignation to the certain approach of age and death. Science, history, poetry – I don't know which draws me most. And there is little time left me for any one of them. I learned Spanish last year but one, and see new vistas everywhere. That makes me think of time thrown away when I was young – time that I should be so glad of now. I could enjoy everything, from arithmetic to antiquarianism, if I had large spaces of life before me.
>
> (IV, 316)

In her early adulthood she translated Strauss's *The Life of Jesus*, Feuerbach's *The Essence of Christianity* and Spinoza's *Ethics*, works which not only sounded the death knell for her own belief in a Christian God, but which represented landmarks in the great shift from religious to secular ethics in the period. As editor of the *Westminster Review* in the early 1850s she was exposed to the most current liberal thinking on religion, philosophy, politics, history, science and the arts, immersed in 'most of the new ideas that have shaped the modern world'.[3] She also established herself as an astute critic on literary topics ranging from *Antigone* to 'Silly Novels by Lady Novelists', and a cultural commentator on matters as various as the history of religion and the future of German philosophy.

Her knowledge of, and interest in, science was deepened through her partnership with George Lewes. She was an enthusiastic companion to Lewes's scientific pursuits, gladly accompanying him on 'zoologizing' trips to the English coast and excitedly noting joint discoveries: 'We had a glorious hunt this morning in the caverns of St Catherine's Rock. Found some specimens of the Alcyonium Digitatum, the Clavellina and the Stag's Horn Polype as well as abundance of Laomedeae and Actiniae.'[4] Similarly, she was so well versed in developments in psychology that she was capable of revising and completing the last two volumes of Lewes's *Problems of Life and Mind* for posthumous publication in 1878.

Though science was rarely an explicit subject for her fiction, it shaped her way of seeing the world, consistently providing her with a vocabulary for analogy and analysis. In this sense Eliot was not a populariser of scientific theory – in the way that Harriet Martineau, for example, was for political economy. Nevertheless, she contributed to the currency of scientific thought, domesticating in particular ideas of evolution and its 'inextricable web of affinities',[5] and effortlessly incorporating its paradigms into her thinking. So, for example, she contemplated the oppressive narrowness faced by Maggie Tulliver in these terms:

> The suffering, whether of martyr or victim, which belongs to every historical advance of mankind, is represented in this way in every town, and by hundreds of obscure hearths; and we need not shrink from this comparison of small things with great; for does not science tell us that its highest striving is after the ascertainment of a unity which shall bind the smallest things with the greatest? In natural science, I have understood, there is nothing petty to the mind that has a large vision of relations, and to which every single object suggests a

vast sum of conditions. It is surely the same with the observation of human life.[6]

Indeed, so pervasive was her scientific vision that her publisher speculated, before her true identity was known, that she may have been 'a man of science', convinced by her 'precision of expression or illustration' that she was at least a writer 'accustomed to scientific definitions' (II, 294).[7]

When Eliot turned to fiction writing at the age of thirty-six, she saw it not as an auxiliary or lesser pursuit, but as the distillation of all her thought and learning. She came to regard her novels as the most adequate representation of her thinking: 'My books are a form of utterance that dissatisfies me less, because they are deliberately, carefully constructed on a basis which even in my doubting mind is never shaken by a doubt, and they are not determined, as conversation inevitably is, by considerations of momentary expediency' (IV, 472). This was more than a preference for the deliberation of the written word over the spontaneity of the spoken, for fiction allowed for a complexity which suited the comprehensiveness and the non-partisan tenor of her mind. It gave scope for the representation of the moral and psychological ambiguity of 'mixed human beings' (II, 299) and offered the opportunity to shift both the focus and perspective through a range of characters, in a way that became a hallmark of her fiction. And it was precisely because fiction enabled the consideration of life 'in its highest complexity' (IV, 300) that it was so suitable for the purposes of aesthetic teaching, which Eliot regarded as potentially the highest form of instruction. That potential was squandered, and aesthetic teaching became 'the most offensive of all', if art merely paid lip-service to didacticism – if it lapsed 'from the picture to the diagram' (IV, 300). However, the great writer could be 'a prophet for his [sic] generation',[8] if he accomplished the difficult task of making his ideas 'thoroughly incarnate' (IV, 300). Then, by virtue of his 'higher sensibility', the artist could bring home to 'our coarser senses what would otherwise be unperceived by us' (SCW, 111). With this enhancement of vision the artist could ensure that his art functioned as a mode of 'amplifying experience and extending our contact with our fellow-men beyond the bounds of our personal lot' (SCW, 264). Far more than other modes – more than 'hundreds of sermons and philosophical dissertations' (SCW, 263) – art had the capacity not simply to call upon pre-existing sympathies but actually to create moral sentiment by surprising readers into the recognition of realities beyond their own: 'Appeals founded on generalizations and statistics require a sympathy ready-made, a moral sentiment already in activity; but a picture of human life such as a great artist can give, surprises even the trivial and the selfish into that attention to what is apart from themselves, which may be called the raw material of moral sentiment' (*SCW*, 263). Eliot became increasingly convinced that if she was to 'help others see at all it must be through that medium of art' (VI, 217), and she regarded her role as aesthetic rather than doctrinal, charged with 'the rousing of the nobler emotions, which make mankind desire the social right, not the prescribing of special measures, concerning which the artistic mind, however strongly moved by social sympathy, is often not the best judge' (VII, 44).

While refusing to use her fiction to speak out on specific 'public topics' (VII, 44), Eliot nonetheless consistently addressed the fundamental question of her age – the death of God and the necessary shift to a secular ethics. The implications of biblical criticism on the one hand and evolutionary theory on the other combined effectively to undermine any confidence in the notion of a divinely inspired and ordained morality. According to Eliot, they compelled one to conclude that all notions of the ethical, and even of the divine, belonged properly to the realm of the human: 'the fellowship between man and man which has been the principle of development, social and moral, is not dependent on conceptions of what is not man: and . . . the idea of God, so far as it has been a high spiritual influence, is the ideal of a goodness entirely human (i.e., an exultation of the human)' (VI, 98).

Eliot began her fiction writing in 1857, that 'year of scientific crisis' in which 'the astounding question had for the first time been propounded with contumely, "What, then, did we come from an orang-outang?" '[9] As Edmund Gosse described the ferment in his autobiographical *Father and Son*, this was 'the great moment in the history of thought when the theory of the mutability of species was preparing to throw a flood of light upon all departments of human speculation and action'.[10] Eliot was acutely aware of the ethical vacuum confronting the period, and claimed that the inspiring principle which alone gave her courage to write was 'that of so presenting our human life as to help my readers in getting a clearer conception and a more active admiration of those vital elements which bind men together and give a higher worthiness to their existence; and also to help them in gradually dissociating these elements from the more transient forms on which an outworn teaching tends to make them dependent' (IV, 472). Having experienced the pain of losing her own faith, and believing that the highest calling of the age was to endure – 'to *do without opium*' (III, 366) in the form of religious consolation – Eliot's determination as a novelist was 'if it were possible to me, to help in satisfying the need of those who want a reason for living in the absence of what has been called consolatory belief' (IX, 201). If, then, Eliot functioned, according to her aspiration, as the prophet of her generation, she did so above all else in her recognition, in the words of Lord Acton, that 'a new code of duty and motive needed to be restored in the midst of the void left by lost sanctions and banished hopes'.[11]

In all, it is hard to imagine a figure more central to the main currents of thought and belief in the nineteenth century. Indeed, as Basil Willey contends, 'Probably no English writer of the time, and certainly no novelist, more fully epitomizes the century; her development is a paradigm, her intellectual biography a graph of its most decided trend.'[12] However, in reading Eliot a century and a half later the question that might well be asked is whether she holds only the limited interest of historical curiosity or whether her work is susceptible to readings which have relevance for contemporary concerns. In many respects, with the advent of the new millennium, George Eliot's reputation, having risen and fallen more than once since her death, lies once more at a crossroad. Feminist literary criticism has boosted Eliot's critical stocks in the last twenty-five years, but the relationship between feminists and Eliot has been marked – with good reason – by deep ambivalence.[13] More generally, Eliot's moralism and her commitment to realism have failed to find much favour with a post-modern age. The case for her irrelevance has been summed up most decisively by John Bayley in a review of a recent Eliot biography by Kathryn Hughes. Referring to the high place that F. R. Leavis ascribed to George Eliot in *The Great Tradition* 'at the front of the greatest practitioners of the novelist's art', Bayley ponders whether such a judgement still stands. He doubts it, and suggests rather that Trollope and Dickens are more congenial and 'less foreign' to our contemporary viewpoint. After damning Eliot with faint praise, he finally consigns her irrevocably to the past:

> The fate of lawgivers and sibyls, in literature if not in life, is to have no lasting influence. George Eliot's precepts can be said to have perished with her. She had tried to turn the novel into too blunt an instrument not only of culture and duty but of what Matthew Arnold called

'sweetness and light' . . . George Eliot can reveal much to us today precisely because she and her mindset and her philosophy of life seem so far off, so irrevocably in a past which has become and will no doubt remain totally a matter of history. Shakespeare may be 'our contemporary', to say nothing of Pushkin or Proust or the Metaphysical poets, but George Eliot is emphatically not. It is true that many young women even today do not feel that Dorothea Brooke or Gwendolen Harleth are remote from them and read about them with passion. But George Eliot herself remains forever the Great Victorian, as well as the last. She lives in a distant and now unrecoverable country of her own.[14]

It is the contention of this book, however, that such a position is wrong – that the landscape of Eliot's fiction is neither so distant, nor so unrecoverable. To begin with, it is hard to imagine that Eliot's central project – 'the extension of our sympathies' (*SCW*, 263) – has been rendered irrelevant simply by the passage of time and the shift of fashion. Indeed, historical distance may in fact provide more of an opportunity than a barrier, for, as Simon Dentith has argued, it provides 'new contexts in which the word may be dialogized and in which unrealized possibilities may be made to speak'.[15] More importantly, Eliot's exploration of ethics in fiction turns not just on the issue of sympathy but, specifically, on the question of difference – and that challenge of difference remains a fundamental concern to a whole range of our contemporary literary and social theories. Indeed, as Eliot explained to her friend Charles Bray, the author of *The Philosophy of Necessity*: 'the only effect I ardently long to produce by my writings, is that those who read them should be better able to *imagine* and to *feel* the pains and joys of those who differ from themselves' (III, 111). Eliot's consequent examination of the essential ethical dilemma of negotiating otherness, conducted over a period of more than twenty years and through eight major works, achieves a complexity and resonance which deserves attention beyond the well-rehearsed arguments of literary studies. If we embrace the comprehensive spirit of Eliot's own scholarship, her work can be seen to speak equally to the post-colonial scholar, the moral philosopher and the psychoanalyst.[16] Eliot herself recognised the liberating '*suggestiveness*' of dialogue between disciplines (*SCW*, 133), and developments in contemporary theory have encouraged us once again to attend to the possibilities for productive exchange. One of the most influential twentieth-century theorists of otherness, Emmanuel Levinas, for example, had no hesitation in recognising the potential for dialogue which exists between philosophy and literature. In 'Time and the Other' he recurs repeatedly to examples from Shakespeare, justifying his 'over-indulgence' with the thought that 'it sometimes seems . . . that the whole of philosophy is only a meditation of Shakespeare'.[17] Similarly, J. Hillis Miller argues in *The Ethics of Reading* that literature and interpretation are fundamental to ethical inquiry:

> Without storytelling there is no theory of ethics. Narratives, examples, stories . . . are indispensable to thinking about ethics. An understanding of ethics as a region of philosophical or conceptual investigation depends, perhaps surprisingly, on mastery of the ability to interpret written stories, that is, on a kind of mastery usually thought to be the province of the literary critic. If this is true it has important implications . . . for my claim that the rhetorical study of literature has important implications for our moral, social, and political lives.[18]

And in confirmation, contra John Bayley, of the breadth of Eliot's relevance, Margot Waddell makes a similar point in a recent special issue of *The American Journal of Psychoanalysis* devoted to Eliot, when she argues that the ideas that George Eliot sought to rescue from speculative detachment and 'to explore in the lived experience of her characters and their relationships were those which have been central to the philosophical and theological inquiries of Western culture from Plato to the present day: How does a person live, or achieve, a good life, and what generates and informs "the good life" '.[19]

II

Eliot's fiction, then, forms an extended, particularised and dramatic investigation of fundamental ethical problems. To the philosophical inquiries that Margot Waddell proposes as central to Eliot we might add the questions, what constitutes sympathy, and what provokes it; how do we apprehend and engage with otherness; what is the basis for, and what are the limits of, ethical responsibility? Eliot's exploration of these issues evolves in a dialogue within, and between, her novels over a twenty-year period – although she herself was ambiguous in her acknowledgement of that development. On the one hand, when an American admirer, Elizabeth Stuart Phelps, suggested that there was a distinction to be made between Eliot's earlier and later fiction, Eliot denied any such differentiation:

> though I trust there is some growth in my appreciation of others and in my self-distrust, there has been no change in the point of view from which I regard our life since I wrote my first fiction – the 'Scenes of Clerical Life'. Any apparent change of spirit must be due to something of which I am unconscious. The principles which are at the root of my effort to paint Dinah Morris are equally at the root of my effort to paint Mordecai. (VI, 318)

Such a denial was in many ways contrary, however, to the way in which she conceived of her work. In keeping with the scientific spirit of the age, she saw her writing as 'a set of experiments' through which she endeavoured 'to see what our thought and emotion may be capable of – what stores of motive, actual or hinted as possible, give promise of a better after which we may strive – what gains from past revelations and discipline we must strive to keep hold of as something more sure than shifting theory' (VI, 216). And underlying that scientific disposition of continuous testing was a belief that there was no 'master-key' to fit a moral universe, but rather a need for a flexible, shifting responsiveness to particular and changing circumstance. Thus, she had an 'instinctive repugnance' to the 'man of maxims', defending instead the spirit, if not the practice, of casuistry: 'The casuists have become a byword of reproach; but their perverted spirit of minute discrimination was the shadow of a truth to which eyes and hearts are too often fatally sealed – the truth, that moral judgments must remain false and hollow, unless they are checked and enlightened by a perpetual reference to the special circumstances that mark the individual lot' (*Mill*, 498).

Rather than the stasis suggested by her reply to Phelps, then, Eliot was far more committed to an evolving body of thought. She wished her work to be published in the order in which it was written because she saw it as belonging 'to successive mental phases' (III, 383). She shrank from the prospect of ' "deliverances" on momentous subjects' (V, 76), not only because she found such inflexibility morally indefensible, but because she also saw it as aesthetically damaging: 'When a novelist is quite sure that she has a theory which suffices to illustrate all the difficulties of our earthly existence, her novels are too likely to illustrate little else than her own theory.'[20] In all, her fiction and thought were shaped by her conviction that the most important sign of spiritual life was the ability 'to be able always to reconsider one's conclusions and go well over the process by which they are arrived at' (V, 58).

This evolution of Eliot's thinking on ethics takes place in the context of a wider contemporary debate about ways of knowing – the adequacy of systems and theories, and the perfectibility of knowledge. In the broadest terms, Eliot moves throughout her fiction-writing career from a position of confidence in the moral efficacy of self-regulation and self-awareness, to a more modest recognition of the limits of agency and subjectivity. Her profound respect for learning was always matched by an equally fundamental apprehension of the limits of the knowable. Thus, for example, she declared herself in complete agreement with Herbert Spencer's assertion of the 'ultimate mystery' which remained, despite the march of science: 'The sincere man of science, content fearlessly to follow wherever the evidence leads him, becomes by each new inquiry more profoundly convinced that the Universe is an insoluble problem . . . He learns at once the greatness and the littleness of human intellect . . . He alone truly *sees* that absolute knowledge is impossible. He alone *knows* that under all things there lies an impenetrable mystery.'[21] And in this, she demonstrated that mental combination which she ascribed to Adam Bede, 'which is at once humble in the region of mystery and keen in the region of knowledge'.[22] Although, as many critics have noted, she was influenced in her thinking by Auguste Comte,[23] she became increasingly sceptical of the 'excessive love of systems' which characterised Positivism, and, arguably, the age.

III

In Eliot's first work of fiction, *Scenes of Clerical Life* (1858), examined in Chapter 3, the nature of her aesthetic endeavour is unusually explicit. She set out to exemplify an artistic credo which, as Chapter 2 reveals, she had previously articulated through a series of reviews and periodical articles. Above all, she sought to achieve a faithful and unheroic realism – a paean to ordinariness. Then, through the transforming eye of the artist, she strove to bring the reader to a recognition of the goodness and tragedy in ordinary life. However, as Eliot herself later acknowledged, she struggled in this first work to 'manipulate' her materials and the result was a flawed and uneven piece of work. In part, she failed to create a narrative voice adequate to the central task of extending the reader's sympathy. More fundamentally, her conception of sympathy at this early stage in her fiction was limited by her concurrence with the Feuerbachian supposition that likeness or recognition was a precondition for the exercise of sympathy. Thus, in *Scenes of Clerical Life* Eliot envisaged only two ways in which the extension of sympathy might be achieved – empathy or pity. Though each functions in a way as the obverse of the other, Chapter 3 argues that both ultimately reinscribe the difference and division they seek to overcome. So, as we see in the relationship between Edgar Tryan and Janet Dempster in 'Janet's Repentance', empathy proves ultimately to be appropriative and self-referential, and fails to meet the challenge, suggested by Levinas, of 'an encounter with an Other which does not entail a return to the self'.[24] As well, it depends, I suggest, upon some level of commensurability between the sympathising subject and the suffering other, to the extent that the possibility of empathetic fellow-feeling breaks down in the face of radical difference, as with Amos Barton's encounter with his congregation in the workhouse.

Pity represents a 'return to the self' in a different form. It relies on a sense of difference, reinscribing the gap between the self and the other, and it invites a focus on the exteriority of suffering. The consequence for Eliot's stories is that they demonstrate a reliance on the idea of suffering as spectacle – seen in a series of affecting tableaux – and they come to depend on the depiction of victimisation as the most effective mode of eliciting response. This leads to a simplification of the characterisation in this first work in a way that runs counter to Eliot's determination to achieve psychological and moral complexity in her fiction.

Eliot's second book, *Adam Bede* (1859), represented a significant advance in her fiction writing. It achieved a level of sophistication in its psychological conception and structure, which marked a departure from the simplicity of melodrama in *Scenes of Clerical Life*, and heralded the complexity of tragedy which was to become a feature of Eliot's mature fiction. Chapter 4 examines the important shift in Eliot's conception of sympathy, which was central to the increasing complexity of her work. In particular, two fundamental aspects of sympathy are revisited in *Adam Bede* and revealed as more problematic than originally conceived. With the extended scrutiny of her first full-length novel, Eliot no longer regards the recognition of commonality as sufficient basis for ethical interaction. The pull of likeness, she now suggests, is attended by the danger of exclusivity and prejudice, which always form one aspect of the 'love of *clan*' (*SCW*, 159). More importantly, whereas in *Scenes of Clerical Life* the appropriative impulse of empathy appears to offer some prospect of amplifying or extending subjectivity, in *Adam Bede* the hope of such extension seems misplaced. Instead, the novel contemplates the limits of subjectivity – the impossibility for even 'the most liberal and expansive mind' of shifting one's point of view 'beyond certain limits' (*AB*, 203). Thus, it is not the recognition of likeness but the confrontation with difference which provides the ethical challenge of this novel, and it is no longer the capacity for identification but rather for imagination, of a kind exercised by Dinah Morris and Mr Irwine, which promises to form the basis for contemplation of the other.

Similarly, in this novel, where the failure to control passion provides the catalyst for a succession of tragedies, Eliot takes a more critical view of the unerring 'truth' of feeling. Influenced by the thinking of Spinoza, Eliot insists in *Adam Bede* that emotion must be regulated by the intellect, and in the face of this necessity for self-reflexive discipline, it is only moral dread, inspired by the recognition of the irrevocability of consequence, which can motivate the requisite self-consciousness and vigilance. In this way, then, Eliot's second work marks a change of emphasis from questions of response to those of responsibility, and from a preoccupation with reaction to one with anticipation.

With the more autobiographical emphasis in *The Mill on the Floss* (1860) Eliot achieved a greater empathy and psychological inwardness with her heroine. This new insight paved the way, as Chapter 5 shows, for a reassessment of the possibility and, more radically, the desirability, of that self-regulation proposed in *Adam Bede*. In many ways Tom Tulliver is the figure who most clearly resembles the Spinozan ideal of self-mastery, and yet it is through the exploration of his character that Eliot reveals the ways in which rigidity and narrowness may be the corollary of the kind of self-control lauded in *Adam Bede*. In contrast, while Maggie is the antithesis of the ideal, repeatedly failing to restrain her passions, the very 'susceptibility' which leaves Maggie vulnerable to irrational and unconscious desires, Chapter 5 argues, also generates the openness and receptivity which Eliot suggests holds the promise of moral and social evolution. Tom's certainty in the world, while attractive in part to the volatile Maggie, is shown to come at too high a cost, leaving him closed to the 'complex, fragmentary, doubt-provoking' (*Mill*, 456) aspects of truth.

More generally, the novel exposes the inadequacy of closed systems, as one character after another attempts unsuccessfully to 'lace [them]selves up in formulas' and thereby ward off 'the mysterious complexity' of life (*Mill*, 498). Against this, the novel explores the forces which exceed regulation – psychological imperatives thrown up by the unconscious, which render self-mastery improbable. The disruptive spectres of violence, madness and desire, set against a pattern of dreaming and forgetting, constantly undermine any faith in the sovereignty of the will, and underscore the vulnerability of conscious intention. The fear of consequence, which seemed to provide the ethical talisman of *Adam Bede*, is revealed in *The Mill on the Floss* to be at best only a partial solution.

Silas Marner (1861) was a transitional text in Eliot's career, bridging the meticulous realism of her earlier studies of English provincial life with the 'empirical freedom' and symbolism of romance, [25] which formed one aspect of a number of the later works. In this fourth work, Eliot explored questions of nature and nurture, which had acquired a particular topicality through the ferment surrounding the publication of Darwin's *On the Origin of Species* two years before. In reversing the usual conventions of the foundling tale, in which the child is recognised and claimed by his or her natural parents, *Silas Marner* refuses the seduction of self-replication, Chapter 6 argues, in favour of a choice of otherness. With the figure of Silas, Eliot contemplates the most alien of all her characters, and in this way she confronts the most radical challenge to her aesthetic determination to produce a capacity in her readers to imagine and to feel with those who are different from themselves. Marner's strangeness isolates him from the narrow world of Raveloe, on whose margins he dwells as an outcast and a hermit, and the stale repetitiveness of his life, protected by the psychological barriers created by his miserliness, mirrors the insular monotony of the ruthlessly endogamous world of the Raveloe community.

In the drama of the tale, the breaking of this impasse of isolation requires a double breach – the entry of the foundling Eppie into Marner's life and the acceptance of the hermit into the village community. In both cases the ethical challenge is to embrace what is not like or known, and that embrace requires more than the empathy or imagination contemplated in earlier novels. It necessitates first of all an instinctive, incipient openness, such as Marner displays in his humble acceptance of the bewildering advent of a child into his life. And, as the exchanges between Marner and Dolly Winthrop illustrate, it also requires a movement beyond cognition – an extrarational leap of affective faith through which the embrace of the other becomes an acceptance of the unknown and unknowable, anticipating Levinas's contention that 'the relationship with the other is a relationship with Mystery'.[26]

Romola (1863) was George Eliot's first, and last, historical novel, and the change to a fifteenth-century setting presented particular difficulties for the author. Underlying the obvious shift in time was a more fundamental change from the narrowly provincial locales of the earlier novels to the quintessentially cosmopolitan world of Florence – from simple environments, untouched by learning and culture, to a complex world enriched by the cross-currents of trade, politics and art. This more complex milieu, Chapter 7 argues, creates a more complex ethical theatre for consideration. The early novels had primarily concerned themselves with the private world of sexual desire, and the ethical microcosm of 'sudden deeds and decisive moments'. Eliot's new novel, in contrast, focuses on the public sphere of political intrigue and a broader context of competing systems of belief and knowledge.

The structuring contrast in the novel is between the Pagan and Christian worlds, creating a tension that leaves the heroine Romola torn between her father Bardo and her brother Dino, and between her husband Tito and her spiritual guide Savonarola. Yet Eliot reveals that these worlds are more disturbingly similar in their absolutism and their desire for supremacy and control than each would ever acknowledge. Chapter 7 explores a more fundamental rift between a world of partisanship and false certainty and one of non-partisan openness and diffidence, opposing ethical worlds which correspond broadly to a divide between a masculine public sphere and a feminine alternative in the novel. Romola is Eliot's most explicit anti-polemicist, constantly seeking out commonality rather than conquest and demonstrating a 'large nature' always conscious 'of possibilities beyond its own horizon'.[27] Her hesitancy and uncertainty in the face of 'the complexities in human things' (420) provide almost the only counterbalance to a masculine tendency toward polarisation and false certitude, in a way that is reminiscent of Maggie Tulliver's painful difference from, and opposition to, her world. It forms part of the tragedy of Savonarola's last days that he, too, is shown to be capable of openness and ambivalence. Yet Chapter 7 concludes that it is an indictment both of him and the masculine world of Florence that there can be no place for such ethical complexity in public life.

Felix Holt (1866) depicts an England in flux, caught up in the debates over radicalism and reform surrounding the first Reform

Bill, and buffeted by a whole series of changes set in train by the Industrial Revolution. While the work is usually regarded as Eliot's most extended and topical examination of politics, Chapter 8 argues that the novel in fact betrays a strange lack of interest in formal politics. The ideological positions adopted by the characters, for example, seem either frivolous and insubstantial in the case of the landed classes, or vague and unconvincing on the part of the alleged radical, Felix Holt, and this lack of substantiality is even more striking at a structural level, where a series of ellipses or lacunae draw attention to a political vacuum in the novel. Rather than parliamentary politics, the real interest of *Felix Holt*, Chapter 8 contends, is with the more informal politics of the everyday, and, in particular, with the nexus between the public sphere and private life.

Even within this broader conception of politics, the changes afoot in the public life of the England of 1832 have a direct bearing on the private ethical life of the country. So, while the spread of literacy and the proliferation of the printed word increase the power and reach of publicity, the extension of the franchise broadens the base of those who sit in judgement, bringing about a commodification of reputation, which creates new pressures on individual morality. And where public reputation comes to matter in such a way, private information acquires a new currency with secrets marking the fault line between public and private, and creating a disjunction between spheres of self-representation.

The most telling contrast in the novel, then, is not, I suggest, between conservatism and radicalism, but between two contrasting ethical milieux, represented by Transome Court and Chapel Yard, and the way in which those worlds negotiate their parallel secrets. Esther Lyon functions as the arbiter between worlds, desired and desirous of both, but finally needing to privilege one. Through her ultimate choice she validates the unadorned openness of the Lyon/Holt sphere over the dissembling ostentation of the Transome world, although, as this chapter concludes, the ethical dichotomy between Harold Transome and Felix Holt breaks down in the realm of sexual politics, where both men seem disturbingly similar.

Just as Darwin recognised 'an inextricable web of affinities' between all living things, *Middlemarch* (1872) demonstrates, both conceptually and structurally, that human lots are 'woven and interwoven'.[28] More than any other novel, it exemplifies that 'exploration of community' which Raymond Williams contends is the distinguishing feature of the Victorian novel.[29] However, as Chapter

9 argues, even at the same time as the novel explores the inevitable engulfment of the individual within the social organisation, it para- doxically highlights the acute isolation of individuals within society. Indeed, if in the earlier figure of Silas Marner Eliot created the most alien of her characters, who presents the most extreme challenge of difference, in *Middlemarch* she addresses a yet more disconcerting and difficult proposition – the intractable otherness of those who seem most familiar, who live in close proximity, and who repeatedly offer themselves for interpretation. This alienation within the closest relationships is explored through the novel's various studies of mar- riage. By underscoring the lack of mutuality within relationships and dramatising the incomprehension which underlies moments of ostensible understanding, Eliot highlights the paradoxical loneliness at the heart of the societal web, and the chronic misreading of the other that constitutes the principal drama of the novel.

This sense of isolation and misunderstanding provides a less fre- quently acknowledged counterbalance to the novel's more famous sense of connectedness. So, too, a sense of 'stupendous fragmentari- ness' (*M*, 190) militates against the organicism of the recurring web metaphor. Characters search for some ordering principle to form a bulwark against this threatening sense of dispersal, whether in the form of the foundational knowledge that both Casaubon and Lydgate pursue in their different ways, or the pervasive shaping force of egoism suggested by the famous metaphor of the scratches on the pier-glass illuminated and patterned by the lighted candle. Repeatedly, characters structure their own narratives around the focal point provided by the 'flattering illusion' (*M*, 262) of ego. However, the reassurance offered by this distorting pattern ultimate- ly reaffirms rather than overcomes the fragmentariness of the world, isolating characters through their incomprehension of the other. The only hope for escape from the solipsism and 'moral stupidity' (*M*, 208) of self-absorption, Eliot suggests, is to live vigilantly, conscious of the fact that the other has 'an equivalent centre of self' (*M*, 208) – to unsettle one's conception of the world and allow for the existence of competing narratives.

This capacity for the reorientation of the ego is first suggested in the character of Mr Irwine in *Adam Bede* and Maggie Tulliver in *The Mill on the Floss*. It culminates with Dorothea Brooke in *Middlemarch*, although even Dorothea's capacity to apprehend the details of the other's narrative is limited. That capability is reserved in the end for art and the artist. It is the constantly shifting perspective of the novel, and the self-conscious redirection of narrative focus, which make *Middlemarch* the pinnacle of achievement for one who began her novel-writing career with the conviction that the extension of sympathy represented the greatest benefit and the highest duty of art.

Whereas *Middlemarch* begins and ends with the regretful acknowledgement that heroic fulfilment is not the realistic lot of characters like Dorothea Brooke, *Daniel Deronda* (1876) startlingly reverses that position, reserving a grand and epic fate for the eponymous hero. In a shift from a determinist belief in the 'invariability of sequence' (*SCW*, 21), Eliot embraces the arbitrary possibilities of prophecy in her final novel, setting up a tension between the realist logic of the Gwendolen Harleth sub-plot and the epic conception of the Jewish section.

This reversal of plot signals a more fundamental volte-face, as Chapter 10 argues, for while Daniel Deronda may seem the culmination of Eliot's ethical heroes, displaying in abundance the qualities of empathy, imagination, humility, receptivity and flexible perspective that distinguish the admirable figures in her earlier work, this novel for the first time evades the challenge presented by the confrontation with the other. The drama of otherness, so central to Eliot's fiction, is transformed by prophetic fiat in this final work, as the fundamental difference between self and other is collapsed, first through Daniel's discovery of his Jewishness, and then through the depiction of his relationship with Mordecai. The vocabulary of that bond places a repeated stress on the fusion of identity, creating the fantasy of a dyadic relationship possible only in the realm of the psychoanalytic Imaginary, where the disturbing divisions between self and other, sameness and difference, are obliterated.

Similarly, Daniel fulfils Mordecai's dream for a prophet because he dissipates difference by incorporation. He is at once an English gentleman *and* a Jew: his old identity merely supplements his new. This fantasy of supplementation operates, too, in the representation of the Zionist project. The new 'Judaea' is imagined as poised between East and West, past and future – with all elements 'perfected together'.[30] Its separateness is achieved, fantastically, with none of the cost of difference, and none of the deficiency of partialness. Thus, whereas Eliot's previous fiction consistently tested the limits of that most fundamental ethical challenge – the negotiation of difference – her final novel ends with an evasion of that problem and a justification of the endogamous embrace of likeness.

2

The Making of a Novelist

I

George Eliot had always nourished a 'vague dream' that she might one day write a novel, although for years her plan never progressed beyond an introductory chapter, 'describing a Staffordshire village and the life of the neighbouring farm houses' (II, 406). When she did finally take up her pen to begin 'The Sad Fortunes of Amos Barton', the first of the *Scenes of Clerical Life*, her life was transformed. She left behind the arduous and largely anonymous life of periodical writing, and embarked on a path which would bring both fame and fortune with remarkable rapidity.[1] And even as she took that first step as a novelist, she recognised the moment as epochal: 'September 1856 made a new era in my life, for it was then I began to write Fiction' (II, 406).

Eliot's detailed account of the event, recorded in her journal in December 1857 as 'How I Came to Write Fiction', is at once revealing and misleading. It lays heavy stress on the almost accidental nature of the process. She records that on a trip to Germany with George Lewes the old introductory chapter just 'happened to be among the papers' she was carrying; a vague 'something' compelled her to read the piece to Lewes; and, despite his encouragement to continue, she 'deferred' the challenge for some months until the subject and the title of her first story came to her in 'a dreamy doze' (II, 407). It seems a curious emphasis from one whose fiction repeatedly underscored the drama and significance of just such decisive moments, and yet its apparent denial of agency provides a clue to Eliot's complex and deeply ambivalent sense of her vocation as an artist.

As we have seen, Eliot could scarcely have made more lofty general claims for the stature and importance of artists. They were for her the 'prophets' of a culture, whose role, as the maestro Herr Klesmer proclaims in *Daniel Deronda*, was no less important to a nation than that of its rulers and legislators:

> A creative artist is no more a mere musician than a great statesman is a mere politician. We are not ingenious puppets, sir, who live in a box and look out on the world only when it is gaping for amusement. We help to rule the nations and make the age as much as any other public men. We count ourselves on level benches with legislators. And a man who speaks effectively through music is compelled to something more difficult than parliamentary eloquence. (*DD*, 206)

Blessed with the superior understanding and revelatory power of a 'higher sensibility' (*SCW*, 111), artists were capable of the 'highest of all teaching' (IV, 300). They constituted an elite, whose gifts deserved reverence and gratitude, as Daniel explains to Gwendolen in *Daniel Deronda*: 'We should have a poor life of it if we were reduced for all our pleasure to our own performances. A little private imitation of what is good is a sort of private devotion to it, and most of us ought to practise art only in the light of private study – preparation to understand and enjoy what the few can do for us' (374). Writers, in particular, had a heavy responsibility, Eliot felt, to practise their craft with a clear appreciation of the 'sacredness' of their art (*SCW*, 319).

Despite nagging insecurities and a much vaunted sensitivity to criticism, Eliot's own artistic ego was fundamentally unshakeable. She was remarkably assured in her sense of her talent and capable of sternly repudiating the judgement of others. Even as a novice author, for example, she was so convinced of both her purpose and her method that she categorically refused the advice of her experienced publisher, when he suggested that in the interests of maintaining reader sympathy, she should modify her portrayal of Caterina in 'Mr Gilfil's Love-Story' by consigning Caterina's murderous impulses to a dream: 'But it would be the death of my story to substitute a dream for the real scene. Dreams usually play an important part in fiction, but rarely, I think, in actual life. So many of us have reason to know that criminal impulses may be felt by a nature which is nevertheless guarded by its entire constitution from the commission of crime, that I can't help hoping my Caterina will not forfeit the sympathy of all my readers' (II, 309). On another occasion she refused to comply with Blackwood's request for an outline of the plot of *Adam Bede*. Her justification was that he might underestimate her power to transform her subject matter into something fine: 'the mere skeleton of my story would probably give rise in your mind to objections which would be suggested by the treatment *other* writers have given to the same tragic incidents in the human lot – objections which would lie far away from my treatment' (VIII, 201). And when she reminded him that Scott's *The Heart of Midlothian* and Sophocles' *Philoctetes* might equally have seemed unpromising on the basis of their subject matter, the exalted nature of the comparison was only half comic. She was, in fact, confident from a very early point in her career not only of her place, but of her rank, in the literary pantheon. Indeed, her self-conception was very much in accord with what Daniel Cottom has called 'the fable of the liberal intellectual', the disinterested figure removed from the vulgar concerns of daily life: 'It is no accident that the same age that invented mass literacy and mass communication also invented an attitude of intellectual distrust toward certain works simply because they were too popular'.[2] So, for example, when in 1860 she was compared in a French journal to her fellow novelist Dinah Mulock, Eliot adamantly set the record straight: 'the most ignorant journalist in England would hardly think of calling me a rival of Miss Mulock – a writer who is read only by novel readers pure and simple, never by people of high culture. A very excellent woman she is, I believe – but we belong to an entirely different order of writers' (III, 302).

It was not that Eliot was incapable of responding to criticism, but rather that she was unusually assured and discerning in her assessment of what was worthy of attention:

> In reference to artistic presentation, much adverse opinion will of course arise from a dislike to the *order* of art rather than from a critical estimate of the execution. Anyone who detests the Dutch school in general will hardly appreciate fairly the merits of a particular Dutch painting. And against this sort of condemnation, one must steel oneself as best one can. But objections which point out to me any vice of manner or any failure in producing an intended effect will be really profitable.   (II, 292)

Although she was complicit in Lewes's arrangements to shield her from all unfavourable criticism, far from being crushed by negative estimates, she was more likely to be scathing and contemptuous.[3] She had 'a very moderate respect' for literary reviewers (II, 291) and a hearty impatience with the 'thrice-breathed breath of criticism' (*DD*, 604). As the exponent of a popular form, she lamented the fact that she was liable to the judgement of fools: 'I should suggest to you all the miseries one's obstinate egoism endures from the fact of being a writer of novels – books which the dullest and silliest reader thinks himself competent to deliver an opinion on' (IV, 300).

Eliot's assurance as an artist, then, sits uneasily with the tentativeness she stresses in describing her assumption of the role. Yet, the discrepancy can be read in part as symptomatic of her deep suspicion of female ambition, and a concomitant unwillingness to assert too readily the egoistic intent of the woman artist. Even at the age of twenty, before she had any taste of public life, Eliot fretted about her own ambitiousness, which she described to her aunt as her 'besetting sin . . . the one of all others most destroying, as it is the fruitful parent of them all' (I, 19). More than thirty years later, she was still ashamed of her 'strong egoism . . . which is traceable simply to a fastidious yet hungry ambition' (V, 125). However, her sense of the desirability of feminine humility was inevitably at odds with the seriousness with which Eliot regarded herself as an artist. Thus, on the one hand, she conducted herself with a sense of self-importance which was galling to some. Eliza Lynn Linton, for example, was affronted by Eliot's aloofness and gravitas: 'But never for one instant did she forget her self-created Self – never did she throw aside the trappings or airs of the benign Sibyl. . . . She was so consciously "George Eliot" – so interpenetrated head and heel, inside and out with the sense of her importance as the great novelist and profound thinker of her generation.'[4] On the other hand, there seems to be a compensatory performative element in the stress she repeatedly placed on her womanliness. She was assiduous, for example, in the presentation of herself as the dutiful wife and 'loving Mutter', emphasising the 'sacred bond' (II, 349) that she shared with Lewes, and the seriousness with which she regarded her familial obligations: 'We shall both be hard workers, for we have three little boys to keep as well as ourselves' (II, 333). And, while privately she pursued her artistic career largely unchecked, supported unflaggingly by Lewes in what Mrs Oliphant jealously characterised as a 'mental greenhouse',[5] she publicly espoused a much more conventional role for women. She decried the encouragement of ambition in women. She was worried, for example, that women's participation in a collegiate system, of the kind being proposed for the new Girton College at Cambridge, could possibly weaken 'the bonds of family affection and family duties',[6] and she wrote to the educational pioneer Emily Davies urging that the 'primary difference' between the sexes should not be lost sight of: 'And there lies just that kernel of truth in the vulgar alarm of men lest women should be "unsexed". We can no more afford to part with that exquisite type of gentleness, tenderness, possible maternity suffusing a woman's being with affectionateness, which makes what we mean by the female character, than we can afford to part with human love' (IV, 468). She was also anxious, as Davies reported, that women should be discouraged from political activism: 'She hoped my friend would teach the girls not to think too much of political measures for improving society – as leading away from individual efforts to be good, I understood her to mean' (VI, 287). Similarly, she wrote to Barbara Bodichon that no good could come to women 'while each aims at doing the highest kind of work'. Cheerful resignation rather than disquieted ambition was the result she hoped for from higher education for women: 'recognition of the great amount of social unproductive labour which needs to be done by women' (IV, 425).

In her fiction, too, she frequently exalted self-sacrifice and self-effacement in women, claiming that the 'best part of a woman's love is worship' and that a 'loving woman's world lies within the four walls of her own home; and it is only through her husband that she is in any electric communication with the world beyond'.[7] Of course, she also created a succession of strong heroines who, as we shall see, demonstrate the frustration and injustice of women's confinement and restraint. Nevertheless, there is a recurrent sense in the novels that endurance is both wiser and more worthy than rebellion for women, and that, as Fedalma claims in The Spanish Gypsy, 'We must be patient in our prison-house / And find our space in loving.'[8]

Eliot's ambivalence is distilled, as one might expect, in her portrayal of female artists in her novels. To begin with, it is revealing that the only artists who are proudly assured in their vocation and live without conflict are male – Piero di Cosimo in Romola, Naumann in Middlemarch and Herr Klesmer in Daniel Deronda. In contrast, Eliot's female artists, Armgart and the Princess Halm-Eberstein, are tragically torn by the disjunction between their gender and their vocation. Both have a fierce sense of their artistic calling. The Princess asserts her 'right to be an artist', established by natural 'charter' (DD, 570). She feels that by virtue of her 'genius' she is entitled to be 'something more than a mere daughter and mother' (DD, 570). Armgart similarly claims to be 'an artist by my birth – / By the same warrant that I am a woman', and she insists that she will be 'more than wife' and refuse the 'oft-taught Gospel: "Woman, thy desire / Shall be that all superlatives on earth / Belong to men, save the

one highest kind – / To be a mother'.[9] Yet both women are 'unwomaned' by their fearsome ambition,[10] led to manipulate those around
them and to betray equally valid 'charters' of affection – the Princess's
to her son and Armgart's to her devoted cousin Walpurga. As though
punished by fate, both women, significantly, are stricken with the
loss of their voice, the essence of their talent.

While the emphasis on the chance nature of the beginning of
Eliot's novelistic career is revealing for what it suggests of her
ambivalence, it is also in many respects misleading. Contrary to the
casual emphasis of Eliot's journal entry, the beginning of Eliot's fiction-writing career was, in fact, one of the most purposeful and self-
conscious debuts in the history of the novel. If it was long delayed, it
was only because it was so fiercely desired:

> I was too proud and ambitious to write: I did not believe I could do any-
> thing fine, and I did not choose to do anything of that mediocre sort
> which I despised when it was done by others. I began, however, by a
> sort of writing which had no great glory belonging to it, but which I felt
> certain I could do faithfully and well. This resolve to work at what did
> not gratify my ambition, and to care only that I worked faithfully, was
> equivalent to the old phrase – 'using the means of grace'.   (VIII, 384)

It was also prompted by pressing financial considerations – a profane
aspect which Eliot's account completely effaces. Having 'married'
Lewes, Eliot now shared responsibility for the very considerable
financial burden of Lewes's continued support for his first wife,
Agnes, and their children. In 1855 Lewes was forced to borrow to
cover Agnes's debts, and again in 1856 he found himself 'agitated'
and 'distressed' by his former wife's debts and by Thornton Hunt's
refusal to contribute, despite his having by that stage fathered three
children by Agnes. Not surprisingly, then, Lewes, according to his
neighbour at Witley, Lady Holland, puts a different emphasis on his
account of Eliot's debut as a novelist:

> The conversation falling on Mrs. Lewes's writings he said, as far as I
> recollect, 'The extraordinary thing is that I never discovered this
> power in her – that she never should have written a line till her 35th
> year. Our friends – Herbert Spencer – and others used to say to me –
> Why doesn't she write a novel? and I used to reply that she was with-
> out the creative power. At last – we were very badly off – I was writing
> for Blackwood – I said to her "My dear – try your hand at something.
> Do not attempt a novel – but try a story. We may get 20 guineas for it
> from Blackwood and that would be something." '   (IX, 197)

Above all, Eliot's journalism in the year prior to the commencement of her 'story' reveals a mind already preoccupied with the fundamentals of fiction writing. Indeed, in a series of reviews in 1856 and 1857 she articulated an artistic credo, which she subsequently set out to exemplify in her first work, *Scenes of Clerical Life*.

II

If, as we have seen, 'the extension of sympathy' (*SCW*, 263) was the goal of Eliot's fiction writing, the primary means to that end in her view was realism.[11] She sought to achieve the natural historian's *veritas* through 'a humble and faithful study of nature' (*SCW*, 248), based on the scrupulous attention to detail that she so admired in Dutch painting. Her aspiration was to make ideas 'incarnate' (IV, 300), and she was unwilling throughout her career to adopt any formula which did not get itself 'clothed for me in some human figure and individual experience' (VI, 216). Underlying her sense of the necessity for fidelity to detail was Eliot's belief that 'emotion links itself with particulars, and only in a faint and secondary manner with abstractions', and the related conviction that 'morality is emotional'.[12] For Eliot, 'truth of feeling' was central to the highest values in ethics and art. So, for example, the greatest failings of the poet Edward Young were, according to her, '*radical insincerity*' and '*want of genuine emotion*' – that is, they were simultaneously aesthetic and moral flaws, and they were born of, or 'closely allied' to, Young's 'adherence to abstractions'.[13]

Realism was, then, much more than an aesthetic preference: it was a 'doctrine' (*SCW*, 263). In 'Silly Novels by Lady Novelists', the essay Eliot completed only days before she began 'Amos Barton', she was scathing in her analysis of the wild improbabilities of a whole 'genus' of women's novels. It was one of the wittiest pieces she ever wrote, but the hilarity of its scorn did nothing to disguise the seriousness with which Eliot regarded the failure of realism – 'unreality of representation' was for her 'a grave evil' (*SCW*, 263). It was most grievous, she felt, when it related to the presentation of the working classes, because these were precisely the people who were 'beyond the bounds' (*SCW*, 264) of Eliot's readers, and on behalf of whom the artist should seek to extend the limits of sympathy:

> Falsification here is far more pernicious than in the more artificial aspects of life. It is not so very serious that we should have false ideas

about evanescent fashions – about the manners and conversation of beaux and duchesses; but it *is* serious that our sympathy with the perennial joys and struggles, the toil, the tragedy, and the humour in the life of our more heavily-laden fellow-men, should be perverted, and turned towards a false object instead of the true one.   (*SCW*, 264)

It is when we understand both Eliot's sense of purpose and her belief in the social consequences of writing that we begin to appreciate the profound seriousness of her conception of the role of novelist. Poor writing, she felt, was 'one of the things that ought never to be done and that everybody is morally the worse for' (IV, 367) – 'bad literature' was 'spiritual gin'.[14] And while the earnestness and high moralism of her position might seem alien at first to modern readers, it is well to remember that such seriousness is not so far removed from our contemporary debates on the representation of race and gender, which equally turn on a belief in the consequentiality of the word or image.

Along with an accuracy and fidelity to detail, realism for Eliot depended on a capacity for psychological veracity. Her belief in an 'undeviating law' which pertained as much to the moral as to the material world – an 'invariability of sequence' which formed the basis of not only science but also social organisation, ethics and religion (*SCW*, 21) – led her to require an internal logic or consistency in the working out of character and plot. She admired Goethe's capacity to form a narrative 'without exaggeration' and with no desire to 'alarm readers into virtue by melodramatic consequences' (*SCW*, 131), and she sought to emulate his mode of treatment in quietly following 'the stream of fact and of life', waiting patiently 'for the moral processes of nature as we all do for her material processes' (*SCW*, 131). Her refusal to modify the character of Caterina in 'Mr Gilfil's Love-Story', for example, was based on a commitment to just such 'process':

> I am unable to alter anything in relation to the delineation or development of character, as my stories grow out of my psychological conception of the dramatis personae. . . . And I cannot stir a step aside from what I *feel* to be *true* in character. If anything strikes you as untrue to human nature in my delineations, I shall be very glad if you will point it out to me, that I may reconsider the matter. But alas! inconsistencies and weaknesses are not untrue.   (II, 299)

Nor did she feel she could deviate from the inevitability of Maggie's demise in *Mill on the Floss*, despite her recognition that the end would be unpalatable to her publisher and public. An unfortunate duck can only lay blue eggs, she told John Blackwood, 'however much white ones may be in demand' (III, 265). Accordingly, Eliot abhorred the tendency of writers like Geraldine Jewsbury to manipulate plot in order to 'make out that this tangled wilderness of life has a plan as easy to trace as a Dutch garden' (SCW, 121), or in an effort to reduce the narrative to a system of rewards and punishments 'distributed according to those notions of justice on which the novel-writer would have recommended that the world should be governed if he had been consulted at the creation' (SCW, 130).

For Eliot the greatest distortion militating against psychological veracity was false simplicity. The obligation of the novelist was to present human nature in all its complexity – 'mixed and erring' (SCW, 131). The notion that characters could be neatly categorised into separate groups of 'the virtuous and the vicious' was 'an immoral fiction' (SCW, 132). For all the brilliance with which Dickens could render the external traits of his characters, his greatness was diminished by his 'frequently false psychology'. Despite the 'delicate accuracy' of his rendition of the idiom and manners of his characters, he failed, in Eliot's judgement, to realise their inwardness, scarcely ever shifting from 'the humorous and external to the emotional and tragic, without becoming as transcendent in his unreality as he was a moment before in his artistic truthfulness' (SCW, 264). Edward Young and Alexander Pope were likewise guilty of oversimplicity, basing their satire on the 'psychological mistake' of 'attributing all forms of folly to one passion – the love of fame, or vanity'.[15]

The manifestation of false simplicity which was perhaps the most common, and yet most unacceptable, according to Eliot, was the idealisation of character. It constituted an affront to reality, a misrepresentation of the damaging nature of oppression and an insult to the intelligence of the reader. In 'The Natural History of German Life', for example, Eliot provides a withering assessment of the conception of the peasantry which underpins their representation in art, and in the political and social theory of the day. She argued that the general view was as ill- informed and unconvincing as 'the idyllic swains and damsels of our chimney ornaments' (SCW, 261). Determined to 'dislodge' the sentimental prejudices of the artistic mind, which represent 'the imagination of the cultivated and town-bred, rather than the truth of rustic life' (SCW, 262), Eliot scornfully concluded that to make men moral, 'something more is requisite than to turn them out to grass' (SCW, 263).

It mattered little to Eliot whether the authorial bias which gave rise to idealisation arose from worthy motives or not. On the one hand, she condemned Geraldine Jewsbury's mean-spiritedness in extracting a kind of literary vengeance in *Constance Herbert* by portraying all her male characters as 'weak, perfidious, or rascally' and all her females as 'models of magnanimity and devotedness': 'The lions, i.e., the ladies, have got the brush in their hands with a vengeance now, and are retaliating for the calumnies of men from Adam downwards' (*SCW*, 121). Yet, on the other, she was no less harsh towards Harriet Beecher Stowe's honourable intentions in exaggerating the nobility of American slaves in her novel *Dred*, and failing to provide 'any proportionate exhibition of the negro character in its less amiable phases'.[16] Beecher Stowe did no service to the cause of Abolition by this distortion, for, in fact, such 'one-sidedness' was 'argumentative suicide': 'If negroes are really so very good, slavery has answered as a moral discipline.'[17] She objected on similar grounds to Dickens's panoply of 'preternaturally virtuous poor children and artisans' (*SCW*, 264), for through such representations Dickens encouraged the 'miserable fallacy that high morality and refined sentiment can grow out of harsh social relations, ignorance, and want; or that the working classes are in a condition to enter at once into a millennial state of *altruism*, wherein everyone is caring for everyone else, and no one for himself' (*SCW*, 265).

If oversimplification ran counter to the reality of the psychological intricacies of human nature, it also offended against the moral complexity that Eliot sought to engender through her fiction. She thought it a sad waste that a novelist of Geraldine Jewsbury's talent 'should have produced three volumes for the sake of teaching such copy-book morality' (*SCW*, 120), and she condemned the 'moral bias' (*SCW*, 129) and 'obstinate one-sidedness' of both Charles Kingsley and Thomas Carlyle (*SCW*, 112). Didactic distortion damaged the art itself, she suggested: 'It is as if a painter in colour were to write "Oh, you villain!" under his Jesuits or murderers; or to have a strip flowing from a hero's mouth, with "Imitate me, my man!" on it. . . . We don't want a man with a wand, going about the gallery and haranguing us. Art is art, and tells its own story.'[18] It was also symptomatic of a failure on the part of the author to engage fully and sympathetically with his subject: 'It is only where moral emotion is comparatively weak that the contemplation of a rule or theory habitually mingles with its action; and in accordance with this, we think experience, both in literature and life, has shown that the minds which are pre-eminently didactic – which insist on a "lesson", and despise everything that will not convey a moral, are deficient in sympathetic emotion.'[19]

It was fundamental to Eliot's ethical and artistic project that the author manage to free 'himself from the spirit of the partisan' (*SCW*, 115) and embrace 'the habit of seeing things as they probably appeared to others' so that a 'strong partisanship' would seem 'an insincerity for him' (*DD*, 307). The capacity to present multiple perspectives and a shifting focus was to become central for Eliot's fiction. Frederick Harrison testified to the successfully non-partisan and comprehensive nature of her sympathetic imagination when he reported that a whole range of often conflicting groups and interests were able to 'see their own side' in *Romola*: 'the religious people, the non-religious people, the various sections of religious people, the educated, the simple, the radicals, the Tories, the socialists, the intellectual reformers, the domestic circle, the critics, the metaphysicians, the artists, the Positivists, the squires, are all quite convinced that it has been conceived from their own point of view' (IV, 285).

For Eliot, 'moral bias' did not make a book moral in its influence (*SCW*, 128). Instead, it was the 'large tolerance' of an author like Goethe which she most admired. In the end, it was not only the exhibition of sympathy in the writer but its *extension* in the reader to which she aspired, and this could only be achieved through the acceptance – and realistic presentation – of psychological and moral complexity, and through the encouragement of that 'vision of others' needs, which is the source of justice, tenderness, sympathy in the fullest sense' (VI, 98).

3

'My first bit of art':
Scenes of Clerical Life

Eliot's determination to exemplify the artistic credo she had so extensively enunciated through her literary journalism is evident at every turn in *Scenes of Clerical Life*. To begin with, the stories are insistently unromantic. The narrator of 'Amos Barton', for example, affects a simplicity of mind and incapacity of invention to explain the mundanity of his tale. He maintains that his 'only merit' lies in 'faithfulness' (50), and warns readers in search of 'thrilling incident' to look elsewhere to the more fashionable novels of 'the last season' (37). Similarly, Eliot's first protagonist, Amos Barton, is adamantly unheroic, 'the quintessential extract of mediocrity' (40). The initial description of Barton stresses the generic rather than the exceptional, thwarting the superficial desire to read character through appearance. He has a narrow face 'of no particular complexion', features of 'no particular shape' and an eye of 'no particular expression' (15). His nondescript visage is complemented by his 'unmistakably commonplace' (36) character, inclining the putative 'lady reader' to declare him 'utterly uninteresting' (36). Yet it is precisely because everything about him is 'so very far from remarkable' (36) that Barton acquires a representative status that warrants attention:

> it is so very large a majority of your fellow-countrymen that are of this insignificant stamp. At least eighty out of a hundred of your adult male fellow-Britons returned in the last census, are neither extraordinarily silly, nor extraordinarily wicked, nor extraordinarily wise; their eyes are neither deep and liquid with sentiment, nor sparkling with suppressed witticisms; they have probably had no hairbreadth escapes

or thrilling adventures; their brains are certainly not pregnant with genius, and their passions have not manifested themselves at all after the fashion of a volcano. They are simply men of complexions more or less muddy, whose conversation is more or less bald and disjointed. (37)

Importantly, the mediocrity of Eliot's protagonists extends to their moral stature, recalling Eliot's conviction that all humanity is 'mixed and erring' (*SCW*, 121). Amos Barton, Mr Gilfil and Mr Tryan all possess a basic goodness, but none conforms to the 'modern demand for an ideal hero' (*SC*, 229). Instead, they are flawed, but 'real': 'Their insight is blended with mere opinion; their sympathy is perhaps confined in narrow conduits of doctrine, instead of flowing forth with the freedom of a stream that blesses every weed in its course; obstinacy or self-assertion will often interfuse itself with their grandest impulses; and their very deeds of self-sacrifice are sometimes only the rebound of a passionate egoism' (229). Their moral and psychological complexities defy the easy categorisation that comes of 'that facile psychology which prejudges individuals by means of formulae, and casts them, without further trouble, into duly lettered pigeon-holes' (219).

Added to the unexceptionalness of both incident and character, the unspectacular Midlands setting of the *Scenes* provides the appropriate backdrop for the ordinary sorrows of its commonplace inhabitants: 'Milby was nothing but dreary prose: a dingy town, surrounded by flat fields, lopped elms, and sprawling manufacturing villages, which crept on and on with their weaving-shops, till they threatened to graft themselves on the town' (181).

Certainly this resolve in Eliot to exhibit 'men and things as they are' (*SCW*, 307) met with immediate recognition and approbation. The *Atlantic Monthly*, for example, saw Eliot as reflecting the temper of the times in her recognition that 'men and women are better than heroes and heroines', and commended her daring in rebelling against 'the old theory of the necessity of perfection'.[1] The *Saturday Review* similarly acclaimed the advent of a new writer who boldly disregarded convention and possessed a rare combination of courage and talent, which enabled the depiction of 'homely every-day life and ordinary characters with great humour and pathos'.[2] Of course, given the insistence with which Eliot signalled her intent in *Scenes*, it is not surprising that her scrupulous realism should have been the focus of contemporary reviews. It is more noteworthy, perhaps, that even so determined a realist as Eliot could not entirely eliminate from this first fictional work the melodrama and sentimentality she criticised so harshly in others. In 'Mr Gilfil's Love-Story', for example, Caterina's homicidal episode, with its exclamatory fervour and its present-tense urgency, betrays all the hallmarks of the lady novelists' striving for thrilling incident:

> See how she rushes noiselessly, like a pale meteor, along the passages and up the gallery stairs! Those gleaming eyes, those bloodless lips, that swift silent tread, make her look like the incarnation of a fierce purpose, rather than a woman . . . Wait, wait, O heart! till she has done this one deed. He will be there – he will be before her in a moment. He will come towards her with that false smile, thinking she does not know his baseness – she will plunge that dagger into his heart. (141)

Similarly, Milly Barton's brood of small children, whose lisping devotedness and unfailing good nature seem unaffected by the crowded poverty of their home, bear as much relation to a likely reality as the idyllic distortions of the English peasantry that Eliot decried in her review of Riehl's *Natural History of German Life*.

The corollary of Eliot's determination to represent life in all its ordinariness is her conviction that through the mediating and transforming eye of the artist the reader might be brought to recognise the tragedy and goodness of common life, or what David Lodge has called 'the significance of the quotidian'.[3] Thus the narrator frequently stresses the inadequacy of first impressions and easy assumptions. It is only to the 'superficial glance' (181), for example, that Milby seems unrelentingly dreary. The goodness of its community is not 'visible on the surface' (180) – 'at first' the life there seems a 'dismal mixture of griping worldliness, vanity, ostrich feathers, and the fumes of brandy' (181). Yet it is in the act of 'looking closer' (181), led to this heightened scrutiny by the exhortation of the narrator, that a truer and more accurate estimate is possible. Such an extension of fellow-feeling is not simply the aim of *Scenes*, it is also the unifying subject of the three tales. Sympathy is central to each story, as misunderstood and ostracised characters – Amos, Caterina, Janet, Tryan – come in the end to be embraced by the communities which have previously judged them so harshly.

The basis for sympathy, Eliot believed, was emotional, not intellectual. The 'large tolerance' that she so admired in Goethe (*SCW*, 131) was the product of the heart, not the mind, and in *Scenes of Clerical Life* she explored that tolerance in relation to religious difference. She endeavoured to get beyond the divisions of 'schools and sects' (229) to a recognition of a more fundamental emotional fellowship. She had long been convinced that opinions were 'a poor cement between human souls' (III, 111), and she knew as a matter of 'heart-cutting experience' (III, 111) the crippling damage done in the name of inflexible dogma. Having come under the influence of the Evangelical wing of the Church of England in her adolescence, Eliot demonstrated a precocious puritanical severity and ostentatious piety. And when that early faith deserted her, at the age of twenty-two, she embraced her new-found atheism with a corresponding fervour. In the face of her father's deep distress at her refusal any longer to attend church, Eliot's response was as unbending and self-righteous as that of any zealot: 'it cannot be a question with any mind of strict integrity, whatever judgement may be passed on their truth, that I could not without vile hypocrisy and a miserable truckling to the smile of the world for the sake of my supposed interests, profess to join in worship which I wholly disapprove' (I, 129).

The painful rift in the emotional fabric of the Evans family caused by Eliot's early religious crisis was not remarkable. It was a familiar drama played out again and again in an age when science was coming to rival religion as the font of truth. What was extraordinary, and revealing, however, was the manner in which Eliot finally resolved the matter. In the space of less than two years, she achieved a perspective on the crisis which was to inform all her subsequent thinking. With great generosity and detachment, she came to recognise the excess of her own position, the inevitability of her father's, and the understanding needful for reconciliation:

> The first impulse of a young and ingenuous mind is to withhold the slightest sanction from all that contains even a mixture of supposed error. When the soul is just liberated from the wretched giant's bed of dogmas on which it has been racked and stretched ever since it began to think there is a feeling of exultation and strong hope . . . But a year or two of reflection and the experience of our own miserable weakness which will ill afford to part even with the crutches of superstition must, I think, effect a change. Speculative truth begins to appear but a shadow of individual minds, agreement between intellects seems unattainable, and we turn to the *truth of feeling* as the only universal bond of union. We find that the intellectual errors which we once fancied were a mere incrustation have grown into the living body and that we cannot in the majority of causes, wrench them away without destroying vitality. We begin to find that with individuals, as with nations, the

only safe revolution is one arising out of the wants which their *own progress* has generated. It is the quackery of infidelity to suppose that it has a nostrum for all mankind, and to say to all and singular, 'Swallow my opinions and you shall be whole.' (I, 162)

This early commitment to moderation, evolutionary growth and anti-polemicism never wavered. By the time she came to write her fiction, she had thoroughly renounced 'the attitude of antagonism' which she believed accompanied the 'renunciation of *any* belief'(III, 230). The experience of the intervening years, and particularly her engagement with the work of Spinoza and Feuerbach, had disposed her toward sympathy with 'any faith in which human sorrow and human longing for purity have expressed themselves' (III, 231). Where once she took pleasure in articulating intellectual difference, she now delighted 'in feeling an emotional agreement' (III, 231).

Thus, in *Scenes of Clerical Life*, Eliot could now admire Evangelicalism for its inculcation of the importance of duty: 'that recognition of something to be lived for beyond the mere satisfaction of self, which is to the moral life what the addition of a great central ganglion is to animal life' (228). Through the figure of Tryan she amplifies the argument she first outlined in her *Westminster Review* article on Evangelical teaching and Dr Cumming – that it is the *idea* of God that is most important. It is an idea, she argued, that is only really moral in its influence when it produces sympathy with 'the pure elements of human feeling' (*SCW*, 168), and it has the potential to bring about 'an extension and multiplication of the effects produced by human sympathy' (*SCW*, 169). Accordingly, it is not a creed but a recognition of a common humanity which enables Tryan to play the decisive role in the redemption of Janet Dempster, and hers is a salvation from alcoholism and despair which is entirely of this world. Indeed, Eliot concedes that Tryan has made the mistake of identifying Christianity with 'a too narrow doctrinal system' (229). Yet she disclaims all interest in the intricacies of dogma, arguing rather that 'surely the only true knowledge of our fellow-man is that which enables us to feel with him – which gives us a fine ear for the heart-pulses that are beating under the mere clothes of circumstance and opinion. Our subtlest analysis of schools and sects must miss the essential truth, unless it be lit up by the love that sees in all forms of human thought and work, the life and death struggles of separate human beings' (229).

II

If the nature of Eliot's task was unusually clear and explicit for her as she approached this first work of fiction, its execution proved much more problematic. Her choice of subject, and to some extent the mode of its treatment, could be a matter of simple resolve, but the success of her project depended much more on skill than will, and in this regard Eliot's inexperience as a novelist limited her achievement in *Scenes of Clerical Life*. She herself looked back on the work as flawed, admitting to her friends, the Brays, 'that was my first bit of art, and my hand was not well in – I did not know so well how to manipulate my materials' (III, 99). The problem with the stories is twofold – first, the narrative voice is uncertain in its tone and compromised by a combination of voyeurism and viciousness. And, secondly, the work's conception of sympathy is too limited, for it contracts in the end into a simpler notion of pity, which, as we shall see, rather than extending fellow-feeling by bridging the gap between the self and other, actually reinscribes difference and distance.

From the outset Eliot struggles to achieve a satisfactory tone for her narrator. The initial address to the reader is strained – overwritten and overly familiar:

> Reader! *did* you ever taste such a cup of tea as Miss Gibbs is this moment handing to Mr Pilgrim? Do you know the dulcet strength, the animating blandness of tea sufficiently blended with real farmhouse cream? No – most likely you are a miserable town-bred reader, who think of cream as a thinnish white fluid, delivered in infinitesimal pennyworths down area steps; or perhaps, from a presentiment of calves' brains, you refrain from any lacteal addition, and rasp your tongue with unmitigated bohea. (8)

Thereafter, the narrative voice vacillates between coercive flattery and hectoring condescension. So, on the one hand, the narrator attempts to enlist agreement by suggesting that 'only the very largest souls' can discern the sincerity of purpose in the bungling figure of Amos Barton. On the other, he chivvies the reader to accept his uplifting instruction: 'Depend upon it, you would gain unspeakably if you would learn with me to see some of the poetry and the pathos, the tragedy and the comedy, lying in the experience of a human soul that looks out through dull grey eyes, and that speaks in a voice of quite ordinary tones' (37).

Such awkwardness of tone may be read as a symptom of inexperience – and certainly subsequent works manage their didacticism with more grace and flexibility. However, there are more fundamental problems with the narrative strategy which arise from contradictions in the role assumed by the narrator. It is essential for Eliot to invest her narrator with a degree of authority in order to give force to the instruction he proffers, and she does this by stressing his capacities as a knowing and reliable judge. He evinces the confidence of the moral cognoscenti, for example, when he advises: 'See to it, friend, before you pronounce a too hasty judgment, that your own moral sensibilities are not of a hoofed or clawed character' (231). He also possesses a sense of perspective endowed by history: 'at Milby, in those distant days, as in all other times and places where the mental atmosphere is changing, and men are inhaling the stimulus of new ideas, folly often mistook itself for wisdom, ignorance gave itself airs of knowledge, and selfishness, turning its eyes upward, called itself religion' (227). He is capable at some moments of the epigrammatic wit of Austen – 'Errors look so very ugly in persons of small means' (285) – and demonstrates at others the worldliness of Thackeray – 'The gentlemen there fall into no other excess at dinner-parties than the perfectly well-bred and virtuous excess of stupidity; and though the ladies are still said sometimes to take too much upon themselves, they are never known to take too much in any other way' (173).

However, in the effort to establish a worldly and witty persona for her narrator, Eliot jeopardises his role as moral instructor. There is a fine line between the knowing and the cynical, and Eliot fails to tread that line when the narrative voice shows signs of being not merely inflected with, but actually infected by, the community viciousness it purports to diagnose. The project of extending sympathy is inevitably compromised when wit becomes insult, as in the description of the one-eyed Mary Higgins, 'who, in spite of nature's apparent safe-guards against that contingency, had contributed to the perpetuation of the Fodge characteristics in the person of a small boy' (21). Similarly, the narrator's role as sympathetic mediator is damaged when ironic detachment gives way to contempt, as when the inhabitants of the Shepperton district are represented as brutes: 'over and above the rustic stupidity furnished by farm-labourers, the miners brought obstreperous animalism, and the weavers an acrid Radicalism and Dissent' (20).

In the depiction of Milby, Eliot portrays gossip as one of the most destructive aspects of community living. Despite this, in a rather crude solution to the narrative challenge of changing scenes, Eliot implicates her narrator in the taint of hearsay by consistently positioning him in the role of voyeur, enthusiastically reporting every detail of village scandal. The narrator, thus, adopts the stance of eavesdropper, inviting the reader to 'over-hear' malicious conversations at Mrs Patten's fireside (8), at the Farquhar's, once the door is closed behind Amos Barton (14), at the Clerical meeting in Barton's absence (49) or at the anti-Tryan gathering at the Red Lion (173). In later works, in contrast, Eliot manages the reporting of the fact and the effect of gossip more summarily and with greater detachment, leaving the narrator of *Middlemarch*, for example, uncontaminated by the depiction of Bulstrode's public ridicule.

In fact, while on the one hand participating vicariously in communal defamation, the narrator in *Scenes* attempts on the other to distance himself from such small-mindedness by appealing to a conspiratorial bond with the reader in which both see the folly of Milby's inhabitants. It is a self-defeating position, however, because it is doubly divisive. We are invited to align ourselves first with the suffering protagonists against the communities which treat them so harshly, and then with the morally superior narrator against the narrow and malicious gossipers. The irony, of course, is that these very moves appeal to the logic of division and run exactly counter to the sympathetic tendencies they ostensibly serve. It is one thing for Charlotte Brontë, for example, to adopt such a narrative strategy in *Jane Eyre*, for there the appeal is precisely, and fiercely, on behalf of the individual against the community. For Eliot, however, such one-sidedness equates with artistic failure. 'Coarse contrasts', she argued, were the stuff of lesser art: she did not believe in the juxtaposition of the 'blameless martyr' against the social tyrant (*SCW*, 245–6). Yet it was not until her more mature work that she could confidently negotiate such freedom from partisanship, recognising in *The Mill on the Floss*, for example, that even while Maggie suffered mightily as a girl in a sexist society, Tom Tulliver, too, was a victim of social constructions of masculinity.

III

Beyond the formal problems with the narrative strategy, there are conceptual limitations, too, with Eliot's consideration of sympathy in *Scenes of Clerical Life*. All three of the stories deal with the fundamental ethical challenge of confronting the difference of the Other, but in this first work Eliot envisages only two ways in which the extension of sympathy might be achieved – empathy or pity.

Although the dynamics of each varies, both ultimately work not to mediate difference, but to reinscribe sameness.

Empathy, for example, depends on recognition – on the perception of commonality between the giver and the recipient. It is, Eliot suggests, 'but a living again through our own past in a new form' (*SC*, 258). Accordingly, Edgar Tryan can help Janet Dempster because he has 'known sorrow' (270), and because Janet's anguish is 'not strange' (258) to him. In this, his character echoes the position taken by Feuerbach in *The Essence of Christianity*, which Eliot had translated three years before: 'I feel only for that which has feeling, only for that which I feel myself, whose sufferings I myself suffer. Sympathy presupposes a like nature.'[4] It requires, then, the imaginative assimilation of another's experience as one's own. It implies a willingness to transport oneself into another's narrative and in that way apparently extend one's subjectivity. At its simplest, it is what Mrs Pettifer does, for instance, in contemplating Janet's drinking problem – 'You and me might do the same, if we were in her place' (191) – and, conversely, what Miss Pratt repudiates: 'Speak for yourself, Mrs Pettifer. . . . Under no circumstances can I imagine myself resorting to a practice so degrading' (191).

However, empathy is limited by the fact that its fundamental reference point is always the self. In the end the aspiration to feel the other's suffering as one's own is appropriative and self-confirming, as we see in the work's ultimate empathetic moment. When Janet Dempster confesses to Edgar Tryan, the clergyman reciprocates with his own narrative of despair in an interchange meant to signal his complete understanding. Yet this exchange, in which 'confession . . . prompts a response of confession' (258), actually highlights the essential return of, and to, the self in the empathetic gesture. So, Tryan's immediate impulse is introspective: 'He had never been in the presence of a sorrow and a self-despair that had sent so strong a thrill *through all the recesses of his saddest experience*' [my italics] (258). And at the conclusion of his confession, he has replaced Janet as the focus of the exchange: 'For a moment he had forgotten Janet, and for a moment she had forgotten her own sorrows' (261). There is, then, in this crucial scene a failure to imagine what Levinas has called a 'relationship with alterity' – 'an inability to envisage an encounter with an Other which does not entail a return to the self'.[5]

Furthermore, if sympathy is seen to depend, like this, on some measure of commensurability, it will inevitably fail when tested against radical difference. This is precisely the case with Amos

Barton's visit to the workhouse, whose inhabitants are 'so unfamiliar' that they remain beyond the reach of any 'leap' that Barton might venture:

> For, to have any chance of success, short of miraculous intervention, he must bring his geographical, chronological, exegetical mind pretty nearly to the pauper point of view, or of no view; he must have some approximate conception of the mode in which the doctrines that have so much vitality in the plenum of his own brain will comport themselves *in vacuo* – that is to say, in a brain that is neither geographical, chronological, nor exegetical.   (22)

As we shall see, Eliot explicitly confronts the ethical challenge posed by the recognition of the limits of empathy in her next work, *Adam Bede*. In *Scenes of Clerical Life*, however, her conception of sympathy remains limited by her concurrence with the Feuerbachian presupposition of the necessity for likeness and recognition: 'it is easy to understand that our discernment of men's motives must depend on the completeness of the elements we can bring from our own susceptibility and our own experience' (231).

Feuerbach's influence is also evident in *Scenes* in the way in which his contention that 'sympathy does not exist without suffering in common' is echoed in the work's stress on the 'fellowship' generated through shared pain.[6] In 'Janet's Repentance', for example, Eliot writes of the man who 'knows sympathy because he has known sorrow' (270) and she describes the sick-room as the place where 'the moral relation of man to man is reduced to its utmost clearness and simplicity' (279). Indeed, Eliot's faith in the instructive and salutary power of suffering was unusually strong. When her fifteen-month-old niece died, for example, she observed that although for the 'poor parents' the death was like 'the breaking off of a sweet melody', for spectators it was 'one of the beauties of this earth' (I, 140). The sorrow of such an occasion, she argued, was 'one of the surest means of subduing and refining the spirit' (I, 140). In much the same vein, she depicts her characters as transformed through suffering – Amos Barton is 'consecrated anew' (59) in the eyes of all who behold him by his wife's death; Maynard Gilfil is likewise 'sanctified' (160) by Tina's breakdown and decline; and Janet Dempster achieves inner peace with a last 'sacred kiss' (300) at Edgar Tryan's death bed. Eliot also relies on the depiction of sorrow to provide the only 'true knowledge of our fellow-man' possible or needful – that is, 'that which enables us to feel with him' (229) – and thereby to prompt a sympathetic transformation in the reader. The danger, however, is that if suffering and sorrow are its only currency, sympathy is debased and simplified, and it comes to exist only as pity.

Although Eliot frequently uses pity and sympathy interchangeably throughout the work, the exercise of pity, in fact, runs counter to the recognition of commonality on which Eliot bases her conception of sympathy in *Scenes*. Pity is a sentiment that appeals implicitly to a sense of difference – to the sense of safe superiority that comes of *not* sharing the fate of the sufferer. Whereas empathy depends, at least, on some notion of connection and exchange – as exemplified in the confessional moment – pity depends on distance rather than mutuality. Eliot herself later suggests as much in *Middlemarch* when she describes 'the remoteness of pure pity' (*M*, 363). It relies not on interiority, but on the exteriority of suffering, and in this way it belongs more to the realm of spectacle, where the sufferer is the object rather than the subject of the narrative focus. So, in these stories we are repeatedly exhorted to observe – to be the spectator at a series of wrenching scenes which are offered like tableaux. On the occasion of Milly Barton's funeral, for example, the reader is aligned with the 'sad eye[s] watching that black procession' (59), as Amos and his children follow the coffin to a snow-covered grave. And similarly the simple burial of Edgar Tryan is presented as an affecting spectacle for the gaze of both the reader and the 'crowd assembled to witness his entrance through the church gates' (224). In the end, as a means of extending sympathy and negotiating otherness, pity remains at most a very partial success. It may evoke compassion, but it does not challenge understanding. So, while Amos Barton's troubles manage to call out his neighbours' 'better sympathies' (62), those feelings of pity do nothing to alter the estimate of, or respect for, the man: none of the onlookers modify their view to reassess his 'spiritual gifts' or 'his ministry' (62).

Eliot's strategic reliance on pity has consequences, too, for the characterisation in *Scenes of Clerical Life*. It leads her to depend on the depiction of victimisation – Milly, Caterina and Edgar Tryan all die, sacrificial lambs to the cause of eliciting the compassion of both the surviving characters and the reader. In order to enhance their status as victims, their innocence is stressed: the characters are simplified and sanitised, relieved of any disconcerting traces of aggression and desire. It is true that Eliot darkly mentions a capacity for explosive anger in each of her clergyman protagonists, but that complexity of character is in each case asserted rather than realised. Perhaps the most striking victim is Milly Barton, who is presented as the epitome of the Angel in the House, nursing children, mending clothes and soothing her husband with unswerving patience. There is, of course, a certain irony in the complacency of the narrator's perspective on Milly, which signals the potential for more searching analysis in later works. His eulogistic account of Milly's existence blithely erases the fact that she is consumed with care and responsibility for her family through fifteen-hour days that are destroying her health: 'Soothing, unspeakable charm of gentle womanhood! which supersedes all acquisitions, all accomplishments. You would never have asked, at any period of Mrs Amos Barton's life, if she sketched or played the piano. You would even perhaps have been rather scandalized if she had descended from the serene dignity of *being* to the assiduous unrest of *doing*' (16). And, similarly, his flippant observation that every man 'is the slave of some woman or other' (34) is reversed in the haunting, and truer, echo of Nanny's complaint that she and Milly are forced 'to "slave" more than ever' (52) to keep the household functioning.

Nevertheless, there is no trace of rebellion in Milly, who shields her husband from all blame and cannot bring herself to evict the thoughtless Countess. Just as tellingly, there is no trace of disruptive desire. Curiously, given the focus on Milly's repeated pregnancies, there is no suggestion of sexuality in the Barton home. Milly's context is unfailingly domestic, and her role as mother completely subsumes her function as lover. Indeed, this triumph of the familial over the sexual extends to the next generation as the daughter, Patty, takes the place of the dead mother. Having served her apprenticeship well, Patty receives the mantle of submission at Milly's death-bed: 'Love your papa. Comfort him; and take care of your little brothers and sisters' (58), and she remains thereafter by her father's side, her 'sweet, grave face' strongly recalling 'the expression of Mrs Barton's' (64).

The character of Caterina initially fits less easily into the category of victim. Consumed with desire, jealous, demanding, even murderous, she blazes through the early part of the story as a 'mad, little thing' (88). However, it is only after her breakdown that she becomes a benign and instructive presence. Never recovering 'beyond passiveness and acquiescence' (163), with a body 'so enfeebled' and a soul 'so bruised' (161), she inspires a 'fresh strength and sanctity' (160) in Gilfil's love. As in 'The Sad Fortunes of the Reverend Amos Barton', sexuality is banished from the ending of this second tale. Caterina submits as a child to Gilfil's affections, 'put[ting] up her little mouth to be kissed' (163), and her 'bodily feebleness' ensures that she does not live long after the 'subdued melancholy' of her wedding day (164). Similarly, in 'Janet's Repentance', the consumptive Edgar Tryan declares that there is nothing that becomes us 'but entire submission, perfect resignation' (261), and his growing affection for Janet is acknowledged and truncated in the death-bed kiss, sanctified by its impossibility: 'She lifted up her face to his, and the full life-breathing lips met the wasted dying ones in a sacred kiss of promise' (300).

In simplifying her characters thus, Eliot was in danger of the kind of failure in aesthetic teaching she found 'the most offensive of all' – that of lapsing 'from the picture to the diagram' (IV, 300). Yet, despite the signs of her inexperience, in *Scenes of Clerical Life* she had begun the fictional exploration of fundamental ethical questions which she was to pursue with increasing complexity and sophistication throughout the whole of her novel-writing career.

4

Self-regulation and the Limits of Subjectivity: *Adam Bede*

I

Encouraged by the modest success of *Scenes of Clerical Life*, and by the assiduous enthusiasm of both her partner, George Lewes, and her publisher, John Blackwood, George Eliot began work on *Adam Bede* in October 1857, less than a fortnight after having despatched the conclusion of 'Janet's Repentance'. From the outset she signalled her intention to continue with the same dedicated realism of *Scenes*, promising Blackwood that her new tale would be 'a country story – full of the breath of cows and the scent of hay' (II, 387).

In the loving, almost excessive, detail of her descriptions of Adam's workshop, the Poysers' dairy, or the Birthday Feast, Eliot aspired to the 'faithful representing of commonplace things' (*AB*, 178), which could provide that 'rare, precious quality of truthfulness' (177) that she so admired in Dutch painting. And, while revealing the same resolve to represent the essentially flawed nature of human beings, *Adam Bede* showed an even greater desire to illuminate the lives of working people, the 'common, coarse' individuals whose lives were untouched by any 'picturesque sentimental wretchedness' (178). In her review of Riehl's *The Natural History of German Life* Eliot had regretted how 'little the real characteristics of the working classes are known to those outside them', and condemned both the art and the social and political theory of her time for their failure adequately to represent this section of the population (*SCW*, 261). In this, her first extended work of fiction, Eliot was determined to broaden the usual middle-class focus of contemporary novels and thus fulfil the duty of the artist, as she saw it, by 'amplifying experience and extending our contact with our fellow-men beyond the bounds of our personal lot'(*SCW*, 264).[1] So, she declared her commitment to the importance of 'insignificant people' (*AB*, 67), and her rejection of 'any aesthetic rules which shall banish from the region of Art those old women scraping carrots with their work-worn hands, those heavy clowns taking holiday in a dingy pot-house, those rounded backs and stupid weather-beaten faces that have bent over the spade and done the rough work of the world' (178).

This new novel was a work of loyalty not only to Eliot's aesthetic creed but also to her past experience. In it she drew heavily on her knowledge of, and affection for, her rural childhood in Warwickshire. The 'germ' of the story came from an anecdote told by Eliot's Aunt Samuel, who as a Methodist preacher had visited a convicted child-murderer prior to her execution and had prayed with her through the night until 'the poor creature at last broke out into tears, and confessed her crime' (II, 502). The character of Dinah 'grew out of my recollections of my aunt' (II, 502) and, similarly, the character of Adam was 'suggested by my Father's early life' (II, 503). More generally, Eliot depicted the aspirations and fears, the virtues and shortcomings, of the provincial farming and working classes – those frequently scorned, as Mrs Poyser points out, as 'dumb creaturs . . . abused and made money on by them as ha' got the lash i' their hands, for want o' knowing how to undo the tackle' (348). Eliot prided herself on her inwardness with country habits and dialect, and she supplemented her knowledge with careful horticultural and sociological research. Accordingly, she professed herself 'both greatly amused and greatly gratified' (III, 10) by her publisher's account of the verdict of a cabinet maker, who read the manuscript with great admiration and declared that 'the writer must have been bred to the business or at all events passed a great deal of time in the workshop listening to the men' (III, 9). It was, as Blackwood observed, 'a curious tribute to one phase of the life-like reality which pervades the whole book' (III, 9).

Despite the similarities and continuities with her first work, however, *Adam Bede* represented more a quantum leap than a gradual step in the development of Eliot's career as a novelist. Perhaps the most obvious advance was the increase in the psychological complexity of the work. In *Adam Bede* the choices that shape the drama are seen to be the result of a complex blend of intention and chance, desire and taboo, self-deception and self-mastery. And whereas in *Scenes* the characters who cause the suffering, like the Countess, Captain Wybrow and Robert Dempster, are largely 'bad' and one-dimensional, in *Adam Bede* no such consoling simplicity exists. Indeed, in this second work Eliot ridicules the desire to see the world ordered so categorically:

> Perhaps you will say, 'Do improve the facts a little, then; make them more accordant with those correct views which it is our privilege to possess. The world is not just what we like; do touch it up with a taste-ful pencil, and make believe it is not quite such a mixed, entangled affair. Let all people who hold unexceptionable opinions act unexcep-tionably. Let your most faulty characters always be on the wrong side, and your virtuous ones on the right. Then we shall see at a glance whom we are to condemn, and whom we are to approve.'   (*AB*, 176)

Instead, the 'good-natured' Arthur Donnithorne, for example, finds himself in the 'wretched position of an open, generous man, who has committed an error' (305). His motives are mixed, inextricably good and bad at once: 'Deeds of kindness were as easy to him as a bad habit: they were the common issue of his weaknesses and good qual-ities, of his egoism and his sympathy' (310). And, Eliot suggests in a passage of remarkable prescience and accuracy, which anticipates a more extended exploration in *The Mill on the Floss*, Donnithorne's weakness in regulating his desires is compounded by his inability to recognise the unconscious motivation at work in his behaviour:

> Was there a motive at work under this strange reluctance of Arthur's which had a sort of backstairs influence, not admitted to himself? Our mental business is carried on much in the same way as the business of the State: a great deal of hard work is done by agents who are not acknowledged. In a piece of machinery, too, I believe there is often a small unnoticeable wheel which has a great deal to do with the motion of the large obvious ones. Possibly, there was some such unrecognised agent secretly busy in Arthur's mind at this moment – possibly it was the fear lest he might hereafter find the fact of having made a confes-sion to the Rector a serious annoyance, in case he should *not* be able quite to carry out his good resolutions? I dare not assert that it was not so. The human soul is a very complex thing.   (173)

John Blackwood had predicted that the extended scope of a novel would benefit Eliot's emerging talent: 'With a larger canvass your exquisite little sketches of character will all come into full life and take their legitimate share in the story' (II, 387). And, indeed, with this coming to 'full life', the simplicity of melodrama in the *Scenes* gave way to the complexity of tragedy in *Adam Bede*.

The refusal of simple categories and opposition is further explored through the process of structural doubling, which is such a feature of this novel. To begin with, Eliot sets up a series of contrasts – between Adam and Seth, Adam and Arthur, and perhaps most strikingly between Dinah and Hetty – in a doubling that prefigures the crucial pairings of Lucy and Maggie in *The Mill on the Floss*, Rosamond and Dorothea in *Middlemarch*, and Mirah and Gwendolen in *Daniel Deronda*. However, rather than simply confirm difference, this set of oppositions is gradually deconstructed to reveal more unsettling points of connection. Eliot was convinced that coarse contrasts were 'not the materials handled by great dramatists' (*SCW*, 245). So, despite her admiration for Mrs Gaskell's *Ruth*, a novel which preceded *Adam Bede* by six years and anticipated its treatment of the theme of the fallen woman,[2] Eliot criticised Gaskell for being 'constantly misled by a love of sharp contrasts – of "dramatic" effects. She is not contented with the subdued colouring – the half tints of real life' (II, 86). Those 'half tints', for Eliot, revealed a more shifting reality, for as she suggested in her essay on 'The Future of German Philosophy', inherent in comparison was a 'perception of likeness in the midst of difference . . . every true judgment inevitably alters the idea both of the subject and predicate' (*SCW*, 136).

The force of this insight is clear in an examination of the doubling of Dinah and Hetty in the novel. The details of the contrast between the two women have been well rehearsed, and at first sight their differences seem stark. Dinah's unfailingly plain appearance in her 'quaker-like costume' (20) is complemented by 'the total absence of self-consciousness in her demeanour' (22). Against this, Hetty's vanity is clear both in her consuming preoccupation with appearance and her constant awareness of the effect her beauty has on others. Hetty is consistently sexualised, while Dinah is seen as the unworldly preacher, 'too good and holy for any man' (33), who desires 'to live and die without husband or children' (35). Dinah is 'moonlight' in contrast to Hetty's 'sunshine' (116). Where Dinah is good with children, patient and attentive, Hetty is careless and resentful of her charges, leaving them to fall behind in the walk to church or spoil their appetites with an excess of currants from the garden. While Dinah's life is ruled by deference to the will of God, the only 'religious rite' of significance to Hetty is the 'worship' she performs in

LIBRARY, UNIVERSITY OF CHESTER

front of the mirror (149). And whereas Dinah counsels Seth 'not lightly to leave your own country and kindred' (36) and remembers her home and past with constant fondness, Hetty has no such attachment to the familiar and 'could have cast all her past behind her and never cared to be reminded of it again' (154). The contrast between the two women is distilled in the famous fifteenth chapter, 'The Two Bed-Chambers', in which Dinah adjourns to her room to look out of the window onto the natural world beyond and contemplate 'all the dear people whom she had learned to care about amongst these peaceful fields' (157), while Hetty in the adjacent chamber is absorbed with her reflection in the mirror. The openness of Dinah's room is contrasted against the guardedness of Hetty's, with its secret drawers and its door bolted against intrusion upon her ritual of self-adornment. The scene culminates with the two women coming together in Hetty's room in a moment that suggests that Dinah represents all things ethereal and Hetty embodies all things corporeal:

> What a strange contrast the two figures made! Visible enough in that mingled twilight and moonlight. Hetty, her cheeks flushed and her eyes glistening from her imaginary drama, her beautiful neck and arms bare, her hair hanging in a curly tangle down her back, and the baubles in her ears. Dinah, covered with her long white dress, her pale face full of subdued emotion, almost like a lovely corpse into which the soul has returned charged with sublimer secrets and a sublimer love.   (159)

However, despite the apparent starkness of the dichotomy, Eliot insists on more than simple opposition in the pairing. Indeed, what unfolds with the narrative is the shifting nature of such polarity. Its instability is ironically foreshadowed in the two episodes where the women's identities are confused. In the first, Adam hears a 'light rapid foot' on the stairs of his family home and is convinced that Hetty has come to visit after the death of his father: 'Adam's imagination saw a dimpled face, with dark bright eyes and roguish smiles looking backward at this brush, and a rounded figure just leaning a little to clasp the handle' (116). He cannot dispel the 'foolish thought' until he leaves the workshop and is confronted by Dinah: 'It was like dreaming of sunshine, and awaking in the moonlight' (116). In the second episode, Hetty creates the unsettling effect of an 'apparition' by dressing herself in Dinah's clothes and appearing like a 'ghost' in the Poysers' kitchen: 'The little minx had found a black gown of her aunt's, and pinned it close round her neck to look like

Dinah's, and made her hair as flat as she could, and had tied on one of Dinah's high-crowned borderless net-caps. The thought of Dinah's pale grave face and mild grave eyes, which the sight of the gown and cap brought with it, made it a laughable surprise enough to see them replaced by Hetty's round rosy cheeks and coquettish dark eyes' (228).

More significantly, the differences which distinguish the two women begin to blur. So, for example, as Hetty's flight from Hayslope becomes an extended nightmare of unfamiliarity, Hetty, the plant with 'hardly any roots' (154), comes to long for the 'familiar fields, the familiar people, the Sundays and holidays with their simple joys of dress and feasting, – all the sweets of her young life [which] rushed before her now, and [which] she seemed to be stretching her arms towards . . . across a great gulf' (386). Under duress, her vanity gives way to complete disregard for her appearance. The young girl at Hayslope who 'would have been glad to hear that she would never see a child again' (155) becomes the woman who cannot stay away from the baby she has abandoned. Finally, the once worldly Hetty is brought in the end to the solace of confession and prayer in the hours preceding her scheduled execution.

In a counter-trajectory Dinah gradually becomes more enmeshed in the material world. Her complete lack of self-consciousness gives way to a sexual bashfulness under Adam's 'dark penetrating glance' (117). She gives up her career as a preacher 'to set th' example o' submitting' (539) and defines herself in the end through her attachments to this world as a wife and mother. Where the 'pretty, round' Hetty becomes the 'pale and thin', corpse-like figure of the court scene (431), the ethereal Dinah of earlier chapters becomes in the end the 'more matronly figure' with 'dazzling' pale auburn hair (537). In this gradual deconstruction Eliot suggests not that the two figures are simply interchangeable, even less that they are the same. Rather she draws attention to the shifting and unstable nature of opposition, even in the apparent dichotomy of likeness and difference.

II

With this greater level of complexity there comes an important shift and development in Eliot's conception of sympathy. In *Adam Bede* Eliot no longer suggests that the recognition of commonality is sufficient basis for the fundamental virtue of sympathy. Rather than aspire to an *extension* of subjectivity, implied, as we have seen, in the self-projection of Mrs Pettifer's response to Janet's drinking or in Edgar Tryan's recognition of Janet's suffering, Eliot concerns herself more in *Adam Bede* with the implications of the limitation of subjectivity, for, as the narrator remarks, 'to shift one's point of view beyond certain limits is impossible to the most liberal and expansive minds: we are none of us aware of the impression we produce on Brazilian monkeys of feeble understanding – it is possible they hardly see anything in us' (203). Sympathetic responsiveness in Eliot's first work, based as it is on the reading of the other as a version of the self, in which one encounters 'our own past in a new form' (*SC*, 258), might be seen as a kind of subjective imperialism, in which, in Levinas's terms, 'the other is another me, an *alter ego* known by empathy, that is a return to the self'.[3] In contrast, the challenge for the protagonists in *Adam Bede* is the challenge of difference. In this novel, even in the midst of resemblance, difference is stressed: the 'family likeness' which 'knits us together by bone and muscle' only serves to disguise 'subtler' divisions of thought and temperament (39). And in this second work there is no longer any suggestion of interchangeable fates, like that previously of Janet Dempster and Edgar Tryan. It is inconceivable, for example, even given the shifting nature of the opposition between them, that the pious and chaste Dinah could find herself in Hetty's predicament, or, for that matter, that the rigidly disciplined and self-righteous Adam could lapse into the moral flaccidness of Arthur.

This challenge of difference is nowhere clearer than in the presentation of the character of Hetty. In a way that has disturbed many critics, Hetty is constantly objectified. She is, for example, repeatedly represented through animal imagery and impugned as both 'shallow-hearted' (319) and unremittingly self-centred. The reader is never invited to divine an inner life in Hetty – as futile a prospect as the study of 'the psychology of a canary bird' (248) – but is exhorted instead 'only [to] watch the movements of this pretty round creature' (248). In this way Hetty's identity is constantly reduced to the realm of the corporeal. Even for herself, Hetty exists as the object of the gaze. She worships her own reflection and comes to regard herself as other: 'As she threw down the letter again, she caught sight of her face in the glass; it was reddened now, and wet with tears; it was almost like a companion that she might complain to – that would pity her' (333). Similarly, she takes her moral bearings from the exterior perspective of shame, which seems to her 'like torture' (336), rather than the inner viewpoint of remorse. Adam, too, reads only

the external signs, confident in his skill and accuracy as a physiogno-
mist:

> Nature, he knows, has a language of her own, which she uses with
> strict veracity, and he considers himself an adept in the language.
> Nature has written out his bride's character for him in those exquis-
> ite lines of cheek and lip and chin, in those eyelids delicate as petals,
> in those long lashes curled like the stamen of a flower, in the dark li-
> quid depths of those wonderful eyes. How she will dote on her chil-
> dren! She is almost like a child herself, and the little pink round
> things will hang about her like florets round the central flower.
> (153)

Hetty's body bears the burden of others' misinterpretation, as character after character reads in her expression what they themselves
wish to find there. Her physicality seems to triumph over her 'little
trivial soul' (340), with her face possessing 'a language that tran-
scended her feelings' (284). In the end, anatomy does become destiny
for Hetty, as her fate is sealed by her body's betrayal, when she can no
longer hide the signs of her pregnancy.

In keeping with such objectification, there is very little attempt
made to understand Hetty's crime or to mitigate judgement by con-
sidering her motives. In fact, Hetty does not do violence to her baby –
she partially covers it with grass and wood-chips, unsure of her own
desires, thinking it may survive and be found, and she later returns to
the place where she abandoned the infant after being haunted by
thoughts of its crying. Yet despite these extenuating circumstances,
no advocacy is offered, and the view of Hetty as an object rather than
an agent persists. Hetty's tragedy functions chiefly as the focus for
others' responses – as Adam wrestles with his feelings of rage and
failure, the Poysers repudiate all family ties, and the community contemplates its responses to Arthur Donnithorne. To the very end, the
terms of Hetty's portrayal repeatedly circumscribe and undercut any
impulse of recognition or sympathy, and her impenetrability constitutes a refusal of even the possibility of empathy:

> Poor wandering Hetty, with the rounded childish face, and the hard
> unloving despairing soul looking out of it – with the narrow heart and
> narrow thoughts, no room in them for any sorrows but her own, and
> tasting that sorrow with the more intense bitterness! . . . What will be
> the end? – the end of her objectless wandering, apart from all love, car-
> ing for human beings only through her pride, clinging to life only as
> the hunted wounded brute clings to it?   (389)

Revealingly, Eliot concludes this description with an exclamation that confirms rather than dispels Hetty's otherness: 'God preserve you and me from being the beginners of such misery!' (389). We are not invited, then, to imagine ourselves in Hetty's position: there is no question of a fellowship of suffering. Instead, we are exhorted to take care how we act, as Eliot's emphasis shifts from the simple desire in her first work to elicit a sympathetic response from the reader to the determination in *Adam Bede* to impress an ethical responsibility.

There are obvious parallels between Hetty Sorrel's predicament in *Adam Bede* and Caterina's in 'Mr Gilfil's Love-Story'. Both women are victims of class and gender; both are ruined by the thoughtless flirtation of the rich, young heir. However, the differences in the unfolding of their fates underscores a change of moral focus for Eliot. In 'Mr Gilfil's Love-Story' Caterina is spared the more dire consequences of her dalliance. Her reputation is never entirely compromised by pregnancy; her murderous desire is never tested, because Captain Wybrow dies before she confronts him. In the end she lives to become the focus of Maynard's love and the reader's pity. Hetty, in contrast, is completely ruined by her affair – disgraced first by her pregnancy and then, irredeemably, by her child-murder. Though arguably the true victim, Hetty dies, while Arthur is left to live with his shame and achieve some final degree of reconciliation. Caterina's is, then, a drama about sympathy, in which the 'long happy days of childhood and girlhood recovered all their rightful predominance over the short interval of sin and sorrow' (163). Hetty's is a much bleaker drama about consequence. The first story seeks to elicit emotional responsiveness, the second to impress the need for moral governance. The ethical focus is now on anticipation, rather than reaction: sympathy is no longer simply a response to suffering but the stimulus to its prevention. Hence, the goal to 'preserve you and me from being the beginners of such misery' (389).

That preservation is made possible both through the anticipation of consequence, keeping before one's mind the 'irrevocableness . . . of wrong-doing' (467), and through the cultivation of a self-consciousness or vigilance in relation to the emotions. We have seen the ways in which Eliot's faith in the *'truth of feeling'* underpins the religious tolerance of *Scenes of Clerical Life*. Similarly, in *Adam Bede* the sectarian difference between Dinah and Mr Irwine causes no disturbance because, as Adam observes with Feuerbachian wisdom, 'It isn't notions sets people doing the right thing – it's feelings' (180). It is not her Methodist creed that gives such power to Dinah's preaching, but rather the fact that she speaks so 'directly from her own emotions' (28). Eliot's second novel does, however, place far greater stress on the conviction that morality depends not just on emotion but on 'the regulation of feeling by intellect' (*SCW*, 144). In this, Eliot draws on Spinoza's notion that man lives in 'bondage' in so far as he fails 'to govern or restrain the emotions', and that feelings need to be mediated through the intellect for 'a passion ceases to be a passion as soon as we form a clear and distinct idea of it'.[4] This is exactly the scrutiny that Mr Irwine urges on the vengeful Adam, when he says: 'Don't suppose I can't enter into the anguish that drives you into this state of revengeful hatred: but think of this: if you were to obey your passion – for it *is* a passion, and you deceive yourself in calling it justice – it may be with you precisely as it has been with Arthur; nay, worse; your passion might lead you yourself into a horrible crime' (423). Adam is ethically liberated, in Spinoza's terms, when he learns to interrogate his emotions and to 'dread the violence of his own feelings' (464).

With this stress on the unpitying nature of consequence, *Adam Bede* offers none of the consolation of 'recovery' that is found in 'Mr Gilfil's Love-Story'. And in keeping with Eliot's long-held desire 'to fire away at the doctrine of Compensation' (II, 258), Eliot shares Adam's indignation at Arthur's 'self-soothing attempt' to repair his wrong by exiling himself from Hayslope: 'The time's past for that, sir. A man should make sacrifices to keep clear of doing wrong; sacrifices won't undo it when it's done' (466). Similarly, though it is clear that Adam's education in the transforming 'knowledge' of feeling (509) has come about through Hetty's tragedy, there is no complacent sense of *quid pro quo*:

> That is a base and selfish, even a blasphemous, spirit, which rejoices and is thankful over the past evil that has blighted or crushed another, because it has been made a source of unforeseen good to ourselves. Adam could never cease to mourn over that mystery of human sorrow which had been brought so close to him: he could never thank God for another's misery. And if I were capable of that narrow-sighted joy in Adam's behalf, I should still know he was not the man to feel it for himself: he would have shaken his head at such a sentiment, and said, 'Evil's evil, and sorrow's sorrow, and you can't alter its nature by wrapping it up in other words. Other folks were not created for my sake, that I should think all square when things turn out well for me.'
>
> (529)

III

The more complex ethical landscape of *Adam Bede*, then, reveals the inadequacy of Eliot's conception of sympathetic relationship in *Scenes of Clerical Life*. If 'truth of feeling' is, as we have seen, more problematic and requires self-reflexive regulation and discipline, so, too, the 'presupposition of likeness' is recognised as no longer a firm basis for that contemplation of the other, which Feuerbach argued was the essence of religion. In her essay 'Evangelical Teaching: Dr Cumming', Eliot had acknowledged the danger of making the self the reference point for engagement with the other. For this reason, she condemned Cumming for his inclination to restrict tolerance and liberality 'within a certain circle', to Christians only: 'the love thus taught is the love of the *clan*, which is the correlative of antagonism to the rest of mankind' (*SCW*, 159). She concluded that the encouragement of generosity only toward the familiar or the same 'may demand a tribute of love, but it gives a charter to hatred; it may enjoin charity, but it fosters uncharitableness' (*SCW*, 159). She explores these issues further in *Adam Bede* in her depiction of a closed and exclusive community. In the world of Hayslope, where a person is judged according to whether he is a 'this-country-man' (341), there is a correspondingly profound xenophobia, to be seen, for example, in Mr Craig's account of the pitiful French army: 'Why it's a sure thing – and there's them ' 'ull bear witness to 't – as i' one regiment where there was one man a-missing, they put the regimentals on a big monkey, and they fit him as the shell fits the walnut, and you couldn't tell the monkey from the mounseers!' (523). A more benign version of the same sentiment is evident, too, in the community's reaction to Dinah, who is subject to constant suspicion and antagonism as an outsider from distant Snowfield.

In this second novel, Eliot suggests that the desire for recognition must be relinquished in favour of the capacity to imagine, and this becomes for her a gauge of goodness. The moral vacuity of Hetty, for example, stems in part from the fact that there is 'not much room for her thoughts to travel in the narrow circle of her imagination' (335). Arthur Donnithorne suffers, similarly, from an imaginative and moral impoverishment. In his compulsion to think well of himself, he is incapable of the moral speculation which might save him from wrong-doing: 'He could no more believe that he should so fall in his own esteem than that he should break both legs and go on crutches all the rest of his life. He couldn't imagine himself in that position – it was too odious, too unlike him' (139). And when that self-transcendence is violently forced upon him in his confrontation with Adam, it is an epiphanic moment:

> The discovery that Adam loved Hetty was a shock which made him for the moment see himself in the light of Adam's indignation, and regard Adam's suffering as not merely a consequence, but an element of his error. The words of hatred and contempt – the first he had ever heard in his life – seemed like scorching missiles that were making ineffaceable scars on him. All screening self-excuse, which rarely falls quite away while others respect us, forsook him for an instant, and he stood face to face with the first great irrevocable evil he had ever committed.   (300)

Arthur's failure is all the more stark when he is compared with his mentor, Mr Irwine, who demonstrates consistently his capacity to enter imaginatively into the other's world. When he hears Will Maskery's criticism of him, he refuses the urging of others to take action against him, and accepts instead that the zealous Will has a legitimate point: 'I *am* a lazy fellow, and get terribly heavy in my saddle; not to mention that I'm always spending more than I can afford in bricks and mortar, so that I get savage at a lame beggar when he asks me for sixpence. Those poor lean cobblers, who think they can help to regenerate mankind by setting out to preach in the morning twilight before they begin their day's work, may well have a poor opinion of me' (64).

Irwine's moral imagination, then, depends on his capacity to shift perspective, and that capacity is underscored structurally in the novel by the shifting point of view of the narrator: 'See the difference between the impression a man makes on you when you walk by his side in familiar talk, or look at him in his home, and the figure he makes when seen from a lofty historical level, or even in the eyes of a critical neighbour who thinks of him as an embodied system or opinion rather than as a man' (68). In *Scenes of Clerical Life* there is little effort made by the narrator to see the world through the eyes of the 'guilty' characters. Scarcely a paragraph is given in each tale to understanding the Countess's self-centredness, Captain Wybrow's emotional irresponsibility or Robert Dempster's brutality. In stark contrast, in *Adam Bede* almost as much attention is given to Arthur's sense of himself and his actions as to Adam's, as the weight of consideration constantly shifts between the two through the fulcrum of their desire for Hetty.

This imaginative capacity to de-centre the self is explored in far greater detail, as we shall see, in *Middlemarch*. In *Adam Bede*, though, Eliot suggests it requires a flexibility that is easier for the less egotistical characters like Dinah and Irwine, both of whom have habits of self-reflexivity, but that is hard learned by those who cling to rigid maxims and an unyielding sense of self to regulate their world. Those who labour unbendingly under 'the yoke of traditional impressions' (413) are incapable of true compassion, as we see in the unforgiving 'severity' of the 'mild' Martin Poyser and his father when they learn of Hetty's disgrace:

> The sense of family dishonour was too keen, even in the kind-hearted Martin Poyser the younger, to leave room for any compassion towards Hetty. He and his father were simple-minded farmers, proud of their untarnished character, proud that they came of a family which had held up its head and paid its way as far back as its name was in the parish register; and Hetty had brought disgrace on them all – disgrace that could never be wiped out. That was the all-conquering feeling in the mind both of father and son – the scorching sense of disgrace, which neutralised all other sensibility. (413)

It is only through the severe lessons of his father's death and Hetty's tragedy that Adam comes to understand the need to consider 'what other people's lives are or might be' (509). The shift in Adam from a simpler, self-confident and self-referential moral universe to the recognition of the need for a more complex blend of discipline, flexibility and imagination reflects the development from Eliot's 'first bit of art' in *Scenes* to the more challenging conception of *Adam Bede*.

5

'A widening psychology':
The Mill on the Floss

I

Adam Bede was a publishing triumph – the work that established George Eliot as both a '*popular*' and a 'great author' (III, 33). Its success was doubly welcome, for not only did it bring a new level of financial security for Eliot, but it provided her with the kind of 'warmly expressed sympathy which only popularity can win', and of which, she confessed to her publisher, she was 'much in need' (III, 6). As well, however, it brought new fears, creating for the first time the pressure of 'immense expectation' (III, 270), and making the writing process for Eliot 'a matter of more anxiety than ever' (III, 185).

Adam Bede was finished in November 1858. Only six weeks later, while still dealing with proofs, Eliot was chafing to begin a new project: 'I have not yet made up my mind what my next story is to be, but I must not lie fallow any longer when the new year is come' (II, 513). True to her word, on 12 January, her journal reveals, planning for *The Mill on the Floss* was under way: 'We went into town today, and looked in the Annual Register for cases of *inundation*.'[1] However, her progress was not unproblematic. Eliot soon found herself unable to face her new project, in the grip of the 'same demon' who tried 'to get hold of [her] again whenever an old work is dismissed and a new one is being meditated'.[2] She took refuge in the distraction of a less demanding proposal, as she was to do on a number of similar occasions throughout her fiction-writing career. Feeling 'too stupid for more important work',[3] she put aside *The Mill on the Floss* and began work on the strange and disturbing story 'The Lifted Veil'.

With its continental setting and its gothic concerns with clairvoyance, murder plots and experimental blood transfusions on the dead, 'The Lifted Veil' seems far removed from Eliot's usual focus on prosaic, provincial life. It is true that there are some points of reference between the protagonist, Latimer, and his creator. Latimer's morbid and 'self-distrusting' desire for sympathy, for example, has echoes of Eliot's own self-doubting and needy character. His gift, or 'curse', of second sight is likened to the visionary capacity of the artist. And his constant perception of others' negative opinions is reminiscent of Eliot's bleaker suspicions about the envy, hatred and malice of 'false and narrow-hearted friends' (III, 124). But perhaps the only significant way in which the tale anticipated the novel to come was in its understanding of the psychological hold that a hard and narrow character might exercise on a sensitive, approval-seeking one: 'there is no tyranny more complete than that which a self-centred negative nature exercises over a morbidly sensitive nature perpetually craving sympathy and support'.[4] The tyranny which this prefigured, of course, was that of the self-righteous and unyielding Tom Tulliver over his loving sister Maggie: 'Her brother was the human being of whom she had been most afraid, from her childhood upwards: afraid with that fear which springs in us when we love one who is inexorable, unbending, unmodifiable – with a mind that we can never mould ourselves upon, and yet that we cannot endure to alienate from us' (*Mill* 483).

Before Eliot had even finished her '*jeu de melancolie*', she was promising her publisher that her new story would 'be a novel as long as Adam Bede, and a sort of companion picture of provincial life' (III, 41). The ways in which the two novels could be regarded as 'companion' pieces are clear enough. *The Mill on the Floss* shows the same preoccupation with rural England, the same commitment to a faithful representation of the 'commonplace', and the Tullivers and Dodsons, 'irradiated by no sublime principles, no romantic visions, no active, self-renouncing faith', are clearly akin to the Poysers of *Adam Bede* in representing 'the most prosaic form of human life' (272). However, if *The Mill on the Floss* was, indeed, another 'close and detailed picture[ ] of English life' (III, 187), it also took Eliot's work a step closer to the autobiographical.

The trajectory towards a more personal fiction is evident in her first three major works. While *Scenes of Clerical Life* drew sketchily on the character of local figures from childhood, and, as we have seen, the portraits of Adam and Dinah in *Adam Bede* were inspired by Eliot's father and aunt, *The Mill on the Floss* provided in the character of Maggie the nearest approach to a self-portrait that Eliot ever produced, and it explored, in the relationship between Maggie and Tom, aspects of her own vexed relationship with her brother Isaac. It was an issue of particular currency and poignancy for Eliot, for even as she was contemplating those early chapters, she received a cruel reminder of the damage done by her brother's implacable opposition to her de facto relationship with George Lewes, and his subsequent prohibition on any contact by the Evans family with Eliot. After nearly two years' silence, Eliot's favourite sister, Chrissey, knowing that she was dying, defied Isaac and wrote to Eliot 'regretting that she had ever ceased to write' (III, 23) to her prodigal sister. It was a letter, Eliot confessed, that 'ploughed up my heart' (III, 23), and her distress was compounded by Chrissey's death three weeks later, without Eliot having seen her sister once more.

Eliot's letters at this time testify to her deep personal involvement with the story she was telling in *The Mill on the Floss*. She confided to her close friend Barbara Bodichon that as the narrative progressed towards Maggie's inevitable demise, 'I have been crying myself almost into stupor, over visions of sorrow' (III, 271). And she later admitted to Blackwood that she had been so beguiled 'by my love of my subject' that the first two volumes acquired an epic breadth, while the third volume seemed rushed and wanting in 'proportionate fullness', a fact which she felt she should 'always regret' (III, 317).

II

Above all, the more autobiographical element in *The Mill on the Floss* led Eliot into greater empathy and psychological inwardness with her heroine, Maggie Tulliver. Maggie's efforts to manage a hostile and unsupportive world had an intimate relevance for her author, and the heroine's fitful struggle with the need for resignation mirrored the conflict closest to Eliot's own heart. So, inspired by her reading of Thomas à Kempis, Maggie recognises the wisdom of acquiescence: 'Our life is determined for us – and it makes the mind very free when we give up wishing, and only think of bearing what is laid upon us, and doing what is given to us to do' (302). Eliot, likewise, sought liberation through the acknowledgement of 'the need for *absolute* resignation' which she repeated to herself like a mantra: 'Never to beat and bruise one's wings against the inevitable but to throw the whole force of one's soul towards the achievement of some possible better, is the brief heading that need never be changed, however often the chapter of more special rules may have to be re-written. I use that summary every day, and could not live without repeating it to myself' (IV, 499). Yet, just as Maggie's embrace of this wisdom was tenuous and imperfect, Eliot, too, recognised the daunting nature of the challenge: 'I know through the experience of more than two thirds of my life', she wrote, 'the immense difficulty, to a passionate nature, of attaining more than a fitful exercise of such resignation, and especially I know . . . the blighting effect on the sympathies of an unsatisfied yearning for a supreme engrossing affection' (IV, 499).

This intimate understanding in *The Mill on the Floss* brings about an important shift in perspective, causing Eliot to revisit and reassess the categories of moral success and failure. In her two previous works, those characters who, like Arthur Donnithorne and Hetty, are unable to negotiate and temper their desires are the moral failures. In contrast, those who struggle with, and largely succeed in, mastering their passions are the moral heroes. Thus, for instance, Seth and Dinah lead exemplary lives, while Adam Bede's moral triumph depends on his learning to use the 'awful' spectre of remorse to ensure the regulation and restraint of his emotions. In *The Mill on the Floss* this reading of the possibility, and the desirability, of such self-regulation is challenged. Tom Tulliver is clearly the character in this novel who most closely resembles the Spinozan ideal of 'regulation of feeling by intellect' evident in the earlier texts. He never exposes himself up to feel that 'bitter sense of the irrevocable' (65) which is almost an everyday experience for Maggie. A figure of great determination and restraint, his is a character 'at unity with itself – that performs what it intends, subdues every counteracting impulse, and has no visions beyond the distinctly possible' (310). Yet now Eliot insists on the more disturbing elements of self-control. Such a character, she recognises, is 'made strong by its very negations' (310), and it is clear that the corollary of Tom's strength is his rigidity. His self-assurance is born of a narrowness which leaves him unable to respond, for example, to the moral complexity of Maggie's suggestion that sometimes wrong-doing arises from feelings that Tom would 'be better for, if [he] had them' (347), and he remains undisturbed throughout by 'that complex, fragmentary, doubt-provoking knowledge which we call truth' (456).

Maggie, in contrast, is the very antithesis of any Spinozan ideal, repeatedly failing to restrain or regulate her passions. There is a 'terrible cutting truth' (393) in Tom's judgement that she is 'always in extremes', and that she is lacking in 'judgment and self-command' (392). However, Eliot refuses to cast Maggie as a moral failure. Instead, she calls for an expansion of ethical categories to take account of an increasing psychological complexity which recognises the limits of individual sovereignty: 'If the ethics of art do not admit the truthful presentation of a character essentially noble but liable to great error – error that is anguish to its own nobleness – *then*, it seems to me, the ethics of art are too narrow, and must be widened to correspond with a widening psychology' (III, 318). It is within the terms of this 'widening psychology' that *The Mill on the Floss* explores the ways in which such self-control is less possible, less probable and – most radically – less desirable, than Eliot's previous fiction suggests.

If this third work is a 'companion picture' to *Adam Bede*'s view of provincial life, it is nonetheless one with a much more acute sense of the 'oppressive narrowness' (272) of its world. The 'prosaic' quality of its 'old-fashioned family life' is no longer quite so quaint or innocuous, and the clear-sighted scrutiny of the failings of individual characters is matched here by a willingness to read individual short-comings more contextually in terms of broader, systemic failure. In this respect, a contrast between Hetty and Maggie is instructive. Hetty's involvement with Arthur Donnithorne is construed within the terms of *Adam Bede* almost entirely as a personal failure, the foolish overreaching of a vain and shallow nature, in a way that largely effaces broader considerations such as the drudgery of her life at Hall Farm, and the demeaning ambiguity of her position as neither simply a servant nor confidently a member of the family. In contrast, Maggie's dissatisfaction with her world, which makes her so vulner-able to the temptation of Stephen Guest, is understood more broadly as a product of the narrowness of her world. The inclination to judge Hetty is overturned with Maggie, replaced with a warning to the reader against precisely such censure:

> You could not live among such people; you are stifled for want of an outlet towards something beautiful, great, or noble; you are irritated with these dull men and women, as a kind of population out of keep-ing with the earth on which they live – with this rich plain where the great river flows for ever onward, and links the small pulse of the old English town with the beatings of the world's mighty heart. A vigor-ous superstition, that lashes its gods or lashes its own back, seems to be more congruous with the mystery of the human lot, than the mental condition of these emmet-like Dodsons and Tullivers. (272)

Eliot's account of the first encounter between Maggie and Stephen, accordingly, makes it perfectly clear that Maggie's intense susceptibility is born of her impoverished existence:

> In poor Maggie's highly-strung, hungry nature – just come away from a third-rate schoolroom, with all its jarring sounds and petty round of tasks – these apparently trivial causes had the effect of rousing and exalting her imagination in a way that was mysterious to herself. It was not that she thought distinctly of Mr Stephen Guest, or dwelt on the indications that he looked at her with admiration; it was rather that she felt the half-remote presence of a world of love and beauty and delight, made up of vague, mingled images from all the poetry and romance she had ever read, or had ever woven in her dreamy reveries. (385)

The longing for a male saviour has been with Maggie since childhood, and in this she is representative of women more generally, faced with the reality that men 'have power, and can do something in the world', and women 'can do nothing [but] submit to those that can' (347). So, for example, when Maggie's initial fantasy of escape to an admiring and congenial community with the gypsies founders in the face of the squalid reality of their camp, she immediately resorts to an alternative fantasy, the specifically gendered longing for some version of a white knight: 'If her father would come by in the gig and take her up! Or even if Jack the Giantkiller, or Mr Greatheart, or St George who slew the dragon on the halfpennies, would happen to pass on that way!' (112).This way of seeing the world leaves Maggie torn in later life between two suitors, facing a hopelessly inadequate choice between Philip and Stephen. And between the poles of the feminised invalid and the shallow Lothario lies the dreadful spectre of Maggie attempting to fend for herself in a 'dreary schoolroom' as a teacher: 'It is with me as I used to think it would be with the poor uneasy white bear I saw at the show. I thought he must have got so stupid with the habit of turning backwards and forwards in that narrow space, that he would keep doing it if they set him free' (373). In all, this is a world which *induces* Maggie's tragedy through the poverty of choice that it provides.[5]

If, then, *The Mill on the Floss* explores the social context which makes intelligent choice and rational self-control seem less possible, it also examines the psychological imperatives thrown up by the unconscious which make the achievement of self-regulation seem less probable. At the simplest level, the novel is charged with a sense of forces which undermine any faith in the sovereignty of the will. Violence and madness – real, incipient or feared – haunt the text. It is not only Maggie who repeatedly rushes into impulsive action. Her father, too, is capable of 'paroxysms of rage' in which he beats his horse (281) and, in a final and decisive 'mad outbreak', he attacks Wakem (357). Even the law-abiding Mrs Glegg is reputed to have a temper which might well 'carry her off her mind' (97). In addition, the vulnerability of good and rational intention to more anarchic forces is expressed on more than one occasion through the images of 'small demons' which take 'possession of Maggie's soul' (98). There are 'passions at war' in Maggie which lead her into self-defeating eruptions like the hair-cutting incident and the pushing of Lucy into the mud. An even more disturbing image of a lack of control was first added to, then deleted from, the manuscript by Eliot, in which she speculated that an ordinary girl like Maggie 'may still hold forces within her as the living plant-seed does, which will make a way for themselves, often in a shattering, violent manner'.[6]

Less dramatically, but no less effectively, the notion of a sovereign will is further undermined by the stress in the text on dreaming and forgetting. The novel, of course, is framed by dream. The narrator's opening description of Dorlcote Mill in Chapter I comes to him as a vision as he dozes by the fire and the final catastrophic flood of the closing chapter has all the unreality of dream: 'Maggie felt nothing, thought of nothing, but that she had suddenly passed away from that life which she had been dreading: it was the transition of death, without its agony – and she was alone in the darkness with God. The whole thing had been so rapid – so dream-like – that the threads of ordinary association were broken' (517). And throughout the work Maggie spends a good part of her life in 'Waking Dreams' (276), subject to 'moments of mental wandering' (293) and 'exasperating acts of forgetfulness' (144) – to forms of vacancy, amnesia and unconsciousness which thwart intention – until the final lapse, 'the partial sleep of thought' which facilitates her 'hardly conscious' flight with Stephen (467). In such a scheme of things, the conscious deliberation and vigilance, which Eliot represented as underpinning ethical behaviour in *Adam Bede*, seem limited. Intention and will can be undermined by more powerful forces, and the fear of consequences, which had seemed such a powerful restraint, is recognised in the more relative terms that Eliot had suggested in her essay on the poet Edward Young as 'only one form of egoism, which will hardly stand against half-a-dozen other forms of egoism bearing down upon it'.[7]

The characters seem acutely afraid of a lack of control in their lives and they resort to various strategies in their attempts to redress such feelings of vulnerability. Most notably, Maggie turns to the teachings of Thomas à Kempis in her search for the 'strength, and conquest' (290) which might provide a bulwark against the 'volcanic upheavings' (293) of desire and dissatisfaction. Eliot offers an astute diagnosis, however, of the pitfalls of Maggie's desire for a 'key' to 'self-conquest'. She recognises the wilfulness and exaggeration of Maggie's excessive humility, reminiscent of her own 'ostentatious affectation of humility' (I, 24). She also acknowledges the sense of gratification in Maggie's self-denial, which causes her to relish Tom's harshness, for that 'is the path we all like when we set out on our abandonment of egoism – the path of martyrdom and endurance, where the palm-branches grow, rather than the steep highway of tolerance, just allowance, and self- blame, where there are no leafy honours to be gathered and worn' (293). And she is alert to the paradoxical indulgence which can form one aspect of renunciation. This self-gratification is betrayed by the sensuous imagery with which she describes Maggie's discovery of Thomas à Kempis. Maggie finds herself shocked by a 'strange thrill of awe', as if 'wakened in the night by a strain of solemn music' (289), and she is drawn to the teachings by the 'long lingering vibrations of such a voice' (292). Indeed, the paradox is further underscored by the way in which the musical imagery anticipates the seductive resonance of Stephen Guest's singing. Most importantly of all, Eliot understands that the dynamics of repression virtually guarantee the counter-productive element of such determined and relentless efforts at self-regulation. Although Maggie greets her discovery of à Kempis as 'the suddenly apprehended solution of a problem' (290), Philip accurately predicts the outcome, when he warns Maggie that 'every rational satisfaction of your nature that you deny now, will assault you like a savage appetite' (329).

The Dodson sisters also attempt to regulate their worlds by evoking a complex series of strictures through codes of dress and domestic ownership. Mrs Glegg, for example, conforms to a strict hierarchy of costume with clear distinctions between the good and the functional: 'Mrs Glegg had doubtless the glossiest and crispest brown curls in her drawers, as well as curls in various degrees of fuzzy laxness; but to look out on the weekday world from under a crisp and glossy front, would be to introduce a most dreamlike and unpleasant confusion between the sacred and the secular' (53). Uncle

Pullet, similarly, orchestrates the suspense surrounding the production of the musical snuff-box, as one who 'had a programme for all great social occasions, and in this way fenced himself in from much painful confusion and perplexing freedom of will' (93). Tom is the very model of 'the man of maxims', who attempts to 'lace up' his world in 'formulas' (498). Mr Tulliver also craves certainty, longing to 'wrap things up' (22) in a world of systems – of law, genetics and language – which might render the world predictable and controllable. Even the preoccupation with inflicting punishment, which is shared by both Tom and his father, might be read as an effort to square the books with Fate – a retrospective attempt to assert mastery over events which have previously eluded their control.

However, every such effort at mastery seems doomed to failure. All the 'treasures' which make the world 'quite comprehensible' (276) for Mrs Tulliver are sold from under her with the family's bankruptcy, leaving her 'bewildered in this empty life' (276). Tom's 'keen and clear' vision is exposed as hopelessly inadequate in his moment of epiphany with Maggie in the rowing-boat. And Mr Tulliver's faith in systems is defeated by the vagaries of the 'crossing o' breeds' (12), the chicanery of the law, a 'sort of cock-fight' (155) he is destined to lose, and the enduring perplexities and 'tricks' (9) of language. He dies with only 'broken words', vexed to the end by 'the painful riddle of this world' (359). In all, there is no protection against the uncertainties of desire and impulse, which, as Philip recognises, will always exceed our determination to understand and regulate: 'I don't think any of the strongest effects our natures are susceptible of can ever be explained. We can neither detect the process by which they are arrived at, nor the mode in which they act on us' (305).

The possibilities for 'self-conquest' seem even more remote given a whole vocabulary stressing the existence of overwhelming and irresistible forces. In particular, the characters are swept away by the twin tides of the river and music. The former suggests the more destructive forces of aggression and vengeance. The latter connotes the equally disruptive forces of desire, with the unsettling, preconscious power of rhythm, recalling Julia Kristeva's theories about the disruptive power of the semiotic, evident in Maggie's acute susceptibility to music and 'rhythmic memories' (293). Both forces are impervious to persuasion or reason – neither can be addressed. So, the river itself is not only 'deaf' (7) but it also creates 'a great curtain of sound' that brings a 'drowsy deafness' to those who have commerce with it (8). And, similarly, 'the inexorable power of sound' (416) that plays on Maggie's soul as she listens to music leaves her trying 'in vain to go on with her work' (416), and finding herself instead 'borne along by a wave too strong for her' (418).

III

Eliot's empathy with Maggie leads, in a departure from her position in *Adam Bede*, to her most radical insight – that the Spinozan ideal of self-regulation may, in fact, be undesirable or, more accurately, may come at too high a price. Such a recognition is played out in the contest between Tom and Maggie, a struggle between 'incompleteness' and multiplicity, the drama of which is encapsulated in the confrontation over Maggie's secret meetings with Philip: 'Tom had his terrible clutch on her conscience and her deepest dread: she writhed under the demonstrable truth of the character he had given to her conduct, and yet her whole soul rebelled against it as unfair from its incompleteness' (344). Tom at one extreme is reconciled to partiality and narrowness. He feels nothing, for example, of the dread that Maggie experiences when Mr Tulliver enjoins the two to immortalise the family hatred for Waken by writing an oath of vengeance in the family bible. With his faith in the simple justice of an eye for an eye, he eliminates the vulnerability of more complex forms of human interaction. He depends on no one and insulates himself from painful expectations by his renunciation of all that 'did not present itself to him as a right to be demanded' (225). He has no hesitation in the face of the loss of possibility that inevitably comes with the 'labour of choice' (151), because for him choice brings closure, clarity and purpose: 'Now, then, Maggie, there are but two courses for you to take; either you vow solemnly to me, with your hand on my father's Bible, that you will never have another meeting or speak another word in private with Philip Wakem, or you refuse, and I tell my father everything. . . . Choose!' (342).

There is only ever room for one version of reality for Tom, yet such certainty comes at the cost of damage to the self, as Eliot once graphically suggested: 'Do you never think of those Caribs', she wrote to her friend Cara Bray, 'who by dint of flattening their foreheads can manage to see perpendicularly above them without so much as lifting their heads? There are some good people who remind me of them. They see everything so clearly and with so little trouble, but at the price of sad self-mutilation' (I, 192). And that suggestion of self-harm is echoed by Philip Waken to Maggie in his definition of self-conquest as 'the blinding and deafening of yourself to all but one train of impressions' (335). Tom has no time for Maggie's 'opium' of refashioning her world, imagining 'it was all different' (48). The fantasies that Maggie generates to alleviate her distress are nothing to him but 'nonsense', for which he has 'profound contempt' (99). Tom guards against indefiniteness by rendering all things quantifiable – debts are repaid and grievances redressed. His obstacles are 'substantial' and his conquests 'definite' (308).

Given the flux and volatility of Maggie's world, it is not surprising that she longs for some aspects of Tom's certainty and lives in awe of his conviction that 'his own motives as well as actions were good' (344). He, like Stephen later, holds out the promise of a 'firm arm' – the temptation of 'the presence of strength' which, Eliot contends, meets a 'continual want of the imagination' in most women (408). Eliot's journals give a further clue to her perception that the world of fixity and clarity has a seductive appeal. In her Recollections of Ilfracombe she writes:

> I never before longed so much to know the names of things. . . . The desire is part of the tendency that is now constantly growing in me to escape from all vagueness & inaccuracy into the daylight of distinct vivid ideas. The mere fact of naming an object tends to give definiteness to our conception of it – we have then a sign which at once calls up in our minds the distinctive qualities which mark out for us that particular object from all others.[8]

Yet just as she recognises the appeal, she repudiates the inherent distortion and 'incompleteness' of such a view. Language, no less than life, is fraught with complexity and multiplicity, and it cannot be rendered mono-dimensional without loss and distortion:

> one word stands for many things, and many words for one thing; the subtle shades of meaning, and still subtler echoes of association, make language an instrument which scarcely anything short of genius can wield with definiteness and certainty. Suppose, then, that the effort which has been again and again made to construct a universal language on a rational basis has at length succeeded, and that you have a language which has no uncertainty, no whims of idiom, no cumbrous forms, no fitful shimmer of many-hued significance, no hoary archaisms 'familiar with forgotten years' – a patent deodorized and nonresonant language, which effects the purpose of communication as perfectly and rapidly as algebraic signs. Your language may be a

perfect medium of expression to science, but will never express *life*, which is a great deal more than science. With the anomalies and inconveniences of historical language, you will have parted with its music and its passion, with its vital qualities as an expression of individual character, with its subtle capabilities of wit, with everything that gives it power over the imagination. (*SCW*, 283)

Revealingly, where Tom feels 'embarrassed alarm' (136) at the doubleness of Mr Stelling's puns, Maggie calmly recognises that words 'may mean several things – almost every word does' (145), and Eliot similarly notes that speech can be 'at once sincere and deceptive' (336).

While Maggie is briefly tempted to aspire to a world of certainty in her single-minded pursuit of 'self-conquest', the very qualities which mark her out as the heroine guarantee that she will not succeed. She is afflicted – *and* blessed – with the 'burthen of larger wants than others seem to feel' (288), and although there are moments when she envies the 'easily satisfied ignorance' of her brother, it is precisely in her yearning for 'something, whatever it was, that was greatest and best on this earth' (208) that any hope of moral progress lies. Tom's 'unimaginative, unsympathetic' (393) mind merely recreates and reconfirms his world at every turn. His is an endogamous world with a longing for sameness and repetition. His vision is 'unmodifiable' (483); he feels a 'superstitious repugnance to everything exceptional' (340); and, like his father, he has 'no room for new feelings' (393). As with all prejudice, Tom's thought is endlessly self-replicating, leaving him 'imprisoned' within the very narrow 'limits of his own nature' (500).

In contrast, Maggie represents not the repetitive, but the disruptive, force upon which moral and social evolution depends. Unlike Tom's closed and xenophobic world, Maggie's is receptive to the 'possibility of a word or a look from a stranger to keep alive the sense of human brotherhood' (435). Her thirst for knowledge is another aspect of that endogamous spirit which puts her at odds with those around her. When she recommends her prized books to the mill-hand Luke, for example, she does so on the grounds that they 'would tell you all about the different sorts of people in the world, and if you didn't understand the readings, the pictures would help you – they show the looks and ways of the people, and what they do' (30). Luke's fearful response encapsulates the circumscription of his world: 'I can't do wi' knowin' so many things besides my work. That's what brings folks to the gallows – knowin' everything but what they'n got to get their bread by' (30). And in this he is, as Maggie accurately observes, 'like my brother Tom' (30).[9]

Her 'longing and wishing' keeps her 'thoroughly alive' (303), for, as Eliot has argued in 'The Lifted Veil', the soul has an absolute need for 'something hidden and uncertain for the maintenance of that doubt and hope and effort which are the breath of life'.[10] It is only because she lives a life 'vivid and intense enough' that she is able to experience a 'wide fellow-feeling with all that is human' (498). Thus, in turning her back on the kind of world represented by Tom, in refusing the 'cowardice' of 'seeking safety in negations' (329), Maggie embodies the possibility of moral progress. It is only this 'enlarged life' (502) which can challenge the 'oppressive narrowness' (272) of Maggie's world. In this sense, the very 'susceptibility' (327) which leaves Maggie prey to the irrationalities of desire, and hence undermines the sovereignty of her will, generates the openness and receptivity through which the 'onward tendency of human things' (273) can counter the static reinscriptions of Tom's world. Eliot had faith in an evolutionary progress, contending that 'the world gets on step by step towards brave clearness and honesty' (III, 227), and confident that 'the tendency towards good in human nature has a force which no creed can utterly counteract, and which ensures the ultimate triumph of that tendency over all dogmatic perversion' (SCW, 170). However, such optimism was tempered by her conviction that the process was both slow and painful: 'the struggle between Antigone and Creon represents that struggle between elemental tendencies and established laws by which the outer life of man is gradually and painfully being brought into harmony with his inward needs' (SCW, 245). In The Mill on the Floss, then, Maggie is the abrasive and oppositional presence who unsettles the world of self-replication – the 'martyr or victim' on whose suffering 'every historical advance of mankind' (273) is built.

IV

Maggie's status as a martyr to progress has been particularly problematic for feminist critics. Ironically, given my argument in this chapter, feminist anger with George Eliot has often been based on the contention that her fiction is not autobiographical or empathetic enough – that having achieved so much in her life, she denied such satisfaction to her heroines. This grievance is crystallised in Elaine Showalter's neat summation: 'The legends attached to Brontë and

Eliot in their lives were reversed in the heroines of their novels. Brontë's Jane Eyre is the heroine of fulfilment; Eliot's Maggie Tulliver is the heroine of renunciation.'[11] Françoise Basch, similarly, lamented that for Eliot renunciation 'is the essence of virtue; and it is the chief moral reality implied by her whole outlook'.[12] And in an earlier work, I, too, have been disappointed by a sense that Eliot 'consistently values the self-sacrificing, passive, acquiescent qualities of her female characters against the self-assertive, combative, and rebellious impulses, upholding Fedalma's claim in *The Spanish Gypsy*: ' "We must be patient in our prison-house, / And find our space in loving" '.[13]

Perhaps this sense of disappointment or betrayal in Eliot's failure to 'reward' her heroines finds particular focus in the discussion of Maggie Tulliver because in *The Mill on the Floss* our hopes for a kind of summary literary justice are raised by Maggie's protest on behalf of the underdog in *Corinne*: 'I'm determined to read no more books where the blond-haired women carry away all the happiness. I should begin to have a prejudice against them. If you could give me some story, now, where the dark woman triumphs, it would restore the balance' (332). Such hopes for a triumphant heroine, however, are born out of political rather than aesthetic considerations, and in this regard are reminiscent, as Toril Moi has pointed out in another context, of the Soviet demand for literary role models: 'Instead of strong, happy tractor drivers and factory workers, we are now, presumably, to demand strong, happy *women* tractor drivers.'[14] In any case, the notion of manipulating the plot to allow the 'dark woman' to triumph runs entirely counter to Eliot's repudiation of any scheme of distributing 'rewards and punishments' according to those 'notions of justice on which the novel-writer [or disappointed feminist critic] would have recommended that the world should be governed if he had been consulted at the creation' (*SCW*, 130).

More importantly, the desire for consolation in some version of a happy ending misses a crucial point. If it is Eliot's scrupulous realism that has provided such a compelling diagnosis of the 'oppressive narrowness' of Maggie's lot, it is only in the abandonment of that realism that Maggie could be 'rewarded' in the end. As the novel itself makes clear, the only realm of happiness for Maggie is fantasy. So, for example, the young Maggie recognises that 'the only way of escaping opprobrium, and being entirely in harmony with circumstances' (104) is through the fantastical scheme of running away to become Queen of the gypsies – and, of course, the test of reality dashes that alternative just as effectively as Tom puts an end to Maggie's earlier make-believe by 'smashing the earwig . . . as a superfluous yet easy means of proving the entire unreality of such a story' (99). For much of her life, Maggie's imagination is her only source of solace, for the 'world outside books was not a happy one' (235).

With this in mind, the implied criticism of Eliot in Showalter's contrast between *Jane Eyre* and *The Mill on the Floss* is more revealing than it first appears. Jane Eyre's 'fulfilment' depends precisely on fantasy. Her happiness-ever-after is achieved not in the socially testing environment of a small town or community, but in the completely asocial retreat of Ferndean. The happiness of her relationship is founded on the doubly fortuitous accidents of Jane's inheritance and Rochester's blinding, both of which arbitrarily serve to bring financial and physical equality to a relationship which has been disturbingly unequal. And the entire tale is founded on a psychological fantasy of the extraordinary and precocious assurance of Jane's ego, which is so markedly at odds with the childhood circumstances which produced it.[15] Such a fantasy is diametrically opposed to Eliot's firm commitment to psychological veracity and 'a widening psychology', which compels the representation of a heroine whose life not only ends tragically, but whose actions are in some ways complicit with that tragedy. More than just a version of her commitment to realism, such veracity was important to her notions of effective critique, for, Eliot was convinced, 'over-zealous champions of women' defeat their own purposes when they argue that women are not damaged by their subjection to 'oppressive laws and restrictions': 'If it were true, then there would be a case in which slavery and ignorance nourished virtue, and so far we should have an argument for the continuation of bondage' (SCW, 185).

It is painfully clear in *The Mill on the Floss* that there are no circumstances in which Maggie can realistically live 'in harmony'. Like Maggie's reading of *The Pirate*, there is no alternative to unhappiness: 'I went on with it in my own head, and I made several endings; but they were all unhappy. I could never make a happy ending out of that beginning' (306). With a similar sense of compulsion, Eliot felt that neither Maggie as the heroine, nor she as the writer, could act out of character. Thus she wrote to her publisher as she was nearing the completion of the novel: 'Jacobi told Jean Paul that unless he altered the denouement of his "Titan", he would withdraw his friendship from him, and I am preparing myself for your lasting enmity on the ground of the tragedy in my third volume. But an unfortunate duck can only lay blue eggs, however much white ones may be in demand' (III, 265).

In the conclusion Eliot has forsworn 'the favourite cant of optimists' – the notion that duty or fate 'looks stern, but all the while has her hands full of sugar-plums, with which she will reward us by and by' (*SCW*, 121). In her commitment to realism there seemed no space for fantastical resolutions or wish-fulfilling rewards. As she argued to Blackwood at the outset of her fiction-writing career: 'Art must be either real and concrete, or ideal and eclectic. Both are good and true in their way, but my stories are of the former kind. I undertake to exhibit nothing as it should be; I only try to exhibit some things as they have been or are' (II, 362). But far from a betrayal, the very distress of the ending is the most telling indictment of a society which has offered the heroine so little outlet, such impoverished choices and such 'false and hollow' (498) moral judgements. The horror of the conclusion lies in the unremitting 'sameness' of Maggie's outlook after her return to St Oggs:

> There is something sustaining in the very agitation that accompanies the first shocks of trouble, just as an acute pain is often a stimulus, and produces an excitement which is transient strength. It is in the slow, changed life that follows – in the time when sorrow has become stale, and has no longer an emotive intensity that counteracts its pain – in the time when day follows day in dull unexpectant sameness, and trial is a dreary routine; – it is then that despair threatens.   (276)

It is a mistake to suggest, as Showalter does, that there is something 'self-destructive' in Maggie's embracing such a fate, and that she is 'the progenitor of a heroine who identifies passivity and renunciation with womanhood'.[16] To begin with, part of the difficulty of Maggie's lot comes from the 'love of independence', which is 'too strong an inheritance and a habit' (493) for her either to accept an invitation to live with Tom, or to fail to endeavour 'to get her bread' (493) in working for Dr Kenn. And Maggie does not undertake renunciation for its own sake. She renounces Stephen out of a sense of loyalty to those she has wronged *and* out of a sense that the relationship would be doomed, for the self-satisfaction involved would be ultimately self-defeating: 'She might as well hope to enjoy walking by maiming her feet, as hope to enjoy an existence in which she set out by maiming the faith and sympathy that were the best organs of her soul' (458). In this sense there is something hard-headed, not mindlessly sacrificial, about Maggie's return to St Ogg's. So, contrary to Françoise Basch's view, this is a renunciation that still has the promise of 'efficacy' (497), or as Felicia Bonaparte has argued: 'renunciation is valuable in so far as it may still have desirable consequences. It is not, therefore – as the religious associations of the word might suggest – a good in itself but a good only if the end it serves is good'.[17]

It is also, one might add, the renunciation of a fate which would be unworthy of the heroine. And in this regard, Eliot is perhaps not entirely true to the standards of her own unflinching realism. In a review of Geraldine Jewsbury's *Constance Herbert*, Eliot criticised the tendency to suggest that 'what duty calls on us to renounce, will invariably prove "not worth keeping" ' (*SCW*, 120). As she points out, were this always the case, 'renunciation would cease to be moral heroism, and would be simply a calculation of prudence' (*SCW*, 120). Although such calculation forms no part of Maggie's thinking, Eliot does seem to hold out some sense of consolation to the reader in the thought that Maggie is well rid of Stephen, when we encounter the whining self-absorption of his final letter: 'Maggie! whose pain can have been like mine? Whose injury is like mine?' (514).

More significantly, having offered us the toughest of visions, the most unflinching of diagnoses, Eliot herself falters in her realism in presenting the denouement.[18] Maggie's death is not so much a punishment, as a form of fantastical euthanasia. Her publisher, John Blackwood, recognised as much in his response to receiving the final instalment of the manuscript: 'The greatest lovers of all ending happily must admit that Providence was kind in removing Maggie. She could not have been happy here' (III, p. 277).

The 'dream-like' flood enables not only the relief of Maggie's escape from the 'stale' sorrow of her fate. It also allows a moment of carnivalesque reversal through which Maggie can take control. In this way, she is finally perceived as 'one who would help to protect, not need to be protected' (516); she reverses the lifetime's power relations in saving Tom; and she redresses the failure of drifting off on the tide in the boat with Stephen by decisively taking the oars and rowing through the torrent. The flood also enables the fantastic punishment of the town, leaving forever the marks of its 'ravages', and recalling Eliot's earlier harshness, which we might read perhaps as displaced, in her assessment of the 'swift river . . . like an angry, destroying god' which swept away the villages on the Rhone:

these dead-tinted, hollow-eyed, angular skeletons of villages on the Rhone oppress me with the feeling that human life – very much of it – is a narrow, ugly, grovelling existence, which even calamity does not elevate, but rather tends to exhibit in all its bare vulgarity of conception; and I have a cruel conviction that the lives these ruins are the traces of, were part of a gross sum of obscure vitality, that will be swept into the same oblivion with the generations of ants and beavers. (*Mill*, 272)

Revealingly, the inadequacy of the concluding fantasy seems to draw attention to itself, almost as though deconstructing its own bad faith. The hopelessly distorting prism of nostalgia, which renders Maggie's and Tom's last embrace as a 'supreme moment' of 'living through again . . . the days when they had clasped their little hands in love, and roamed the daisied fields together' (521), does nothing to counterbalance the truth of that conflict-ridden, unhappy childhood so meticulously documented for more than half the novel.[19] And similarly, the epiphany in which Tom supposedly experiences 'a new revelation to his spirit, of the depths in life, that had lain beyond his vision which he had fancied so keen and clear' (520) is entirely undermined by the repeated stress on the silent, unacknowledged, and so untested, nature of Tom's realisation: 'he was unable to ask a question'; they sit 'mutely gazing at each other'; while thought was busy, 'the lips were silent'; Tom asks 'no question'; and finally offers up only the 'old childish – "Maggsie" ' (520). One is tempted to put this reconciliation, then, to the test of Eliot's own question to Sara Hennell: 'What is anything worth until it is uttered?. . . . Utterance there must be in word or deed to make life of any worth' (I, 279). But perhaps Tom's contrite 'new revelation' is beyond the realm even of fantasy.

Whatever the distortions of the conclusion, however, in *The Mill on the Floss* Eliot has created a work in which both the possibility, and the desirability, of self-conquest are radically called into question and the exogamous spirit of Maggie's receptive temperament holds out the only hope of social and ethical progress.

6

The Mystery of Otherness: *Silas Marner*

I

George Eliot left England for Italy within forty-eight hours of despatching the proofs of *The Mill on the Floss*. She had looked forward to this trip for a number of years, not, as she pointed out with characteristic earnestness, in 'the hope of immediate pleasure' but 'rather with the hope of the new elements it would bring to my culture'.[1] She was also anxious to leave the country before her new novel appeared, determined to escape the 'chorus, pleasant or harsh' (III, 270) which would greet it. Her anxiety to escape the critical storm arose in part from her sense that there was a 'very strong disposition' to see *The Mill on the Floss* as a 'falling off' after her triumph with *Adam Bede* (III, 270). But this was also the first book to appear after Eliot's true identity had become public knowledge and hence her pseudonym could no longer protect her from the censure arising from her unorthodox relationship with George Lewes.

The trip lasted for three months and was, in Eliot's estimation, both delightful and epochal – 'one of those journeys that seem to divide one's life in two by the new ideas they suggest and the new veins of interest they open' (III, 311). This division in Eliot's life was marked out in personal as well as creative terms. She returned to London to give up her 'wandering life', establish a household for the first time with Lewes's oldest son Charles, and 'buy pots and kettles and keep a dog' (II, 339). She also returned resolved to take a new direction in her fiction. Inspired by Florence, and prompted by a suggestion from Lewes, Eliot was determined to move away from her previous studies of English provincial life, set in the recent past, and undertake an historical romance based on the life of the fifteenth-century Italian monk, Girolamo Savonarola.

In the event, the writing of Eliot's Italian novel was to give way to two other projects. The first was 'a slight Tale',[2] called 'Mr. David Faux, confectioner' (and subsequently published as 'Brother Jacob'), a minor piece which Eliot used to ease her way back into writing. The second was *Silas Marner: The Weaver of Raveloe*, a story that came to her as a 'sudden inspiration' and compelled her to set her 'other plans' aside (III, 371). In her Journal of November, 1860, she stressed the peremptory force of her new idea, noting that it had 'thrust itself between me and the other book I was meditating'.[3]

There is little in 'Brother Jacob' to indicate the direction she was to take in *Silas Marner*, beyond some superficial points of connection at the narrative level. The short story, like the novel, for example, features the fetishisation and theft of a stash of gold coins. And the Godfrey–Dunsey sub-plot in *Silas Marner* is anticipated in 'Brother Jacob' by the unfolding story of a vexed relationship between two brothers, which sees the fraudulent David Faux exposed by the re-appearance, after a long separation, of his idiot brother Jacob, thus providing, as the tale concludes, 'an admirable instance of the unexpected forms in which great Nemesis hides herself'.[4] Yet the story suggests nothing of the poetic concentration, the resonance of metaphor, and the complex doubling of plot, which gives *Silas Marner* the force of parable.

In many ways *Silas Marner* seems at first to represent a return to old ground for Eliot, a retreat from the new directions of historical romance she had contemplated in Italy. Indeed, the novel is usually seen as consistent with her previous work, regarded variously as 'the last of her "early" novels' or the final work 'in what has been called George Eliot's Natural History of English Life'.[5] And yet it is probably more accurate to see the work as occupying the middle ground between the familiar, meticulous studies of English provincial life, set in the recent past, and what Gillian Beer has characterised as the 'empirical freedom' and 'unanalytical symbolism' of romance.[6] The transitional aspect of the enterprise was suggested by Eliot herself in her account of the tension between realism and legend in the novel's genesis. As she explained to John Blackwood, the story came to her 'quite suddenly, as a sort of legendary tale', one that she felt 'lent itself best to metrical rather than prose fiction, especially in all that relates to the psychology of Silas' (III, 382). However, this new impulse towards the distilled clarity of poetry was checked by the desire to accommodate more familiar features. So, in the end she forswore verse, because it seemed to preclude the possibility of 'an equal play of humour', and as her mind dwelt on the subject, she became increasingly 'inclined to a more realistic treatment'(III, 382).

Clearly, one break that *Silas Marner* did effect from the earlier work was its disruption of the autobiographical trajectory of Eliot's previous fiction. Its only reference point with the author's past was the 'merest millet seed' (III, 371) of a thought, Eliot's recollection 'of having once, in early childhood, seen a linen-weaver with a bag on his back' (III, 382), a man whose expression 'led her to think that he was an alien from his fellows' (III, 427). That said, however, in less direct ways the autobiographical context does have its relevance for a reading of the novel. The timing of the 'sudden inspiration' for this new work, for example, is revealing. The idea came to her as she was reluctantly moving back into inner London, a relocation which left Eliot physically unwell and mentally depressed.[7] It is hardly surprising, then, that this pastoral tale, redolent with nostalgia for 'old-fashioned village life' (III, 371), should have commandeered her imagination precisely at a time when she was languishing 'sadly for the fields and the broad sky' (III, 363).

Furthermore, Eliot's reluctant move back into central London was prompted by the need to establish a suitable home for her stepson, Charles, who had returned from boarding school in Germany to live with Eliot and Lewes for the first time. When Charles obtained a position as a supplementary clerk in the Post Office, following the helpful intercession of Anthony Trollope, Eliot felt there was no choice but to relocate: 'duties must be done, and Charles's moral education requires that he should have a home near to his business and the means of recreation easily within his reach' (III, 363). A parallel can clearly be drawn between this moment of Eliot's initiation into 'parental joys and anxieties' (III, 373) and the simultaneous exploration of the relationship between child and foster-parent in *Silas Marner*, the first extended treatment of this issue which recurs frequently in her subsequent fiction. However, there is more at stake in this connection than mere topicality. For all Eliot's insistence on the delight and good cheer that Charles brought to the domestic scene, the truth is that she felt a deep ambivalence about the intrusion of a child into her shared life with Lewes. Eliot had deliberately chosen not to have children with Lewes[8] and, as she once observed to Mrs Mark Pattison, she 'profoundly rejoice[d] that I never brought a child into the world' (V, 52). Instead, throughout her career, Eliot regarded her books as her offspring, referring, for example, to *The Mill on the Floss* as her 'youngest child' (III, 335) and to her fictional characters as 'spiritual children', and trembling, according to John Blackwood, at the idea of handing over the incomplete manuscript of *Daniel Deronda* 'as if it were her baby' (VI, 136).

The arrival of Charles threatened to interfere with her devotion to her own 'progeny'. In her Journal epilogue to 1860, for example, Eliot revealingly juxtaposed comments about the welcome advent of Charles with observations concerning the diminution of her literary output: 'This year has been marked by many blessings, and above all by the comfort we have found in having Charles with us. Since we set out on our journey to Italy on March 25 the time has not been fruitful in work: distractions about our change of residence have run away with many days, and since I have been in London my state of health has been depressing to all effort. May the next year be more fruitful.'[9] Writing to her publisher about the progress of *Silas Marner* a fortnight later, the causal connection is made more starkly: 'I think I get slower and more timid in my writing, but perhaps worry about houses and servants and boys, with want of bodily strength, may have something to do with that' (III, 372).

She continually chafed at the restraints entailed by her new domesticity: 'I can't tell you how hateful this sort of time-frittering work is to me, who every year care less for houses and detest shops more' (III, 364). And even as she buckled to the yoke of her new duties, she did so with a determination that such constraint must be temporary. Accordingly, the lease that she and Lewes took on their Blandford Square home was only for three years. In her Journal Eliot expressed the hope that 'by the end of that time' she would have 'so far done our duty by the boys as to be free to live where we list'.[10] This was a curiously truncated period of parenthood envisaged by Eliot, since Lewes's younger sons, Thornton and Herbert, were both still in boarding school, aged sixteen and fourteen respectively. However, in keeping with her determination, the younger boys never lived with Eliot and Lewes for more than a few months and they were in due course despatched to Natal in South Africa, where they failed miserably at trading and farming, and both died before the age of thirty.[11]

Given this context, then, Eliot's portrayal of the blessed redemption brought by the sudden advent of a child into Silas Marner's obsessively ordered and industrious life might well be read as the expiation of a sense of guilt at the deep ambivalence she felt about her role as a stepmother. In fact, this would not have been the first time that Eliot had effected an expiatory reversal in fiction of autobiographical fact, for in writing her previous novel, *The Mill on the Floss*, at a time when her scandalous liaison with Lewes had first become public knowledge, she created a heroine in Maggie, who, in direct contrast to her author, renounced all hope of personal happiness by stepping back from the brink of her elopement with Stephen Guest. Here, in *Silas Marner*, she imagines another reversal of her own circumstances, so that Silas wholeheartedly embraces the disruption in his life, and child and step-parent become inseparable in a lifetime bond of love and devotion.

II

In more general terms, Eliot's focus on the foster-parenthood of Silas Marner allowed her to explore questions of nature and nurture, which had particular currency, given the appearance of Charles Darwin's widely read and highly influential study *On the Origin of Species* (1859) two years previously. Eliot's response to Darwin had been balanced and judicious, in a way characteristic of the 'active dialogue' in which she engaged with a broad range of contemporary scientific thought.[12] As one of the consummate intellectuals of her age and as the enthusiastic partner of a leading amateur naturalist, she was herself sufficiently immersed in the world of scientific exploration to recognise both the original contribution of Darwin's study and its more derivative dependence on a long line of previous thinkers. Even more characteristically, her assessment of Darwin was formed on the basis not only of scientific considerations but on questions of literary and philosophical merit as well. Thus, while acknowledging the work as a genuine step forward in the progress of knowledge, she also saw it as badly written and finally unsatisfactory as a theory of ontology:

> We have been reading Darwin's book on the 'Origin of Species' just now: it makes an epoch, as the expression of his thorough adhesion, after long years of study, to the Doctrine of Development – and not the adhesion of an anonym like the author of the 'Vestiges', but of a long-celebrated naturalist. The book is ill-written and sadly wanting in illustrative facts – of which he has collected a vast number, but reserves them for a future book of which this smaller one is the avant-courier. This will prevent the work from becoming popular, as the 'Vestiges' did, but it will have a great effect in the scientific world, causing a thorough and open discussion of a question about which people have

hitherto felt timid. So the world gets on step by step towards brave clearness and honesty! But to me the Development theory and all other explanations of processes by which things came to be, produce a feeble impression compared with the mystery that lies under the process.   (III, 227)

Eliot's reservations about Darwin's theory are not surprising. In *The Mill on the Floss*, as we have seen, expectations that the world might be rendered safely 'comprehensible' by systems of knowledge are constantly thwarted by the perplexities and vagaries which exceed prediction. Similarly, even as Eliot participated with Lewes in the scientific endeavour of sample collection, rejoicing over 'the wonderful Cydippes that we found yesterday floating in the sunny sea', she confessed to feeling 'every day a greater disinclination for theories and arguments about the origin of things in the presence of all this mystery and beauty and pain and ugliness, that floods one with conflicting emotions' (II, 341).

As Gillian Beer has pointed out, Eliot's 'disinclination' towards the search for origins finds expression in her fiction thematically in a concern for fostering and foster-parenting, and formally in her pervasive use of metaphor, which operates by adopting 'the unkinned as kin'.[13] Ironically, though, this stress on the affinity of lateral kinship rather than the more patriarchal emphasis on origins had been immensely reinforced in this period precisely by 'Darwin's insistence on the "infinite web" of connection between all living forms'.[14]

While Eliot's exploration of fostering, then, had both an autobiographical and intellectual topicality, it is also true that tales of foundlings, who are eventually recognised and claimed by their natural parents, represent 'one of the oldest and most potent kinds of story'.[15] Yet, *Silas Marner* reverses the conventions of the genre, for, as Terence Cave notes: 'In virtually every case the recognition restores a genealogy, a true-blood line, for good or ill.'[16] Eppie's choice of her foster-father ahead of her biological father is seen by Cave as important for its class implications, representing a choice of 'lowly social status rather than instant gentrification', which is repeated in the denouement of *Felix Holt*.[17] Gillian Beer, in contrast, sees Eppie's choice as anti-patriarchal, for in privileging nurture above nature, the novel highlights and questions 'the assumption that origins, fathers, law and descent have some rational connections'.[18] Another way of seeing that choice, and the focus of this chapter, is as a refusal of the seduction of self-replication, a choice of otherness, which calls into being an ethics of contiguity rather than of genealogy or identity.

III

As we have seen, the ethical question of the relation to the Other pre-occupies Eliot throughout all her early fiction. After an initial faith in the possibility of extending subjectivity through a recognition of commonality in *Scenes of Clerical Life*, Eliot begins to recognise the impossibility, 'even for the most liberal and expansive mind', of extending empathetic connection 'beyond certain limits' (*AB*, 203). In *Adam Bede*, recognition gives way to imagination as the mode of sympathetic response. In *Silas Marner* Eliot takes her exploration a step further, recognising not only the limits of cognition but also of imagination. In the figure of Marner she contemplates the most alien of her characters, the least susceptible to sympathetic accommodation – the one who, in embodying Levinas's 'constitutive strangeness',[19] is the most intractably other. In this sense Marner represents the most extreme challenge to Eliot's fundamental writerly determination to produce in her readers a capacity 'to *imagine* and to *feel* the pains and joys of those who differ from themselves'(III, lll), the severity of which did not escape the reviewer of *Silas Marner* in *The Westminster Review*: 'There is nothing so difficult to a cultivated intellect as to enter into the mental states of the ignorant and uninformed.'[20]

Silas Marner's difference is marked in every way. His past is opaque, and he comes from an 'unknown region called "North'ard" ' (6). With his pallid complexion, small, bent body and large, unseeing 'protuberant eyes' (4), his freakish appearance inspires fear and 'repulsion' (18). The patrons of the Rainbow Inn have 'only [to] look at him' to know that he is 'half-crazy' (61). Like Wordsworth's Old Cumberland Beggar, he is so 'alien' (4) that he seems scarcely human.[21] Like a 'spider', he weaves from pure impulse, and he has minimised all thought, human contact and need to such a point that his life is reduced to the 'unquestioning activity of a spinning insect' (19). Just as his body is seated every day inside his loom, his identity is likewise subsumed into his obsession, so that he becomes barely distinguishable from the tools of his trade: 'Strangely Marner's face and figure shrank and bent themselves into a constant mechanical relation to the objects of his trade, so that he produced the same sort of impression as a handle or a crooked tube, which has no meaning standing apart' (19).

The perception of Marner's strangeness is compounded by his unwillingness to offer himself for assimilation. So, for example, he does not fraternise in any way with the community, never inviting anyone into his home or seeking anyone out except for business, and never entering the Rainbow Inn or the church, the two social centres of Raveloe. He defies interpretation, barely listening to the villagers, who offer comfort and admonition after the theft of his gold, and remaining uncommunicative even in his grief: 'all the evening, as he sat in his loneliness by his dull fire, he leaned his elbows on his knees, and clasped his head with his hands, and moaned very low – not as one who seeks to be heard' (74). Indeed, in one sense, regardless of inclination, Marner cannot bridge the gap between himself and the villagers because his catalepsy guarantees that he cannot explain himself, even to himself. The three decisive events in his life – the disappearance of the church money at Lantern Yard, the theft of his gold at Raveloe and the appearance of Eppie on his hearth – are as much mysteries to him as to anyone else.

On the one occasion when Marner does reach out to the community, moved by pity to produce a simple preparation of foxglove to ease Sally Oates's breathlessness, his mysterious expertise in herbal medicine, rather than creating some 'fellowship' with his neighbours, confirms for everyone his strange and alien nature: 'and now it was all clear how he should have come from unknown parts, and be so "comical-looking" ' (17).

Marner's strangeness, then, provides one of the two crucial components at play in this drama of otherness. The second is the narrowness and insularity of the world of Raveloe into which he comes. George Eliot sets up the terms of this fearfully – and ruthlessly – endogamous world in the opening paragraph of the novel: 'To the peasants of old times, the world outside their own direct experience was a region of vagueness and mystery: to their untravelled thought a state of wandering was a conception as dim as the winter life of the swallows that came back with the spring; and even a settler, if he came from distant parts, hardly ever ceased to be viewed with a remnant of distrust' (3).[22] Anything that does not fall within the limited ken of Raveloe understanding becomes the subject of superstition and suspicion. 'Singularities' of any kind invite 'persecution' (7). Wandering tradesmen, in general, are viewed with apprehension, and Marner, in particular, is regarded variously as a madman, a ghost, and as one in league with the devil.

The closed world of Raveloe has never been made 'various' by learning or culture and its security depends on familiarity in the narrowest of terms – on a knowledge of origins through which identity can be established and behaviour can be predicted. Thus, the most unsettling thing about the itinerant tradesmen is that 'No one knew where wandering men had their homes or their origin; and how was a man to be explained unless you at least knew somebody who knew his father and mother' (3). Suspicion is not warranted, in contrast, for 'honest folks' who were 'born and bred in a visible manner' (4). The absurdity of this pursuit of sameness, this faith in self-replication, is exemplified in the history of Mr Kimble, the town doctor, who pursues his profession not by virtue of training or knowledge, but as a hereditary right:

> Doctor Kimble (country apothecaries in old days enjoyed that title without authority of diploma), being a thin and agile man, was flitting about the room with his hands in his pockets, making himself agreeable to his feminine patients, with medical impartiality, and was being welcomed everywhere as a doctor by hereditary right – not one of those miserable apothecaries who canvass for practice in strange neighbourhoods . . . Time out of mind the Raveloe doctor had been a Kimble; Kimble was inherently a doctor's name; and it was difficult to contemplate firmly the melancholy fact that the actual Kimble had no son, so that his practice might one day be handed over to a successor, with the incongruous name of Taylor or Johnson. (96)

At the righteous centre of Raveloe, the Lammeter family put their trust explicitly and insistently in the familiar. Nancy insists, for example, that her sister Priscilla dress identically to her, despite the unsuitability of the clothes Nancy chooses for them both, because she believes the family tie should be evident and acknowledged at all times: 'Would you have us go about looking as if we were no kin to one another?' (93). Nancy lives by an 'unalterable little code' (151) which regulates all the duties and proprieties of life. With a rigidity that is reminiscent of Tom Tulliver in *The Mill on the Floss*, and of the moral inadequacy of that novel's inflexible men of maxims (*AB*, 498), Nancy's opinions always take the form of 'principles to be unwaveringly acted upon' (151). Revealingly, one of those rigid principles is against adoption. While the rationale for such opposition is based on acceptance of the will of Providence, it confirms the endogamous instinct that stems from a faith in the known, and a trust in the security and control that comes with a knowledge of origins. That instinct finds its most extreme expression in Priscilla Lammeter, for whom the idea of acceptable clan or tribe barely extends beyond the family hearth. Confronted by Nancy's anxiety about her husband's discontent, for example, Priscilla contemplates a fantasy of familial self-sufficiency: 'if it had pleased God to make you ugly, like me, so as the men wouldn't ha' run after you, we might have kept to our own family, and had nothing to do with folks as have got uneasy blood in their veins' (148).

The Lammeter sisters share their father's conviction that nature takes precedence over nurture, or, in the words of his favourite saying, that 'breed was stronger than pasture' (96). It is not surprising, then, that in the novel's dramatic climax, when Eppie is confronted with the true circumstances of her birth, Nancy sides without compunction with her husband Godfrey in the 'contest' between biological and foster-father. Where Eppie and Marner depend on the authority of emotion for their sense of right, Godfrey and Nancy appeal to a language of patriarchal law. So, Godfrey sees his genetic tie as 'the strongest of all claims' (164), while in Nancy's eyes any 'natural', affective claim is outweighed by 'a duty you owe to your lawful father' (167). Nancy is not unaware of the sacrifice being asked of Marner, 'but her code allowed no question that a father by blood must have a claim above that of any foster-father' (166).

In the end, the irony of such faith in endogamy is that the known proves to be no guarantee of security, for Godfrey is blackmailed by his brother Dunsey and Marner is betrayed by his 'own famil'ar friend" (139). Concomitantly, Marner is redeemed by his willingness to embrace the unknown, while Godfrey's tragedy is set in motion by his repudiation of the outsider, his first wife Molly.

IV

In many ways, as we have seen, Marner is trapped in his seclusion, 'his life narrowing and hardening itself more and more into a mere pulsation of desire and satisfaction that had no relation to any other being' (19). And yet, as James McLaverty has noted, for all the deprivation of his life, Silas 'retains in a perverted form the life of feeling which typifies [Comtean] fetishism'.[23] Eliot urges that we be 'tolerant of that fetishism' (137), for it keeps open the channels of emotional responsiveness. Thus, for example, Marner demonstrates that 'the sap of affection was not all gone', when, after breaking his brown water pot, he assuages the 'grief' at the loss of his 'companion' by sticking the pieces together and propping the 'ruin' back in its old place (20). Similarly, while his gold provides a sterile substitute for human affection, it nonetheless creates forms of affective exchange. He takes pleasure in the 'bright faces' (16) of his coins, thinks that his money is 'conscious of him' and feels a sense of loyalty to it, so that he would not on any account 'have exchanged those coins, which had become his familiars, for other coins with unknown faces' (18). The forms and habits of responsiveness which are created around the fetish object provide the foundation for the transference of affection, when the right moment comes. This dynamic is clearly underlined when Silas catches sight of what he takes to be his gold glinting on the hearth, reaches out with violently beating heart to grasp his 'restored treasure' (109), only to touch instead his new treasure in the form of Eppie's golden curls.

Marner's life before the advent of Eppie lacks any newness 'to keep alive in him the idea of the unexpected and the changeful' (39). Its stale familiarity is protected by the psychological barriers created by his miserliness, which 'fenced him in from the wide, cheerless unknown' (74) and kept his heart like a 'locked casket' (79). In its repetitive sameness, Marner's life reflects *in extremis* the insular monotony, 'independent of variety' (29), of the wider community. And yet the saving grace which marks Marner out is his incipient openness. The preliminary intrusion of the thief into his cottage prepares the ground for the more decisive entrance of the child. The 'fence' around his life and the 'lock' upon his heart are both 'broken' (74, 79), leaving him susceptible to the blessing of the child. As Eliot repeats three times for emphasis, Eppie is able to make her way into Marner's cottage, and life, because 'the door was open' (119). Similarly, Marner's instinctive response when stricken by the pain of loss is fundamentally exogamous: 'Left groping in darkness, with his prop utterly gone, Silas had *inevitably* [my italics] a sense, though a dull and half-despairing one, that if any help came to him it must come from without' (79). Appropriately, then, the blessing Eppie brings, and the reversal she effects, is expansion in every aspect of Marner's life:

> Unlike the gold which needed nothing, and must be worshipped in close-locked solitude – which was hidden away from the daylight, was deaf to the song of birds, and started to no human tones – Eppie was a creature of endless claims and ever-growing desires, seeking and loving sunshine, and living sounds, and living movements; making trial of everything, with trust in new joy, and stirring the human kindness

in all eyes that looked on her. The gold had kept his thoughts in an ever-repeating circle, leading to nothing beyond itself; but Eppie was an object compacted of changes and hopes that forced his thoughts onward, and carried them from their old eager pacing towards the same blank limit – carried them far away to the new things that would come with the coming years.   (124)

V

Marner's exogamous impulse can be compared with Maggie's in *The Mill on the Floss*. It is that movement outward which, as we have seen, is necessary for moral progress. In embracing Eppie, Marner accepts the mystery of her origins. Revealingly, his initial instinct is to assimilate her history into the familiar. So, his first thought is that she is the same – his little sister come back to him in a dream – and, then, that she is similar – 'a lone thing – and I'm a lone thing' (116). But in the end he can only confess that he is 'partly mazed' (116) by her advent, and take her into his lap 'trembling with an emotion mysterious to himself, at something unknown dawning on his life' (120).

This ethical challenge – to embrace what is not known or like – is played out not just in Marner's adoption of Eppie, but also in Raveloe's eventual accommodation of Marner. Like Marner in his solitary life, Raveloe is withering under the grip of a 'communal exclusiveness' (*SCW*, 276) which must gradually be loosened. The challenge that Marner represents, however, is greater than that presented by the unknown child, because, as we have seen, Marner's otherness is so intractable it exposes the limits of empathy and understanding. It was a problem that Eliot had anticipated in her recognition in *Adam Bede* that 'to shift one's point of view beyond certain limits is impossible to the most liberal and expansive mind' (*AB*, 203). And it echoes the dilemma which Feuerbach contemplated in his *The Essence of Christianity*, which Eliot translated in 1854 and with which Eliot claimed 'everywhere to agree' (II, 153). While Feuerbach saw the essence of religion as the 'involuntary, unconscious contemplation of human nature as another, a distinct nature', he also argued that it was impossible for man to transcend his subjectivity because sympathy presupposed likeness:

> Man cannot get beyond his true nature. He may indeed by means of the imagination conceive individuals of another so-called higher kind, but he can never get loose from his species, his nature; the conditions of being, the positive final predicates which he gives to these other

individuals, are always determinations or qualities drawn from his own nature – qualities in which he in truth only images and projects himself.[24]

In this novel Eliot strives to imagine something beyond the ethical possibilities opened up by empathy, or by the exercise of moral imagination, skill and discipline, as she had contemplated them in her earlier novels, for if the other is unknowable, and exceeds the efforts of cognition, then something more, or different, is required. In *Silas Marner* she moves beyond Feuerbach's sense of limitation to propose something more akin to Levinas's conception of ethics as 'not a sympathy through which we put ourselves in the other's place' but rather a recognising 'the other as resembling us, but exterior to us; the relationship with the other is a relationship with a Mystery'.[25]

Such a relationship obviously requires a movement beyond the known and knowable – an extra-rational leap which has parallels with the religious leap of faith. However, whereas in religion that leap is enabled by belief, in Eliot's humanist scheme of things such a leap depends on an instinctive, extra-rational welling-up of emotion. So, for example, Marner's embrace of Eppie is born of a 'sudden impulse', which comes 'like a revelation to himself', and is, significantly, an impulse at odds with his rational self, 'a minute before, he had no distinct intention about the child' (113). Those who are wedded to the known, to origins, to the closed world of familiarity, and the certainty of maxims cannot hope to be receptive at the providential moment to the 'something given',[26] whether it be Marner's child, or Maggie Tulliver's 'possibility of a word or a look from a stranger' (435). Marner, in contrast, demonstrates a 'humble sort of acquiescence' in the face of the bewildering gift which has been 'sent to him out of the darkness' (138).

The one character who is capable of breaching Raveloe's insularity in reaching out to Marner is Dolly Winthrop. Notably, she is the character who is least unsettled by the mystery of Marner, for she, like Marner, is capable of 'humble acquiescence' in the face of the unknown. To her, life is a 'big puzzle', and meaning eludes her frequently because she lacks the 'big words' necessary for rational explanation (140). Despite the goodwill that develops between Dolly and Marner, it is clear that they remain largely uncomprehending of each other: 'The communication was necessarily a slow and difficult process, for Silas's meagre power of explanation was not aided by any readiness of interpretation in Dolly, whose narrow outward

experience gave her no key to strange customs, and made every nov-
elty a source of wonder that arrested them at every step of the narrative' (138). Dolly cannot help Marner to understand the abiding
puzzle of his life – how the drawing of lots at Lantern Yard failed to
support his innocence. She can 'make nothing' (140) of it. But when
she gives up trying to think through the problem, the resolution
comes to her as a feeling rather than a thought.[27] Her advice to
Marner is 'to do the right thing as far as we know and to trusten'
(141) – that is, to act morally according to the limits of knowledge or
rationality and *then* to make a leap of affective faith. It is in this way
that it becomes possible to stay connected, despite incomprehension,
in human fellowship. As Dolly admonishes Marner, 'if you could but
ha' gone on trustening, Master Marner, you wouldn't ha' run away
from your fellow-creaturs and been so lone' (141). Dolly's prescription of trust is a recognition of the need for connection or relation
that exceeds understanding or calculation – that, in effect, accepts
the relationship with mystery of which Levinas speaks. Not surprisingly, Dolly is the one character who is capable of looking beyond the
claims of origin to acknowledge Marner's affective claim to Eppie,
insisting he has 'a right to her, if [he's] a father to her' (121).

The otherness of Marner is not entirely dissipated with his acceptance into the Raveloe community. He cannot ever be fully assimilat-
ed, for both the fact of his catalepsy and the complete disappearance
of the location of his past at Lantern Yard ensure that the mystery of
his origins must remain. He never becomes at one – or *as* one – with
Raveloe. For his part, he remains 'quite unable' to 'identify' with the
religious observances he undertakes in Raveloe, but he can by virtue
of 'sharing the effect that everything produced on her . . . come to
appropriate the forms of custom and belief which were the mould of
Raveloe life' (138). Thus, through the mediating power of his bond
with Eppie, he is drawn into a relationship with the community that
is based on proximity rather than absorption. No child, for example,
was afraid of approaching Silas '*when* [my italics] Eppie was near
him', and 'everywhere' people are ready to engage Silas in conversation, but always 'about the child' (128). She provides the 'link'
between Marner and the 'whole world' (129), and while in himself
Marner remains a mystery, his actions in fostering Eppie render him,
to a degree at least, comprehensible and acceptable. In the resolution, love becomes the force that dismantles the barriers between self
and other: 'There was love between him and the child that blent them
into one, and there was love between the child and the world' (129).

Emotion, then, is the *lingua franca* through which otherness can be negotiated – or, as Feuerbach puts it, the 'Paraclete',[28] the symbol of a force that transcends difference by allowing men of every nation to hear each other as though in their native tongue.

In *Silas Marner* Eliot confronts the limits of human sympathy through the contemplation of the hero's intractable otherness. She also confronts the limits of moral agency both through the fact of Marner's catalepsy and through the idea of moral luck played out in the novel in the workings of chance. In the face of these limits any version of willed or rational moral choice will only take us so far. Beyond that we are left with the necessity for openness, a willingness to embrace the unknown and a preparedness to make the affective leap of faith through trust.

7

Between Two Worlds: *Romola*

I

When George Eliot became 'fired' with the idea of writing an historical romance set in fifteenth-century Florence, she contemplated this leap into unfamiliar creative territory with a mixture of trepidation and determination. So conscious was she of the risk of producing 'something else than what was expected' (III, 339), that she considered publishing her 'Italian story' anonymously in *Blackwood's Magazine*.[1] Nonetheless, Eliot was resolved to sacrifice popularity – 'Of necessity, the book is addressed to fewer readers than my previous work' – in the interests of extending and diversifying her creative range: 'If one is to have the freedom to write out one's own varying unfolding self, and not be a machine always grinding out the same material or spinning the same sort of web, one cannot always write for the same public' (IV, 49).

By the time Eliot put 'the last stroke to Romola'[2] in June 1863, the novel had been eighteen months in composition, and a further eighteen months in contemplation and research. It was the most ambitious and difficult task that she had ever undertaken, and the one that took her closest to the brink of failure. Eliot was well accustomed to grappling with the recurring 'demon' of despair and insecurity, which gripped her whenever she had completed one work and was contemplating a new project, and yet she was so 'dreadfully depressed' and 'utterly dejected' at the possibility of successfully executing her plan for her Italian story that she 'almost resolved to give up'.[3] Having agreed to serial publication with a new publisher, George Smith, she struggled to produce each Part, unable to recall ever having felt so 'despairing' or 'so chilled and oppressed'.[4] In retrospect, though, she saw the writing of *Romola* not only as an ordeal – 'I began it a young woman, – I finished it an old woman'[5] – but also as a triumph. She felt that there was no other book of hers about which she could more thoroughly 'swear by every sentence as having been written with my best blood, such as it is, and with the most ardent care for veracity of which my nature is capable. It has made me often sob with a sort of painful joy as I have read the sentences which had faded from my memory' (VI, 336).

Certainly, the effort that Eliot put into the preparation for her novel was prodigious. She was conscious of the pitfalls of any attempt to 'reanimate the past', having been especially critical of the '*modern-antique* species' of silly women's novels as the most 'leaden' of all (*SCW*, 316). Success in such an endeavour required the rarest form of imaginative power, she recognised, and demanded 'as much accurate and minute knowledge as creative vigour' (*SCW*, 317). Accordingly, she took 'unspeakable pains' (IV, 301), immersing herself in scholarly research, as though to compensate with erudite detail for the unfamiliarity of her subject. A diary entry for November, 1861, offers a glimpse of her extraordinary zeal: 'This week I have read a satire of Juvenal, some of Cicero *De Officiis*, part of Epictetus' Enchiridion, two cantos of Pulci, part of the Canti Carnascialeschi, and finished Manni's Veglie Piacevole, besides looking up various things in the classical antiquities and peeping into Theocritus.'[6] She was, as she wrote to Fredrick Harrison, determined to neglect nothing that she could find that would help her 'to what I may call the "Idiom" of Florence, in the largest sense one could stretch the word to. . . . I felt that the necessary idealization could only be attained by adopting the clothing of the past' (IV, 301). Not surprisingly, then, John Blackwood reported that she was 'studying her subject as subject never was studied before' (III, 474), and Anthony Trollope, having read the first number of *Romola*, expressed 'wonder' at the toil Eliot must have 'endured in getting up [the] work' (VIII, 304). Yet even as he congratulated Eliot, he sounded a note of caution about the excessive erudition she seemed to be bringing to her task. Echoing George Lewes's anxiety that the novel was in danger of 'being the product of an Encyclopaedia' (III, 474), Trollope urged Eliot not to 'fire too much over the heads of your readers' (VIII, 304). Despite her gratitude for his 'delightful, generous letter',[7] Eliot was unswayed. In consequence, most readers, then and since, have felt burdened by the sheer weight of historical detail in the novel. *The Westminster Review*, for example, acknowledged that 'no care and labour have been spared', but lamented that such care 'has resulted only in an accumulation of details'.[8] And Henry James concluded that a 'twentieth part of the erudition would have sufficed'.[9]

When one of her most enthusiastic and intelligent critics, R. H. Hutton, made much the same criticism in his review in *The Spectator*, Eliot wrote to him and conceded that her 'presentation of details' was perhaps 'somewhat excessive'. Interestingly, however, she explained this 'tendency to excess' not in terms of the anxiety produced by the effort to bring to life a new and alien milieu, but rather in terms of her habitual commitment to realism: 'It is the habit of my imagination to strive after as full a vision of the medium in which a character moves as of the character itself. The psychological causes which prompted me to give such details of Florentine life and history as I have given, are precisely the same as those which determined me in giving the details of English village life in "Silas Marner", or the "Dodson" life, out of which were developed the destinies of poor Tom and Maggie' (IV, 97).

Of course, fullness of vision could not be guaranteed simply through the 'accumulation of details', for as Eliot herself argued, there were limits to what any 'real observation of life and character' could achieve, and the 'imagination must fill in and give life to the picture' (III, 427). Furthermore, what Eliot's explanation to Hutton failed to take into account was the fact that in setting her novel in fifteenth-century Florence, her capacity to 'give life' to her 'medium' was compromised by a loss of idiom. In writing her earlier novels, Eliot was accustomed to 'hearing' her characters talking (III, 427), and she demonstrated a command of dialogue that had been justly celebrated. With *Romola*, however, she was at a loss to capture that immediacy of the speaking voice, and, as she confided to Blackwood, she felt a weight upon her mind 'as if Savonarola and friends ought to be speaking Italian instead of English' (III, 427). The unhappy result for the novel was a great deal of unlikely dialogue from minor characters – colloquially accurate, densely allusive, and dramatically moribund.

Despite Eliot's appeal to realist criteria in her defence to Hutton, one of the most telling developments in the writing of *Romola* was the move towards romance. It was a progression anticipated, as we have seen, by the 'transitional' text, *Silas Marner*, but one which was extended significantly in Eliot's Italian story. The seemingly organic development of narrative in Eliot's earlier fiction, which was sub-servient usually to the unfolding of character, gives way in *Romola* to a far greater sense of 'premeditation and contrivance,'[10] in which the narrative predominates over character. Thus, this novel relies far more for its effect on the determinations of a plot elaborately shaped by coincidences, parallels and patterning, and informed by an intri-cacy of symbolism and allusion more usually associated with poetry.[11]

Romola, then, is a hybrid, unable quite to loose its realist moor-ings, yet ambitiously experimental in non-realist ways that variously derive from poetry, fable, epic and romance. Indeed, it is precisely this hybrid quality which has so disconcerted critics, and the novel's failures of realism have provided the stick with which it has been beaten by a succession of commentators from Henry James onward.[12] George Levine has diagnosed the tension in the novel cogently, arguing that the difficulty with *Romola* 'is not so much that it is as strictly controlled by fabulous and symbolic events as *Silas Marner*, but that it seems to be struggling to be a different kind of work – to be, that is, a traditional novel'.[13] While Levine conceded that the two aspects of the novel never 'mesh', he convincingly argued that *Romola* can be read as a far better, or at least far more interesting, novel, if we give up a determination to judge it as a con-ventional, realist text.[14]

II

The shift of setting may have been the most obvious change in Eliot's determinedly new venture, and the one that caused her the greatest headaches of execution, but its real importance has perhaps been underestimated. Certainly, whether from conviction, or for the pur-poses of encouraging his diffident partner, George Lewes insisted that the change to an 'historical' setting had negligible implications: 'As I often tell her most of the scenes and characters of her books are quite as *historical* to her direct personal experience, as the 15th cen-tury of Florence; and she knows infinitely more about Savonarola than she knew of Silas, besides having deep personal sympathies with the old reforming priest which she did not have with the miser' (III, 420). And, indeed, the opening paragraph of the novel insists on the relative superficiality of the change. So, no sooner does it announce a chronological gulf of 'three centuries and a half', than it asserts a continuity of universal experience with 'the broad sameness of the human lot, which never alters in the main headings of its history – hunger and labour, seed-time and harvest, love and death' (3).[15]

Furthermore, it has been plausibly argued that the travails of late fifteenth-century Florence – a city grappling both with the conflicting claims of religious and secular worlds, and with the demands and threats of a broadening democratic base – had clear contemporary relevance for Eliot's England. Felicia Bonaparte, for example, has noted that in its turbulence and transition, Florence closely reflected England: 'Philosophically confused, morally uncertain, and culturally uprooted, the city was a prototype of the upheaval of nineteenth-century England.'[16] In the same vein, Bonaparte contends, the heroine, Romola, might be seen as 'a thoroughly contemporary figure, the Victorian intellectual struggling to resolve the dilemmas of the modern age'.[17]

Such discussions of topicality, however, can easily obscure more fundamental issues. It is important to recognise that the shift in *Romola* is not just one from *circa* 1800 to 1492, but, equally, a move from a narrowly provincial England to the cultural capital of Renaissance Europe; from the endogamous worlds of St Oggs and Raveloe to the quintessentially exogamous world of Florence; from simple worlds not remotely 'made various' (*SM*, 13) by learning and culture to a complex world enriched by the myriad cross-currents of Western culture, politics and trade.

With the greater complexity of milieu comes a greater complexity of ethical interrogation. Certainly, the novel still demonstrates the same fascination with the moment of choice as the cornerstone of ethical life. Tito Melema, for example, is in many ways a familiar figure in Eliot's fiction, reminiscent of the earlier study of Arthur Donnithorne in *Adam Bede*. Both men have an easy charm and enjoy the admiration that comes to them freely. Each man would, all other things being equal, choose virtue over evil, not from any firmly grounded moral conviction, but rather because such a choice concurs with a pleasing self-image. Tito's gradual loss of 'moral youthfulness' (205) mirrors Arthur's, his innocence contaminated by a sequence of deceit and betrayal, his integrity 'slowly strangled . . . by the successive falsities of his life' (331). The relentless nature of that sequence underscores Eliot's belief in the efficacy and necessity of habits of goodness, and both men exemplify 'that inexorable law of human souls, that we prepare ourselves for sudden deeds by the reiterated choice of good or evil which gradually determines character' (212). Each man is blinded by his ego into a belief in his own sovereignty. Both come to rely increasingly – and disastrously – on their blessed relation to Fortune and their immunity to Nemesis.

In the end, though, Tito's moral demise is more complete than Arthur's, because he remains untouched by remorse. He knows the egoistic fear of being exposed, but he is destitute of the moral dread which might compel him to right action. When he feels a 'strong reaction of regret' (125) at the realisation that by his actions he has rendered himself unworthy of Romola's unquestioning love, that regret prompts not contrition, but the fervent hope that Romola's brother will die before he can disclose any information harmful to Tito's reputation. The erosion of Tito's moral bearings is so total that by the end of the novel he has repudiated all claims upon him and is reduced to the ultimately egocentric conviction that there is no motive that any man could really have 'except his own interest' (449).

However, even though Tito Melema is familiar as a type, there is much that is new in *Romola*. While, as we have seen, *The Mill on the Floss* gestures towards a concern with the wider context against which Maggie's individual drama is played out, *Romola*, as Eliot's first political novel, broadens the ethical focus decisively so that the ideological context itself becomes central. Whereas the tragedy of each of her earlier works centred on the private world of sexual desire, the libidinal investments in this novel revolve far more around the public desire for power and glory. In contrast to earlier erotically charged scenes of secret trysts, domestic piano recitals and country-house dances, the decisive scenes in *Romola* take place in the more open, and more masculine, spaces of the marketplace, the Rucellai Gardens or the barber shop, and the animating force is provided not by sexual desire, but by political intrigue and intellectual sparring.

In this regard, even the romantic attachments in the novel are curiously desexualised. On the one hand, Romola is so idealised as the aloof madonna that she seems untouched, and untouchable, by sexual desire. Symptomatically, for example, the moment of Tito and Romola's mutual declaration of love takes place in the arid setting of Bardo's library, a place of 'lifeless objects . . . the parchment backs, the unchanging mutilated marble, the bits of obsolete bronze and clay' (50). It is marked by only the most fleeting physical contact: 'The faces just met, and the dark curls mingled for an instant with the rippling gold. Quick as lightning after that, Tito set his foot on a projecting ledge of the book-shelves and reached down the needful volumes' (116). Subsequently, Romola's lofty bearing eliminates any possibility for furtive contact in the presence of her blind father:

'there was no finesse to secure an additional look or touch. Each woman creates in her own likeness the love tokens that are offered to her; and Romola's deep calm happiness encompassed Tito like the rich but quiet evening light which dissipates all unrest' (117).

On the other hand, even Tessa, Tito's mistress, for all the emphasis on her corporeality, has nothing of the calculating self-consciousness of a character like Hetty in *Adam Bede*, and seems exempt from the taint of sexuality by the stress on her almost preternatural innocence and child-like qualities. Tito's attraction to Tessa, correspondingly, has nothing of the irresistible and disruptive force of Arthur's for Hetty, or Stephen's for Maggie, but rather stems from a more complacent and enervated attraction to Tessa's *naïveté* and lack of judgement. Tessa's most pertinent asset is her 'ignorant lovingness' (287), which provides Tito with a comforting ethical vacuum, 'a refuge from a standard disagreeably rigorous' (288), a world 'completely cushioned with goodwill' (292).

Accordingly, too, there is never any suggestion of sexual jealousy between Romola and Tessa as rivals for Tito's affection, in a way that there is, for example, in the destructive and competitive intensity played out between Gwendolen and Lydia Glasher in *Daniel Deronda*. It is not Tessa who comes between Romola and Tito, for in the end their marriage founders on his lust for power, prestige and wealth. It is political manoeuvring and intrigue, much more than occasional visits to Tessa, which keep Tito from the marital home. And it is politics and not sex that introduces the rupture in their marriage. Thus, in a brilliantly emblematic moment, it is not his mistress but his chain-mail vest, worn to ward off the assassin's knife, which physically alienates Romola from her husband, as if 'some malignant fiend had changed [his] sensitive human skin into a hard shell' (238).

Against the wider Italian canvas, then, Eliot extends her focus beyond the ethical microcosm of 'sudden deeds and decisive moments' to explore not only different kinds of desire, as we have been suggesting, but also different, and competing, systems of belief and knowledge. The novel's most apparent contrast is that between the pagan and the Christian worlds. In the opening pages we are introduced to the generic 'old Florentine', who negotiates these opposing traditions of belief – their 'conflicting sentiments and contradictory opinions' (7) – with canny impartiality:

> It was his pride, besides, that he was duly tinctured with the learning of his age, and judged not altogether with the vulgar, but in harmony

with the ancients: he, too, in his prime, had been eager for the most correct manuscripts, and had paid many florins for antique vases and for disinterred busts of the ancient immortals – some, perhaps, *truncis naribus*, wanting as to the nose, but not the less authentic; and in his old age he had made haste to look at the first sheets of that fine Homer which was among the early glories of the Florentine press. But he had not, for all that, neglected to hang up a waxen image or double of himself under the protection of the Madonna Annunziata, or to do penance for his sins in large gifts to the shrines of saints whose lives had not been modelled on the study of the classics; he had not even neglected making liberal bequests towards buildings for the *Frati*, against whom he levelled many a jest.   (7)

The tension of this divided world runs like a fault line through Romola's family, fracturing the bonds between father and son. Bardo is scornfully dismissive of Dino's Christian conversion, seeing only a son who has abandoned his father and their shared and honourable scholarly endeavour so that he might 'lash himself and howl at midnight with besotted friars – that he might go wandering on pilgrimages befitting men who know of no past older than the missal and the crucifix' (51). And for his part, Dino is no less withering in his assessment of his father's classical world: 'the studies he wished me to live for were either childish trifling – dead toys – or else they must be made warm and living by pulses that beat to worldly ambitions and fleshly lusts: for worldly ambitions and fleshly lusts made all the substance of the poetry and history he wanted me to bend my eyes on continually' (149).

The two other significant men in Romola's life – her husband, Tito, and her spiritual guide, Savonarola – similarly represent the poles of pagan and Christian belief, and both are equally bound up in a dynamic of antagonism and conquest. Savonarola dismisses classical scholarship as 'vain discourse', a spurious projection of 'fancied wisdom' onto times past (341), while Tito has no time for the 'monkish visions, bred of fasting and fanatical ideas' (171). Both men assume a mastery derived from their beliefs. So, despite Romola's pagan heritage, Savonarola claims the authority of a 'divine warrant' (340) in imperiously directing her to return to Florence, and Tito assumes that he can banish the resonances of the Christian world, which unsettle Romola, by locking away the crucifix given to her by Dino within a cabinet that he has designed and had decorated with pagan images of himself as Bacchus and Romola as Ariadne.[18]

This contrast between worlds, though, is not as stark as it seems, for while the male characters differ in creed, they resemble each other in conduct. Whatever the beliefs that divide Bardo and Dino, for example, father and son are as one in their fanatical absolutism. And, similarly, despite the gulf in ideology between Tito and Savonarola, they are alike in their desire for supremacy and control. Thus, while the structuring contrast in the novel may seem to be between Christian and pagan worlds, *Romola* actually explores a more fundamental divide between a world of partisanship and false simplicities and one of non-partisan openness and diffidence. These opposing ethical worlds broadly correspond to a divide between a distinctively masculine sphere and a feminine alternative, of which Romola stands as the crucial representative. Thus, Romola, unlike the men in her life, knows neither the affliction – nor the protection – that comes from the certainty of polemicism. She is unable either simply to repudiate, or to reconcile, the 'clashing deities' represented by Dino and Tito respectively. Instead, she is both burdened by a vertiginous sense of ambivalence, and blessed with a longing – a 'questioning need' (172) – always to fathom some point of connection or common ground. She seeks, like her creator, 'to know if possible, the lasting meaning that lies in all religious doctrine from the beginning till now' (IV, 65).

Romola's concern to seek out commonality places her outside the masculine logic of conquest. Whereas all the men around her use their creeds to insulate and bolster a sense of self, the impulse behind Romola's receptiveness to Savonarola is one of self-extension, born of a 'strange sympathy with something apart from all the definable interests of her life' (235). Unlike Dino, Romola is never drawn in her 'conversion' to the dogma of Christianity, nor does she feel impelled to repudiate her past. Indeed, she is repelled by the narrowness of the Church, and its 'denunciatory exclusiveness' (420), and attracted instead to an inclusive concern for 'universal regeneration' (367) and the expansive sense of 'large breathing-room which she found in [Savonarola's] grand view of human duties' (420).

The values that Romola cherishes in the Christian message are those that connect her to others – fellowship, duty and sympathy. In stark contrast to Tito's gospel of self-interest, Romola follows Savonarola in the hope of finding a way of transcending self-interest, 'a reason for living, apart from personal enjoyment and personal affection' (367), and she is led by him from the isolation of her father's library, a world obsessed with ownership, seclusion and privacy, into philanthropic service in the public streets. Where once the 'religion of her life' had simply been attachment to 'the near and the loved' (305), at Savonarola's urging she comes to recognise her place as a 'citizen', her particular affections 'transformed . . . into an enthusiasm of sympathy with general life' (366).

In this world of factions, controversy and contest hold no interest for Romola. She is, in fact, the least political of animals. It is not only her sense of loyalty and candour which equip her ill for the necessary intrigue, but her instinctive repugnance for the polemical and the divisive. Thus, the quality she most respects in her beloved godfather, Bernardo del Nero, is 'the power of respecting a feeling which he does not share or understand' (173) – a quality that leaves him fatally vulnerable in this Florentine world.

In this regard, Romola is, ironically, a poor choice to model for Piero's painting of Antigone. The points of connection between Eliot's heroine and her classical counterpart are clear enough. They share an intense pride and a remarkable capacity for personal affection, loyalty, courage and integrity. The differences between them, however, are even more telling. Romola is admirable precisely because she lacks the 'defiant hardness' of Antigone, a hardness which allows Sophocles' heroine to pursue her cause until death, despite the fact that even while she contends for what she believes to be right, she is conscious that 'in following out one principle', she is laying herself open 'to just blame for transgressing another' (SCW, 245). Where the essence of the drama may be the same for both heroines, in that each faces 'the antagonism between valid claims' (SCW, 245), their responses are markedly different. For Antigone, the polemicist, the perception of the other's point of view serves only to heighten and harden the extremity of her own position. For Romola, Eliot's anti-polemicist, such antagonism causes her repeatedly to seek a middle ground.

Romola's capacity to negotiate extremes arises in part from her respect for, and openness to, others. Just as importantly, however, it is grounded on her capacity for doubt. Faced with conflict or opposition, Romola's impulse is self-questioning rather than self-justificatory. Indeed, it is a measure of the nobility and generosity of her mind that she is given to uncertainty: 'It belongs to every large nature, when it is not under the immediate power of some strong unquestioning emotion, to suspect itself, and doubt the truth of its own impressions, conscious of possibilities beyond its own horizon' (232).

Such a disposition makes Romola unwilling to submit to the 'false certitude' (223) of polemical positions. Thus, her development, as she attempts to negotiate the broadest questions of belief and being, is heroic, not in conventional terms of decisiveness and forward momentum, but in its struggle with confusion and uncertainty:

> No radiant angel came across the gloom with a clear message for her. In those times, as now, there were human beings who never saw angels or heard perfectly clear messages. Such truth as came to them was brought confusedly in the voices and deeds of men not at all like the seraphs of unfailing wing and piercing vision – men who believed falsities as well as truths, and did the wrong as well as the right. The helping hands stretched out to them were the hands of men who stumbled and often saw dimly, so that these beings unvisited by angels had no other choice than to grasp that stumbling guidance along the path of reliance and action which is the path of life, or else to pause in loneliness and disbelief, which is no path, but the arrest of inaction and death.   (310)

The trajectory of her journey, then, is sporadic, marked by false starts, departures and returns. Even her epiphanic meeting with Savonarola on the road outside Florence provides less the certainty of revelation, than the fragile and tenuous hope of a 'fresh clue' with which to 'thread' life (348).

Tito, in contrast, is as decisive as Romola is hesitant. Although, like hers, his plans are subject to change, such fluctuation for him is prompted by external circumstance, carefully calibrated to the likelihood of success, and never influenced by personal scruple or hesitation. Tito lacks the moral imagination to be self-questioning: 'His conduct did not look ugly to himself, and his imagination did not suffice to show him exactly how it would look to Romola' (269). His is a political intelligence, his acuity employed in the service of worldly ambition and brought to bear in the judgement of others – their motives, their dispositions, their likely behaviour. Romola's intellect, in contrast, is ethical, using her capability of 'discerning the complexities in human things' (420) to ascertain the truthful rather than the opportune.

Romola's hesitancy and uncertainty are more than just the markers of a large and generous mind. They are the only counterbalance to a masculine way of perceiving the world that is at once destructive and dangerous. None of the men in Romola's life admits to doubt; each lives out of an absolute conviction of right. In this, they bring to mind the hard inflexibility of the 'man of maxims' (498) in *The Mill on the Floss*, but whereas the rigidity of Tom Tulliver gives rise to personal tragedy in the domestic drama of *The Mill*, on the wider political stage of *Romola* such unbending certitude leads to widespread persecution, and to the deaths of honourable and dishonourable men alike.

Such rigidity can be seen in microcosm, for example, in the way in which the rigour and exactitude of Bardo's life of scholarship becomes reduced to the fetishisation of accuracy in his translations. Although even the child Maggie, struggling with Latin in *The Mill on the Floss*, recognises that a word 'may mean several things – almost every word does' (145), Bardo allows no such complexity or fluidity. He pursues accuracy as a form of power over others, asserting his exclusive authoritativeness and scorning the endeavour of fellow scholars. Where the act of translation should highlight the difficulty of simple correspondence, for Bardo, and the squabbling and jealous scholars of Florence, it inspires a quest for the dominance of univocalism.

The competing creeds of Florence lay claim to different kinds of knowledge, the pagan world espousing the rationality of the philosophers, the Christian world the visionary wisdom of the mystics. However, in this masculine world these ways of knowing only operate oppositionally. For Bardo, Dino's turn to mysticism puts him incontrovertibly at odds with his heritage, and beyond the bounds of communication: 'I have disowned him for ever. He was a ready scholar . . . showing a disposition from the very first to turn away his eyes from the clear lights of reason and philosophy, and to prostrate himself under the influences of a dim mysticism which eludes all rules of human duty as it eludes all argument' (123). Ironically, it is not only mysticism which enables the evasion of duty: the example of Tito shows us precisely how rational 'argument' can be used just as effectively to elude all 'human duty'. So, it is his philosophical training which Tito uses to excuse himself from all obligation to his father:

> could any philosophy prove to him that he was bound to care for another's suffering more than for his own? To do so, he must have loved Baldassarre devotedly, and he did *not* love him: was that his own fault? Gratitude! seen closely, it made no valid claim: his father's life would have been dreary without him: are we convicted of a debt to men for the pleasures they give themselves? (112)

Similarly, when Tito seeks to persuade Romola of the foolishness of her concern for her father's dying wish, he does so through the explicit appeal to rationality or 'argument':

> But a little philosophy should teach us to rid ourselves of those air-woven fetters that mortals hang round themselves, spending their lives in misery under the mere imagination of their weight. Your mind, which seizes ideas so readily, my Romola, is able to discriminate between substantial good and these brain-wrought fantasies. Ask yourself, dearest, what possible good can these books and antiquities do stowed together under your father's name in Florence, more than they would do if they were divided or carried elsewhere? Nay, is not the very dispersion of such things in hands that know how to value them, one means of extending their usefulness? (270)

Tito's 'erudite familiarity with the disputes concerning the chief good' allows him to regard the discourse of ethics as little more than a game and 'a matter of taste' (113). And he uses his rationality like a weapon, levelling the charge of madness against those who oppose or threaten him – Dino, Romola, and, most cruelly, Baldassarre.

Just as Eliot suggests a commonality between the enemies Tito and Savanarola, so too she indicates that Tito and Dino are alike in the way that their modes of thinking are bankrupted in their alienation from, and disregard for, feeling. Tito's rationalising, for example, constitutes a lethal assault on his emotions: his 'thought showed itself as active as virulent acid, eating its rapid way through all the tissues of sentiment' (112). Similarly, Romola is shocked to find that Dino has come to see the world through a prism which excludes all affective ties. His visionary knowledge has no place for sentiment, and comes rather 'from the shadowy region where human souls seek wisdom apart from the human sympathies which are the very life and substance of our wisdom' (155). In this dichotomised world, only Romola, in the face of the unfamiliar, unknown or oppositional, shows the generosity and humility to contemplate the possibility 'that there is some truth in what moves them – some truth of which I know nothing' (171).

When Savonarola turns Romola back in her flight from Florence, he accuses her of a sin that is recognisable to pagan and Christian alike: 'you yourself are breaking the simplest law that lies at the foundation of the trust which binds man to man – faithfulness to the spoken word' (340). Yet if utterance is potentially the unifying force that binds men together, its use and misuse in the Florentine world ensures that rather than the 'foundation of trust', speech becomes the battleground for competing creeds and factions – much more a weapon of opposition than a tool of unity.

Florentines in *Romola* are untroubled by the apparent contradiction between their fervid desire for truth and their cynical awareness of duplicity. Thus, on the one hand, while Nello boasts of the scepticism and sophistication of the Florentines' 'liberal ideas about speech' (36) and 'wise dissimulation' (327), the populace flocks to hear the 'certitude' of Savonarola's sermons. It is a milieu that thrives on 'concise alternatives' (494), on the fixity and clarity that makes opposition possible. In such a world, a figure like Baldassarre – a man confused and unable 'to seize the words that would convey the thought he wanted to utter' (422) – is bound to be outcast. Hence, the struggle between the fluent, rational Tito and the rambling, crazed Baldassarre is no contest at all. Blinded by their love of the elegant utterance, the Florentines embrace the traitor and the lie, and cast out the victim and the truth. Only Romola resists the sway of Tito's narrative to read an emotional truth behind the rhetoric, guided by her alertness both to Tito's dread and Baldassarre's passionate conviction.

In such a context, both Savonarola and Tito are performers *par excellence*. Just as Savonarola is a man 'accustomed to make [his] power felt by speech' (496), Tito also depends for his position and advancement on his verbal acumen. Tito's misuse of language is, of course, more egregious. His 'fluent talk' (270) is as disingenuous as it is contemptible; he uses 'all the resources of lying' (213) to further his own ambitions; and, like all good liars, he comes in the end to deceive even himself.

Yet Savonarola, too, is guilty of misusing his rhetorical power, seduced into false simplicity and artificial certainty by the dynamics of rhetorical performance. From the outset Savonarola is carried away by the drama of his sermons, offering himself up for martyrdom with a bravado that proves humiliatingly hollow when put to the test. More damagingly, he is transformed by his audience, drawn by a need to dominate them into a debasement of his message: 'for the mass of his audience all the pregnancy of his preaching lay in his strong assertion of supernatural claims, in his denunciatory visions, in the false certitude which gave his sermons the interest of a political bulletin; and having once held that audience in his mastery, it was necessary to his nature – it was necessary for their welfare – that he should *keep* the mastery. The effect was inevitable' (223). His performances acquire a momentum which sees him 'hurried into self-justifying evasiveness' (459) and 'driven into . . . excesses of speech' (454). The inner struggles of an honourable man are artificially clarified, exposed and 'brought into terrible evidence' (417) by his speech. And he succumbs to the false simplicities required both by his polemical position and by the demands of oratory: 'To the common run of mankind it has always seemed a proof of mental vigour to find moral questions easy, and judge conduct according to concise alternatives' (494). In Eliot's reckoning, Savonarola has paid the inevitable price of political life: 'No man ever struggled to retain power over a mixed multitude without suffering vitiation: his standard must be their lower needs, and not his own best insight' (223).

It is a grim testimony to the destructiveness of that polemical world that by the end of the novel all the men in Romola's life – Bardo, Dino, Tito, Baldassarre, Bernardo del Nero and Savonarola – are dead, each to some extent the victim of a public and masculine world of enmities and opposition. In contrast, Romola has retreated to a domestic feminine space where she lives in harmony with her aunt, Tessa and Tessa's children. Yet while making her point in such a contrast, in keeping with the spirit of a novel which abhors 'simple judgment' and 'facile knowingness' (223), Eliot does not allow this last opposition to stand unmodified. In the final confrontation between Romola and Savonarola, over the death sentence for Bernardo del Nero, where they seem most at odds as representatives of opposing ways of seeing the world, we discover that they are in fact most alike. For her part, Romola, swayed by the immediate power of strong emotion, succumbs to harsh and ungenerous judgement of her opponent, allowing her love for her godfather to arouse unfair antagonism: 'she saw all the repulsive and inconsistent details in his teaching with a painful lucidity which exaggerated their proportions' (472).

Accordingly, she judges him 'unfairly on a question of individual suffering at which *she* looked with the eyes of personal tenderness, and *he* with the eyes of theoretic conviction' (472). In the face of Romola's temporary blindness, Eliot insists on a complexity of judgement:

> In that declaration of his, that the Cause of his party was the Cause of God's kingdom, she heard only the ring of egoism. Perhaps such words have rarely been uttered without that meaner ring in them; yet they are the implicit formula of all energetic belief. And if such energetic belief, pursuing a grand and remote end, is often in danger of

becoming a demon-worship, in which the votary lets his son and daughter pass through the fire with a readiness that hardly looks like sacrifice; tender fellow-feeling for the nearest has its dangers too, and is apt to be timid and sceptical towards the larger aims without which life cannot rise into religion. In this way poor Romola was being blinded by her tears.   (472)

Perhaps more important than Romola's momentary failure to tread the middle ground, Eliot demonstrates that whatever the rigidity of his outward resolve, Savonarola is haunted by the complexities of a fine moral intelligence. When Romola confronts him with the injustice of her godfather's sentence, he is reluctant to address her arguments, not out of any simple conviction of his rightness, but out of a sense of familiarity with her position: '[he was] strongly disinclined to reopen externally a debate which he had already gone through inwardly' (459). For this moment, his is not the arrogance of certainty, but the humility of doubt: Romola's position merely reiterates the 'inner voices' that he fears 'might become loud again when encouraged from without' (459). And where Romola sees only 'one ground of action', he is tormented by 'many' (464). Indeed, unlike all the other males who die unshaken in their rigid antipathies, it is a measure both of his nobility and of his tragedy that Savonarola cannot hold on to the sureness either of his vision or of his rhetoric. The certitude with which he swayed the multitude degenerates into the humiliating vacillations and contradictions of his forced confessions, and in the end at his execution a 'last silence' (541) defies all expectation of momentous utterance.

George Eliot insisted that Savonarola and Romola were much alike. More than their shared love of homage, their 'passionate sympathy' and 'the splendour of [their] aims' (366), Eliot suggested that the 'great problem' of Romola's life 'essentially coincides with a chief problem in Savonarola's' (IV, 97). Although she was not more specific, it seems reasonable to assume that what Savonarola and Romola have in common above all is their struggle with the 'question of where the duty of obedience ends, and the duty of resistance begins' (431). If Romola seems to avoid the more agonising consequences of that struggle, it is, perhaps, because she is never fully tested. Unlike Savonarola, Romola, with her dream-like escape to the plague village and her return to matriarchal contentment, seems to be – in the terms suggested by George Levine[19] – shielded from the harsh test of realism and sheltered by the idealism of romance. Yet if one argues on the one hand that Romola is spared the temptation and corruption of public life, one must acknowledge on the other that her deliverance stems from the fact, as Maggie Tulliver has observed, that it is men who occupy the public domain, 'who have the power, and can do something in the world' (*Mill*, 347). And whereas Savanarola's *capacity* for openness and doubt renders him a more tragic figure, it is an indictment both of him, and of the masculine world of Florence, that there is no place for the expression of such ethical complexity in public life.

8

A Politics of Morality: *Felix Holt*

I

George Eliot's prediction that *Romola* was destined to be less popular than her earlier works proved to be all too accurate for her new publisher George Smith, whose gamble in paying £7000 for the serialisation of the novel in his *Cornhill Magazine* failed to pay dividends in the form of increased sales. Undeterred, however, Eliot continued to experiment with new forms, determined with her next project, *The Spanish Gypsy*, to write 'rather to please myself than the public', and uncertain as to whether her new work would ever be published (IV, 176). For the first time in her 'serious authorship' Eliot was attempting to write in verse,[1] and, almost perversely, after the 'unspeakable pains' (IV, 301) she suffered in the preparation of *Romola*, Eliot chose once again to set her new work in a distant place and time – Spain in the fifteenth century. Accordingly, the end of 1864 saw her immersing herself in Spanish history and learning Spanish grammar.

Eliot struggled with *The Spanish Gypsy* for eight months before she allowed the project to be halted by Lewes's intervention, simply noting in her Journal in February 1865, '*George has taken my drama away from me.*'[2] Unable to proceed, Eliot once again changed direction. Just as she had retreated from the difficulties of her Italian story to the more familiar territory of *Silas Marner*'s England, once again she switched projects, setting aside her Spanish drama to take up another 'English' novel, *Felix Holt*, set in provincial England in 1832. She returned as well to her original publisher, John Blackwood, who rejoiced in the assurance of Eliot's reversion to a familiar idiom: 'The book is a perfect marvel. The time is just after the passing of the Reform Bill and surely such a picture or rather series of pictures of English Life, manners, and conversation never was drawn. You seem to hear and see the people speaking. Every individual character stands out a distinct figure' (IV, 247).

Indeed, that confident facility is evident in the novel's opening pages which represent a *tour de force* of familiarity. Through the imaginative device of a coach journey, Eliot offers a sweeping panorama of continuity and change. Just as the coach moves inexorably through the Midlands, so, too, a whole range of developments, set in train by the Industrial Revolution, are seen to have moved through the countryside, intruding upon the pastoral world of provincial England. The movement of the coach distils the movement of history, as the traveller passes 'rapidly from one phase of English life to another' (*FH*, 8). History becomes 'incarnate' (*SCW*, 284), as geographic proximity provides a visual equivalent to the layers of historical chronology. Thus, for example, a 'village dingy with coal-dust, noisy with the shaking of looms' gives way in another ten minutes of travel to a rural region where 'the neighbourhood of the town was only felt in the advantages of a near market for corn, cheese, and hay' (8). Through the metaphor of the journey, and through the unifying force of the coachman's memory, Eliot stresses a sense of organic continuity, a recognition of the 'vital connexion with the past' (*SCW*, 283). Or, as Peter Coveney has claimed, with the opening of the novel 'we feel at once the presence of a mind which possesses the power of all creative history, to see any present in the context of an accumulated past'.[3]

On the face of it, Eliot's new novel seems to intensify the focus on politics begun in *Romola*. The novel's full title, *Felix Holt, the Radical*, heralds its concern with radicalism and reform, and the opening of its first chapter announces its preoccupation with 'the memorable year of 1832' (13), the year of the first Reform Bill. Moreover, written between March 1865 and May 1866, at a time of heightened agitation leading up to the passage of the second Reform Bill in 1867, *Felix Holt* represents Eliot's most direct foray into matters of the day. Indeed, both her publisher and her husband were excited by the novel's topical resonance. Finding himself in complete agreement with the political tenor of the novel, John Blackwood wrote to his London manager declaring, 'Her politics are excellent and will attract all parties. Her sayings would be invaluable in the present debate' (IV, 247).[4] Similarly, George Lewes was alert to both the public benefit and the commercial potential of the book's relevance to the contemporary debate:

> It is a great pity that it isn't quite ready for publication just in the thick of the reform discussion so many good quotable 'bits' would be furnished to M.P.'s. However the subject will not grow cold. She expects to be entirely finished by the end of May; so as to appear at the beginning of June. – Would it be too late to insert a slip into Maga this month announcing it for June – *with* the title?   (VIII, 374)

So, unlike the remote Renaissance world of *Romola*, the change that this novel contemplates is, to use Eliot's own words from *Middlemarch*, 'here – now – in England' (*M*, 28). Whereas in Eliot's earlier England novels the spectre of change haunts the margins of the text in the form of the dystopic worlds of Snowfield in *Adam Bede* and Lantern Yard in *Silas Marner*, their industrial bleakness never really impinges on the rural idylls in which the texts are set, and both Dinah and Silas respectively are recuperated back into domestic bliss in a safer agrarian world. In contrast, the 'eager unrest' of the industrial towns in *Felix Holt* is never far away. No longer on the margins, the manufacturing towns – 'the scene of riots and trade-union meetings' – now form 'crowded nests *in the midst* [my italics] of the large-spaced, slow-moving life of homesteads and far-away cottages and oak-sheltered parks' (8).

Just as the countryside is now penetrated by the threatening force of the railway, 'shot, like a bullet through a tube' (5), the 'old England', represented by Treby Magna's 'old-fashioned, grazing, brewing, wool-packing, cheese-loading life', is not immune to the contagion of the 'new' (40). In a paradigmatic fall from grace, Treby Magna has lost its innocence and simple respectability through being drawn into the more complex and compromised world of industrial capitalism. Emblematically, Sir Maximus Debarry, the lord of the manor, has been seduced by the grandiose and greedy plans of the persuasive outsider, Matthew Jermyn, not a 'native Trebian' but a lawyer 'from a distance' (40), to invest in plans to turn Treby Magna into a spa and fashionable watering-place. When the venture fails, Debarry lets his 'useless hotel' on a long lease, supposing that it will be turned into a benevolent college. He is then powerless to prevent its transformation into a tape manufactory, unable to halt the march of change. The safely localised community, 'where the trade was only such as had close relations with the local landed interest', is thus thrown open to the wider world as the town takes on 'the more complex life brought by mines and manufactures, which belong more directly to the great circulating system of the nation than to the local system to which they have been superadded' (41).

The more insistent and inescapable sense of change in this novel and the relevance of the work's deliberations to the contemporary debate combine to alter Eliot's treatment of politics in *Felix Holt*. Where the outcome of the political machinations of Renaissance Florence were fixed in the historical record, the developments of reform in nineteenth-century England were an unfolding reality for Eliot. Indeed, the novel can be read, as Peter Coveney has argued, as 'part of a mid-Victorian dialogue between culture . . . and the rising democracy'.[5] In this light, it is not surprising that unlike the more detached perspective of *Romola*, in which the political outcome is of far less interest than the political process, in *Felix Holt* Eliot's assessments are more partisan and didactic, her agenda more transparent.

It is precisely this agenda which has attracted a great deal of critical attention, troubling many commentators on the novel.[6] It has become a critical truism, for example, to note that despite the title, Felix Holt is no radical. There is only the slightest underpinning to any claim for radicalism in the novel, which rests with Eliot's conviction that change was at once inevitable and desirable. Whatever her nostalgia for the past, the tenor of Eliot's Introduction to *Felix Holt* makes it clear that she does not share the conviction 'that old England was as good as possible' (8). She disdained any tendency towards a 'poetic fanaticism for the past', and, like Wilhelm Riehl, she had a mind 'capable of discerning the grander evolution of things' (*SCW*, 294). Yet for Eliot, everything turned not on the nature but on the pace of change. Her concern was that organic growth was being jeopardised by too rapid a transformation – that 'the discontinuities in English society arising from the economic and social developments we call the Industrial Revolution would be compounded by the processes of a too swift and unconsidered political change, among which the concept of society as an organic continuum and of culture as an organic inheritance would become submerged and lost'.[7] That fear of a loss of continuity informs Eliot's reading of the Reform debate, and gives rise in the novel to a faith in gradualism and meliorism that amounts almost to political quietism in the end. Thus, Felix Holt's prescriptions for change are so vague and so minimal – harsh words and good books for the 'few within [his] reach' (223) – that they hold out scant prospect of reform, especially when they are considered in conjunction with the novel's general mistrust of the working classes and of their capacity for self-regeneration.[8]

II

In the end, however, the most fundamental concerns of the novel are not directed at the world of party politics. Indeed, it is remarkable that for all the overt interest in formal politics in *Felix Holt*, and for all the critical attention afforded that aspect of the novel, there is a strange tenuity about the novel's political exploration. It is not simply, as many critics have noted, that the imaginative intensity of the novel inheres in the Transome sub-plot. It is that the parliamentary politics in this novel seem ultimately insignificant and unimportant, suggesting most often a realm of bathos rather than tragedy. Whereas, as we have seen, in *Romola* the most powerful libidinal investments of that world are bound up with a desire for power and glory in a public and political sphere, in *Felix Holt* political allegiances seem far more trivial and contingent. Harold Transome's radicalism, for example, is 'not defined by theory' (93), but is born rather of personal reaction, a calculated definition of himself against a home and a system which has never accorded him the status his ego requires. As the second son, who has cut 'no great figure' (92) at Eton, he is determined to return and 'thrash a lord or two who thrashed me at Eton' (19). Having confirmed his social illegitimacy by acquiring a fortune through mercantilism in foreign climes, Harold has nourished over time 'an inclination to as much opposition as would enable him to assert his own independence and power without throwing himself into that tabooed condition which robs power of its triumph . . . He was addicted at once to rebellion and to conformity, and only an intimate personal knowledge could enable any one to predict where his conformity would begin' (93).

Mrs Transome's outraged opposition to her son's radical candidature is equally unimpressive. Her objection to radicalism amounts to nothing more than the expression of arrant snobbery: 'I always thought Radicals' houses stood staring above poor sticks of young trees and iron hurdles' (21). And her adherence to conservatism stems simply from the complacency of privilege: 'she believed all the while that truth and safety lay in due attendance on prayers and sermons, in the admirable doctrines and ritual of the Church of England, equally remote from Puritanism and Popery; in fact, in such a view of this world and the next as would preserve the existing arrangements of English society quite unshaken, keeping down the obtrusiveness of the vulgar and the discontent of the poor' (27).

The shallowness of political convictions is epitomised in the novel by the comic figure of the Reverend Lingon, a 'born' Tory who, after his initial alarm at discovering his nephew Harold's political intentions, convinces himself in the course of half an hour that it 'followed plainly enough that, in these hopeless times, nothing was left to men of sense and good family but to retard the national ruin by declaring themselves Radicals, and take the inevitable process of changing everything out of the hands of beggarly demagogues and purse-proud tradesmen' (31). Amid the general bankruptcy of political conviction, the main players in the election get the servants they deserve – the fickle and self-interested figures of Jermyn, Johnson and Scaddon.

Whereas in *Romola* political principle can be a matter of life and death, in *Felix Holt* the consequence of party allegiance is mere social awkwardness. So, Mrs Transome's dire warning to Harold is that 'No one will visit you' (34) and Sir Maximus Debarry's disgust finds expression in the cancellation of a dinner invitation: 'Dine with me? I should think not. I'd sooner he should dine off me' (82). Even so, those social rifts are quickly healed when a more fundamental class solidarity leads Sir Maximus to take Harold's side on the occasion of Jermyn's public announcement that he is Harold's father. Demanding that the interloper leave, Sir Maximus reconfirms loyalties which transcend party politics, declaring 'This is a meeting of gentlemen' (381).

Similarly, the political process which is seen to be so powerfully corrosive in *Romola*, where Savonarola's fate tragically bears out the dictum that 'No man ever struggled to retain power over a mixed multitude without suffering vitiation' (223), seems simply contemptible in *Felix Holt*. Harold's enmeshment in the petty corruption of electioneering is only disturbing to him in so far as he is irritated by the prospect of public exposure. He consoles himself with a sense of the moral insignificance of Felix's condemnation of his campaign tactics: 'A practical man must seek a good end by the only possible means; that is to say, if he is to get into Parliament he must not be too particular. It was not disgraceful to be neither a Quixote nor a theorist, aiming to correct the moral rules of the world' (158).

The striking exception to this lack of principle and seriousness in the novel's political world is, of course, Felix Holt. He is the earnest, outspoken, moral centre of the novel, and yet his gravitas does not function as a sufficient counterbalance to the general insubstantiality. To begin with, his political convictions are based on the vaguest of conversions in a 'Scotch garret', brought on rather puzzlingly 'by six weeks' debauchery' (53). Furthermore, his avowed class solidarity sits uneasily with his supercilious disdain for his fellow workers, whose greatest need, in Felix's judgement, is to be told that they are 'blind and foolish' (223). His scepticism about the efficacy of parliamentary reform and his more generally quietist agenda culminate, unsurprisingly, in his professed indifference to the outcome of the election. Indeed, this indifference is reflected more broadly in the novel where the election result is barely noted. So, Harold feels his loss as a mere 'annoyance', Reverend Lingon easily reverts to his prior Tory convictions, and the tone of Eliot's political epilogue for Treby Magna bespeaks an almost cynical disinterest:

> As to all that wide parish of Treby Magna, it has since prospered as the rest of England has prospered. Doubtless there is more enlightenment now. Whether the farmers are all public-spirited, the shopkeepers nobly independent, the Sproxton men entirely sober and judicious, the Dissenters quite without narrowness or asperity in religion and politics, and the publicans all fit, like Gaius, to be the friends of an apostle – these things I have not heard, not having correspondence in those parts. Whether any presumption may be drawn from the fact that North Loamshire does not yet return a Radical candidate, I leave to the all-wise – I mean the newspapers. (398)

If there is a strange lack of substantiality about the politics in *Felix Holt*, that vacancy in the novel is even more strikingly evident at a structural level through a series of ellipses or lacunae. Repeatedly, the opportunity for the articulation of a programme of radicalism and reform is set up, and framed specifically as a moment of audition, only to collapse into non-performance. Thus, for example, on the first occasion that we actually encounter Felix at the Sugar Loaf Inn, the site of his Sunday 'preaching' to the miners, after the briefest of contretemps with the slick Mr Johnson, he judges it best not to say any more, and leaves. Similarly, on the occasion of Harold's maiden speech on market-day, the audience is assembled, the introduction is provided by Reverend Lingon, Harold's voice is described as 'full and penetrating' and then we are presented with the most anti-climatic summation, informed simply that 'Harold's speech "did"' (171). The absence is underscored further by the series of negatives which describe it: 'it was not of the glib-nonsensical sort, not ponder-ous, not hesitating' (171). And again, after several anticipatory chap-ters, Reverend Lyon's debate against Mr Sherlock comes to nothing, as Lyon is left on stage facing an expectant audience, only to discover that Sherlock has absconded, and the debate is 'adjourned' (205), never to be rescheduled.

This succession of thwarted expectations creates a certain political muteness in the novel, which is compounded by the obliqueness of the two political speeches of any consequence which do occur. The first, the most elaborate exposition of a credo that Felix offers, is telling in that it is delivered not in the context of the public, urban world of the Radical politician but in the most private of settings, a tête-à-tête with Esther, secluded away from the agitation of the city in an idyllic natural world. It is the vaguest and most unconvincing of manifestos. Beyond a general rejection of the 'struggle for success' (220), which Felix unquestioningly sees as synonymous with corrup-tion, Felix's only plan of action is to take himself off to 'some ugly, wicked, miserable place' and set himself up as a 'demagogue of a new sort' (223).

The second speech, delivered to a gathering assembled to hear the 'hard-lipped antagonism' of the trade-unionist, constitutes Felix's one genuine moment of formal political utterance. Yet where the unionist at least speaks a language of rights and demands, Felix dissi-pates that focus to urge instead the possibility of 'another sort of power' for working men, a power 'without votes' (248), and he con-signs the prospect of 'political power' to an amorphous future date; 'some time, whether we live to see it or not' (247). His ultimate rec-ommendation is that workers pursue the 'the greatest power under heaven', the power of 'public opinion' (248), but his tortuous ana-logy between the driving power of opinion and the water in a steam engine does nothing either to clarify the vagueness of his conception or to convince us of its efficacy. In fact, what is most striking in this, his only real political speech, is the fact that Felix in effect repudiates the whole political process.[9]

III

Paradoxically, then, there seems to be a lack of interest in formal pol-itics in this, Eliot's most avowedly political novel. Nonetheless polit-ics does provide a key to *Felix Holt* – but it is politics understood in a broader and more informal sense as the politics of the everyday, the process or principle according to which decisions are made. In particular, Eliot explores the nexus between the public sphere and the private life, which underscores the novel's contention that 'there is no private life which has not been determined by a wider public life' (43). By shifting the focus in this way we can challenge the common critical perception that the novel lacks structural cohesion. Peter Coveney exemplifies such a view when he complains of a 'sense of alternation' between 'two loosely connected parts', which creates only a 'tenuous connection between the personal tragedy of Mrs Transome and the political theme of Felix Holt'.[10] However, the novel no longer seems so fractured, when we recognise the way in which Eliot consistently explores the *inter-relation* between on the one hand the public construction of opinion, reputation and shame, and on the other the private experience of integrity, conscience and guilt. More than a novel about reform, this is a novel about secrets; it is less concerned with the machinations of party politics than the working out of a politics of morality.

Even within this broader conception of politics, the crucial issues of change and continuity remain pertinent. The 'more complex' life that has come to Treby Magna with industrialisation has brought not just religious dissent and reformist ferment. The circumstances of public life which regulate and inform private life have changed too. The greater mobility of the population has led to a greater preponderance of strangers in Treby Magna – people whose pasts are unknown, and therefore susceptible to various kinds of misrepresentation. Mr Christian, for example, comes 'from nobody knows where' (87), and neither Mr Scales's hints at a criminal background nor the gardener's report of his nobility comes close to divining the truth of Christian's assumed identity. In a similar way mobility can also divide personal histories – as in the case, for instance, of Harold's mysterious sojourn in Smyrna – offering the individual considerable scope for concealment. In this more cosmopolitan world, speculation and rumour replace the localised knowledge and certainty displayed in the opening by the coachman, who could 'tell the names of sites and persons, and explain the meaning of groups', and who knew 'whose the land was wherever he drove; what noblemen had half-ruined themselves by gambling; who made handsome returns of rent; and who was at daggers-drawn with his eldest son' (9).

Where once the population of 'old' England was kept 'safely in the *via media* of indifference' (6) by their inability to read, and reputations were made and lost through the personal transmission of gossip, with the increase of literacy and the proliferation of the printed word, public reputation has entered the realm of mass production.[11] Thus, in *Felix Holt*, the newspapers act as the 'guides of public opinion', depicting Harold Transome variously as a 'dissolute cosmopolitan' and an 'intellectual giant' (92), and the suspicion of the illegitimacy of Harold's claim to the Transome estate is propagated by the handbills which the disgruntled Johnson writes and posts around the town.

Furthermore, at the same time as technology is increasing the reach and power of publicity, the extension of the franchise is broadening the base of those who sit in judgement on an individual's public reputation. Where once Harold Transome would not have been expected either to know or to care about the common man's estimate of his character, now he must participate in an orchestrated campaign of courting popular approval. And where public reputation has come to matter in such a way, private information acquires a new currency. Thus, secrets become, potentially, 'a source of profit' (208), and the 'possession of facts', rightly interpreted and cunningly managed, can promise a character like Jermyn 'new power' over others (165). Similarly, public opinion and support become things to be purchased, as in the bribery of the miners at the Sugar Loaf Inn. With this commodification of reputation in the public sphere, the stakes are raised in the private sphere of moral choice, as virtues such as integrity and rectitude come under new pressure.

Secrets mark a fault line between the public and private worlds of morality, as they create a disjunction between public and private self-representation. They have the potential to breach the fabric both of the communal and the individual history because they impede and distort the narrative through which we make sense of the world and the self. We can see this in operation in the novel's opening. The coachman through his narrative names and explains the world, acting at once as historian and guide. He is the custodian of social memory and, by his tale, he creates a sense of continuity. Significantly, though, his narrative breaks down at the point at which he broaches the Transome history, and the surety with which he has hitherto accounted for his community gives way to uncertainty. In the face of the Transome secrets he is forced to try to 'make out' the story, a tale with so many 'ins and outs' that it defies interpretation: 'you couldn't look into it straight backward' (10). His narrative is baffled; from the ready and fulsome proffering of his story 'without being questioned', the coachman is reduced to silence: 'If the passenger was curious for further knowledge concerning the Transome affairs, Sampson would shake his head and say there had been fine stories in his time; but he never condescended to state what the stories were. Some attributed this reticence to a wise incredulity, others to a want of memory, others to simple ignorance' (10). In this way it is not simply political change, as we have seen, which threatens the organic inheritance of culture, but the narrative discontinuities created by secrets and subterfuge which sever 'the vital connexion with the past' (*SCW*, 283).

The same dynamic in which secrets undermine the unifying interpretative power of narrative is played out at an individual level. Mrs Transome, for example, is cut off from all around her by secret deeds and secret desires. Her tenants, who rely only on 'glimpses of her outward life' (28), have no way of understanding or forgiving her haughty behaviour because none 'divined what was hidden under that outward life – a woman's keen sensibility and dread, which lay screened behind all her petty habits and narrow notions, as some quivering thing with eyes and throbbing heart may lie crouching behind withered rubbish' (28). Significantly, the one person to whom Mrs Transome remains connected, and from whom she receives meagre solace, her maid Denner, is the only person who 'knew all her mistress's secrets' (25). Conversely, Mrs Transome's alienation from her son, which strikes her like a 'terror' (16), is the result not so much of his absence abroad as of her inability to offer an account of herself which might engender understanding. She is forced to dissemble because 'there were secrets which her son must never know' (17). Her silence is damaging for both. Harold, for example, expects to know himself in terms of his history. Yet because he labours under a delusion about his past, his present remains a puzzle: ' "How is it I have the trick of getting fat?" (Here Harold lifted his arm and spread out his plump hand.) "I remember my father was as thin as a herring" ' (17). And it is not until the shattering public revelation of her deceptions that Harold understands 'as he had never understood before, the neglected solitariness of his mother's life' (382). Similarly, when Reverend Lyon reveals the secret of Esther's parentage, she too comes to 'see things I was blind to before – depths in my father's nature' (218). In all, secrets militate against understanding, isolate individuals and breach the sense of continuity between the past and the present through which we make sense of the world.

IV

In her consideration of the nexus between public and private in a politics of morality Eliot makes use of structural contrast, as she had before in the fifteenth chapter of *Adam Bede* and in the more extended contrast between worlds in *Romola*. Indeed, rather than a merely 'tenuous connection' between the 'personal tragedy' of the Transome sub-plot and the 'political theme' of the Holt/Lyon plot,[12] it is possible to see the two worlds of the novel held together through a complex web of comparisons and contrasts. The connection between the two parts is underscored initially by the symmetry of the secret which is central to each – that is, the deception of both Harold and Esther as to the true identity of their biological fathers. The difference, however, in the ways those secrets are managed underlines the strikingly different ethical milieu of the two worlds. On the one hand, when Jermyn threatens Mrs Transome with exposure, she rebels against the impending shame and notoriety, resolving never to tell her secret, and thus confirming the isolating fear of disclosure which has tormented her adult life. On the other hand, when Reverend Lyon's secret similarly comes under scrutiny, his response is not directed to the public prospect of shame, but rather to the private experience of guilt at the 'one act of deception' (135) in his life. And in his resolution to tell Esther, even when the threat of disclosure is removed, he recognises the potential for liberation from the isolation of the lie: 'then I shall fear nothing' (212).

The contrast between Mrs Transome's and Reverend Lyon's responses to imminent disclosure is suggestive of a broader contrast between a world of artifice and subterfuge and a world of simplicity and directness. Transome Court is a realm obsessed with keeping up appearances. Mrs Transome's determination to cut a fine figure, despite her reduced circumstance, is evident from the moment of her first entry into the novel. Dressed in worn black cloth and 'visibly mended' lace, she nevertheless sports the 'rare jewels' (14) that confirm her station with a 'high-born imperious air' (26). Her vanity strikes an answering chord in her son Harold who is struck both by her distinguished bearing and by the 'wreck' his father has become (15). Without concern for any substantial relationship with his mother, he is nevertheless 'bent on seeing her make as good a figure in the neighbourhood as any other woman of her rank' (94). Harold himself dresses impeccably, frets about his weight and is concerned above all with the impression he makes on others:

The blockheads must be forced to respect him. Hence, in proportion as he foresaw that his equals in the neighbourhood would be indignant with him for his political choice, he cared keenly about making a good figure before them in every other way. His conduct as a landholder was to be judicious, his establishment was to be kept up generously, his imbecile father treated with careful regard, his family relations entirely without scandal. (31)

In a similar way, the family portraits in the Transome Court drawing-room record, as Esther notes, a history of self-conscious affectation (321).

In contrast to the ostentatious and decorative Transome Court, the Reverend Lyon's house at Chapel Yard is humble and functional. As his surroundings suggest, the minister is as unself-conscious as he is unfashionable. Although every aspect of his person is 'so irrelevant' to a 'fashionable view of things' that he is an object of derision to well-dressed ladies and gentlemen (68), he is too short-sighted and too unworldly either to notice or to care. And in his disregard for appearances, Reverend Lyon finds a fellow-traveller in the figure of Felix Holt, who appears in Lyon's house like a 'roughly written page', 'shaggy-headed' and disdainful of conventional notions of respectable attire (52).

The transparency of Chapel Yard makes it a place unconducive to secrets, whereas the careful management of appearances at Transome Court encourages dissembling. This difference is reflected in the disparate linguistic style of the two groups. Reverend Lyon is as unfashionable in his speech as in his appearance, finding himself corrected by Esther 'on the grounds of niceties' which are incomprehensible to him: 'I am eager for precision, and would fain find language subtle enough to follow the utmost intricacies of the soul's pathways, but I see not why a round word that means some object, made and blessed by the Creator, should be branded and banished as a malefactor' (60). Felix's language is similarly unadorned. Impatient of 'roundabout euphemisms' (60), Felix is frank to the point of offensiveness. Yet beyond his self-righteousness, there is a striving for accuracy: 'But you do look ill . . . Or rather – for that's a false way of putting it – you look as if you had been very much distressed' (218). And in this he resembles Reverend Lyon's eagerness for precision, evident too in Lyon's life-long quest to 'fathom' the 'great texts' through careful study (45). Felix Holt's characteristic bluntness provides a marked contrast with Harold Transome's smooth sophistry. The clash of styles between the two men is distilled

in their attitudes to the court proceedings against Holt. Felix for-
swears 'legal adroitness' (298), scorning a defence in which truth
might be 'screened or avoided' (308) in favour of giving a 'perfectly
simple' (298) account of his actions. Harold, on the other hand, is
appalled by the unworldliness of Felix's attitude, dismissing his 'singular directness and simplicity of speech' as 'fanatical' (308).

The commitment of Felix and Reverend Lyon to simplicity and
accuracy in language provides the cornerstone of their integrity, for it
is the slippage in language which readily accommodates moral laxity,
as Eliot makes clear in her epigraph to Chapter XXXVI:

> See now the virtue living in a word!
> Hobson will think of swearing it was noon
> When he saw Dobson at the May-day fair,
> To prove poor Dobson did not rob the mail.
> 'Tis neighbourly to save a neighbour's neck:
> What harm in lying when you mean no harm?
> But say 'tis perjury, then Hobson quakes –
> He'll none of perjury.
>   Thus words embalm
> The conscience of mankind; and Roman laws
> Bring still a conscience to poor Hobson's aid.   (284)

Much more than a matter of style, the use of language in the world
of Chapel Yard bespeaks a commitment to disclosure. In contrast to
the prevalence of the hidden and the unspoken at Transome Court,
Chapel Yard is an environment in which the Reverend Lyon feels a
compulsion towards articulation and hence exposition, as he confesses to Felix: 'I have a need of utterance which makes the thought
within me seem as pent-up fire, until I have shot it forth' (56). Hence,
as we have seen, in his crisis over his secret, his prayer is simply 'to
know' and 'to declare' (135).

In this scheme of contrast Esther, of course, functions as a go-
between and, ultimately, as the arbiter between the two worlds. She
is fitted for that role by her chameleon-like qualities. With her 'surprisingly distinguished manners and appearance' (289), cultivated
tastes and aspirations toward gentility, Esther seems an 'incongru-
ous' (58) presence in her father's humble household. The prospect of
a radical 'change of condition' in the move from Chapel Yard to
Transome Court is immediately 'tempting' (307) to her, and she is
gratified to find herself taken in to a world which, at least for a time,

approximates the 'delightful aristocratic dwelling in her Utopia' (317). Esther's gradual disenchantment leads in the end to a choice not just between rival lovers but, explicitly, between two worlds. Her decision to return to Chapel Yard and to marry Felix represents a more complex and considered choice than Eppie's comparable decision to refuse Godfrey Cass's adoption and 'stay among poor folks' (167) in *Silas Marner*. Esther's decision is based on more than affectionate loyalty: where Eppie decides passively to stay, Esther must choose actively to return. While she has a clear-sighted sense of the implications of her choice, knowing through her 'previous' existence 'the dim life of the back street, the contact with sordid vulgarity, the lack of refinement for the senses, the summons to a daily task' (388), she has scrutinised the features of Transome Court with equal sharpness: 'If I had not, I should not have left what I did leave. I made a deliberate choice' (395).

V

There is, however, one curiously discordant detail in the account of Esther's heroic act of renunciation. Having announced her determination not to 'be rich' and to give 'it all up' (395), Esther resiles from that position to declare that she means to have 'some wealth' (395). The two pounds a week which she intends to retain from the Transome estate to ensure that there is always 'money to spare' (395), and which Felix accepts without demur, raises the prospect of an on-going commerce – and contagion – between the two worlds, which undermines the dichotomy which, as we have seen, so much in the novel seems to affirm. This moment of irresolution in the conclusion points to a more generally disturbing and unresolved aspect of the novel, for it would seem that the contrast and arbitration between worlds which forms the basis of the novel's moral equation breaks down in the area of gender or sexual politics.

Thus, for example, for all their differences as representatives of the contrasting worlds, Harold Transome and Felix Holt are uncannily alike in their entrenched misogyny. They share a casual contempt for women's intelligence, evident in the condescending relationship each has with his mother. Harold regards women as 'slight things' (149) with 'weak minds' (91), whose opinions are insignificant because irrelevant: 'they are not called upon to judge or to act' (35). Similarly, Felix disdains to place them on a level with 'intelligent fleas' (63), and, more vehement even than Harold, characterises women as the 'curse' of men's lives, moral pygmies for whom 'all life is stunted to suit their littleness' (105).

Both men seek to dominate women. Harold's 'sense of mastery' (280) is reflected in his choice of a 'slave' (352) for his first wife and his attraction to the prospect of 'conquest' (341) over Esther. A similar impulse is echoed in Felix's fantasies of imposing his will on Esther. After their first meeting he finds himself wishing he could 'scold her every day, and make her cry and cut her fine hair off' (62), and he feels a challenge 'to see if she could be made ashamed of herself' (63). The disconcerting note of sadism in Felix's fantasy is evident, too, in the way Felix 'often amuse[s] himself' in his dealings with his mother by giving Mrs Holt 'answers that were unintelligible to her' (189).

Such diversion, of course, sits very uneasily with his much-proclaimed commitment to accuracy and simplicity in speech, but it passes without judgement in the novel. Indeed, more generally, a double standard seems to operate in Eliot's characterisation of men's and women's speech. Felix's outspokenness is, as we have seen, part of his 'nobleness of character' (349) and it frequently takes the form of forthright, unwelcome and unheeded disapproval, expressed variously to Esther, his mother, Harold and his working-class audience. In contrast, when either Mrs Holt or Mrs Transome speak their minds in criticism of their sons, it is seen as self-defeating, for 'half the sorrows of women would be averted if they could repress the speech they know to be useless' (35). Felix is not guiltless of gratuitous and provocative utterance, as we see in his intemperate defence of himself in court: 'I consider that I should be making an unworthy defence, if I let the Court infer from what I say myself, or from what is said by my witnesses, that because I am a man who hate drunken motiveless disorder, or any wanton harm, therefore I am a man who would never fight against authority. I hold it blasphemy to say a man ought not to fight against authority: there is no great religion and no great freedom that has not done it, in the beginning' (369). Yet where Felix's performance is represented as heroic, Mrs Transome's blunt outspokenness regarding the election is construed very differently. Her failure to resist the 'temptation' to comment on Harold's loss contributes 'with feminine self-defeat, to exclude herself more completely from any consultation by him. In this way poor women, whose power lies solely in their influence, make themselves like music out of tune, and only move men to run away' (277). Similarly,

Mrs Holt's determination to 'make the gentry know their duty' (346), which leads her to arrive unannounced at Transome Court and confront Harold with his responsibility regarding her imprisoned son, could be read as comparable to Felix's earlier confrontation with Harold in which he insists on Transome recognising his duty in the matter of the dishonest electioneering tactics. Instead, her intervention is dismissed as merely comical, defying the polite efforts at 'gravity' of all her listeners (347).

An examination of the sexual politics in the novel, then, uncovers an unexpected similarity between the two worlds and an ambiguity in the authorial judgement which seems otherwise so clear. Most damaging of all, the neat equilibrium and closure achieved through the contrast of ethical frameworks gives way to fractured irresolution in the area of sexual politics, as two disparate voices are set up in unsettling counterpoint, with the sacrilising idealism of Esther's conception of heterosexual relationships juxtaposed against the trenchant cynicism of Mrs Transome's views.

Esther embraces her love for Felix as a project of self-improvement. She is enlivened by Felix's challenge that she be 'something better than she actually was' (60) and correspondingly afraid that the acceptance of Harold Transome's love would give 'an air of moral mediocrity to all her prospects' (340). Indeed, there is a curious way in which Felix's failed public mission is replicated and rehabilitated in the private sphere, as his disastrous political demagoguery is rewritten as triumphant sexual demagoguery. Thus, Felix's determination to instruct the working class in the error of their ways finds its parallel in the way in which he conducts his courtship with Esther, 'always oppos[ing] and critiz[ing] her' (101). However, whereas the Sproxton miners remain recalcitrant, Esther comes to like 'best in the world [the] one who did nothing but scold me and tell me my faults' (322).

The overtones of a secular ministry to the working class, suggested by the parallels between Felix's Sunday 'preaching' and Reverend Lyon's, and the proposed venue of the Church Hall for his meetings, is amplified inordinately in the characterisation of the relationship between Esther and Felix. Repeatedly, the relationship is portrayed through the vocabulary of religion. Esther feels that if she can attain Felix's love, for example, 'her life would be exalted into something quite new – into a sort of difficult blessedness' (194). She offers 'devotion' (359); she longs to be 'worthy' of what she 'reverenced' in Felix, and that reverence holds out the prospect of her salvation, for,

Eliot contends, the 'best part of a woman's love is worship' (299). Her relationship with Felix provides 'the first religious experience of her life' (225) and her prospects for fulfilment depend entirely on her eventual union with Felix: 'She was "a fair divided excellence, whose fullness of perfection" must be in marriage' (359).

Intrinsic to this construction is the notion of female subjection and inferiority. From the outset, Esther has a secret consciousness 'that [Felix] was superior' (101). She ultimately rejects Harold Transome because in relation to him she has 'no sense of inferiority and just subjection' (340), and she comes to recognise that only Felix can call forth 'her best feeling, her most precious dependence' (358).

This constitutes Eliot's most extreme, conservative and repellent reading of heterosexual relationships. Yet, revealingly, it does not go unchallenged within the novel. Unlike Felix's 'radical' politics, which are spared any unsettling critique within the text, this version of sexual politics is subjected to the jarring counterpoint of Mrs Transome's pronouncements. There is no suggestion, of course, that Mrs Transome's jaundiced view has the weight of authorial endorsement that Esther's carries. Nevertheless, like the subversive voice of many 'doubles' in women's literature,[13] Mrs Transome's observations, for all their bitterness, have an accuracy which, at the very least, unsettles the authority of Esther's position. So, for example, her assessment of Harold's conduct as a 'good son' resonates with insight into his condescension and trivialisation of her life: 'O, to be sure – good as men are disposed to be to women, giving them cushions and carriages, and recommending them to enjoy themselves, and then expecting them to be contented under contempt and neglect' (97). Similarly, she provides a telling diagnosis of the power dynamic involved in the masculine will to mastery, which is as pertinent to Felix's fascination with Esther as it is to Harold's: 'This girl has a fine spirit – plenty of fire and pride and wit. Men like such captives, as they like horses that champ the bit and paw the ground: they feel more triumph in their mastery' (313). And Mrs Transome's relationship with the ruthless John Jermyn provides a glimpse of the darker side to feminine dependence. She is forced to confront the fact that by his financial opportunism and dishonesty Jermyn has exploited their sexual relationship, to recognise that his tenderness has become a 'calculation' and their love made into a 'good bargain' (336). In her dependence, she has become hopelessly compromised: 'I suppose if a lover picked one's pocket, there's no woman would like to own it' (336).

The dark presence of Mrs Transome, then, shadows the idealised bliss of Esther and Felix's union. And as if Eliot herself is unconvinced, she concludes her novel for the first – but not last – time by despatching her lovers off-stage, asserting, rather than observing, their future happiness in some 'secret' (398) location.

9

The 'difficult task of knowing another soul': *Middlemarch*

I

Having finished *Felix Holt* on the last day of May 1866, Eliot left almost immediately for the Continent, according to her now well-established custom of seeking both refuge from the fuss of publication, and restoration of her health and well-being after the 'dreadful nervousness and depression' (IV, 265) of composition. It was to be five and a half years before she published another novel, the longest gap in her novelistic career. In the intervening period she turned her attention to poetry, first taking up once more her verse drama, *The Spanish Gypsy*, which appeared in April 1868, and subsequently producing a number of poems, which formed the bulk of her 1874 volume, *The Legend of Jubal and Other Poems*.

Eliot had already demonstrated her determination to experiment and extend her range in writing *Romola*, and *The Spanish Gypsy* represented a new testing of limits, aspiring to the grand sweep of epic and tragedy. The work was inspired by a painting of the Annunciation of the Virgin Mary by Titian, which had led Eliot to conclude that the theme provided 'a great dramatic motive of the same class as those used by the Greek dramatists . . . a subject grander than Iphigenia, and it has never been used'.[1] Substituting the claims of race for those of religion, Eliot produced in the story of her heroine Fedalma, the Gypsy Queen, a secular version of the Christian narrative which left the basic template unchanged:

A young maiden, believing herself to be on the eve of the chief event of her life – marriage – about to share in the ordinary lot of womanhood, full of young hope, has suddenly announced to her that she is chosen to fulfil a great destiny, entailing a terribly different experience from that of ordinary womanhood. She is chosen, not by any arbitrariness, but as a result of foregoing hereditary conditions: she obeys.[2]

Despite two-and-a-half years of research, labour and revision, *The Spanish Gypsy*, which marked her public 'debut as a Poet' (IV, 442), was both a critical and aesthetic failure, confirming the judgement of one of her most sympathetic and astute contemporary critics that verse was to Eliot 'a fetter, and not a stimulus'.[3] One might almost have predicted from her prose that poetry would never provide the right métier for Eliot. The weight of her intellect, which was well served by her lengthy and intricate sentences, proved too burdensome for the strictures of the poetic line, which seemed to confound rather than clarify her thought. Too often self-conscious and sentimental, her poetry rarely rose above the laboured and the earnest.

The exception to this was provided by Eliot's short dramatic poem 'Armgart', written in August and September 1870, after she had begun 'the Featherstone–Vincy part' of *Middlemarch* and just before she commenced the 'Miss Brooke' section of her novel. Perhaps the key to the poem's success was its choice of a subject – the dilemmas facing the female artist – which was of more compelling and immediate interest to Eliot. Certainly, 'Armgart' is written with a directness and incision which is missing from her treatment of the more self-consciously 'poetic' historical and mythical themes which characterise the majority of the poems in *The Legend of Jubal*, and which seem to constitute a repudiation of Eliot's original determination to devote her art to 'the faithful representing of commonplace things' (*AB*, 178).

In fact, in its negotiation of the issues of ambition and devotion, 'Armgart' can be read as a transitional text, operating at once as a coda to *Felix Holt* and anticipating Eliot's last novels, *Middlemarch* and *Daniel Deronda*. Providing something of a strident afterword to the sexual politics of *Felix Holt*, Armgart categorically refuses the role of helpmeet. Choosing instead an operatic career, Armgart stands in marked contrast to Esther Lyon, who, as we have seen, imagines that fulfilment lies in being subsumed into the life and purpose of Felix Holt. Armgart's scornful advice to her suitor, Graf Dornberg, echoes like a riposte to Esther's self-effacement:

> seek the woman you deserve,
> All grace, all goodness, who has not yet found
> A meaning in her life, nor any end
> Beyond fulfilling yours. The type abounds.   (133)

Similarly, with a trenchant bitterness reminiscent of Mrs Transome, she exposes the sexism inherent in her suitor's proposal: 'You claim to be / More than a husband, but could not rejoice / That I were more than wife' (131). And with the psychological acuity of Mrs Transome, she accurately diagnoses the baser motives in Graf's suit: 'my charm / Was half that I could win fame and yet renounce!' (140).

The poem's connection with *Daniel Deronda* is clear, for the character of Armgart closely anticipates Eliot's only other depiction of the female artist, the opera-singing Princess Halm-Eberstein in that novel. Both women assert the claim to their careers as a 'right', established by 'natural' charter in the case of the Princess, and by 'birth' for Armgart: 'By the same warrant that I am a woman' (129). And both feel justified, by virtue of their talents, in repudiating conventional claims and ties. So, the Princess refuses to be 'a mere daughter and mother' (*DD*, 570) and Armgart insists that she will be 'more than wife' and not accept:

> The oft-taught Gospel: 'Woman, thy desire
> Shall be that all superlatives on earth
> Belong to men, save the one highest kind –
> To be a mother'.   (128)

However, the foreshadowing of *Middlemarch* is less immediately clear. Armgart seems at first glance to have little in common with Dorothea Brooke, the heroine Eliot turns to within weeks of finishing 'Armgart'. Nevertheless the two women represent sides of the one coin, the figure of the 'passionate, ideal nature' (*M*, 3), yearning for a transcendent purpose in life. The difference between them lies in the degree to which egoism, and its concomitant, ambition, inform the pursuit of their goals. As an artist, Armgart has much in common with her creator. The seriousness with which she regards her 'Supreme vocation' (129) echoes Eliot's own intense dedication, as does the discernment and assuredness with which she judges her achievement: 'I am only glad / Being praised for what I know is worth the praise' (122). Eliot's aversion and disdain for the prurient interest of the public, which condemned her to a socially reclusive life for the better part of her career, finds vent in Armgart's protest:

> Were I the Virgin Mother and my stage
> The opening heavens at the Judgement-day:
> Gossips would peep, jog elbows, rate the price
> Of such a woman in the social mart.   (120)

And finally the artistic pride which gives rise to Armgart's resolve to forsake the stage – 'I will not feed on doing great tasks ill, / Dull the world's sense with mediocrity, / And live by trash that smothers excellence' (150) – has its parallel in Eliot's own hesitation at beginning her writing career: 'I was too proud and ambitious to write: I did not believe that I could do anything fine, and I did not choose to do anything of that mediocre sort which I despised when it was done by others' (VIII, 384).

Eliot's sense of herself as an artist was tempered, however, as we have seen, by feelings of guilt and self-censure. She felt unease at her 'strong egoism', which she saw as 'traceable simply to a fastidious yet hungry ambition' (V, 125), and she characteristically compensated for that anxiety by zealously espousing the virtues of feminine duty and domestic engagement. Her ambivalence finds expression in 'Armgart' in Graf's judgement that 'Too much ambition has unwomaned her' (117), and Armgart's character is placed in stark contrast to the humble and selfless devotion of her attendant and cousin, Walpurga. In the end, Armgart, like the Princess Halm-Eberstein in *Daniel Deronda*, is punished by the loss of her voice. Yet while the resolution of the narrative seems to endorse the harshest assessment of her egoism, like the summary retribution meted out to the subversive female character in so many women's texts, it provides a meagre counterbalance to the daring, force and logic of Armgart's position.

II

Having in one sense exorcised the demon of the egoistic, ambitious woman with Armgart, Eliot turned immediately to the creation of her more benign counterpart, Dorothea Brooke, the woman whose lofty aspiration is not fuelled by self-absorption but rather informed by a determined self-forgetfulness. Just as importantly, she moved away from the satisfactions of the more conventionally heroic narrative, with its consoling fictions of self-determination and self-sufficiency, to confront the challenges and frustrations of a novelistic world in which self-determination is impossible and 'interdependence' (93) inescapable.[4] Armgart's artistic triumph relies on her repudiation of a relational self: her spurning of her suitor and her thoughtless acceptance of the sacrifices of others. At her strongest, she is magnificently solipsistic, representing an essentially infantile fantasy of individual completeness. *Middlemarch*, in contrast, as 'one of the few English novels written for grown-up people',[5] insists on the impossibility of such insularity: 'there is no creature whose inward being is so strong that it is not greatly determined by what lies outside it' (821).

Indeed, if, as Raymond Williams has argued, the distinguishing feature of the Victorian novel is the 'exploration of community',[6] then *Middlemarch* is the quintessence of the form. The novel has been justly celebrated for the intelligence and complexity of its depiction of the 'hampering thread-like pressure' (178) that comes with community living. Echoing Darwin's recognition of an 'inextricable web of affinities' between all living and extinct forms,[7] Eliot demonstrates both conceptually and structurally that human lots are 'woven and interwoven' (139), and that no individual escapes the 'retarding friction' that comes from having 'to walk on earth among neighbours' (144). In a shrinking world of increasing urbanisation, 'fresh threads of connexion' ensure that no one lives 'blamelessly afar', immune from the 'faultiness of closer acquaintanceship' (94).

Lydgate, for example, makes the grave mistake of imagining he can avoid entrapment by keeping away from 'London intrigues, jealousies and social truckling' (143). And in envisaging Middlemarch contemptuously as no rival to his 'pursuit of a great idea' (145), he sorely underestimates its power of 'swallowing . . . and assimilating him very comfortably' (152). Through his character, Eliot shows us the hubris of a man determined to shape his own fate, and the futility of his plans to insulate himself against the inevitable demands for conformity. Ironically, in this regard, Lydgate's scientific awareness does not inform his social intelligence. Indeed, he is incapable of extrapolating his understanding of the interconnectedness of the biological organism to reflect on its equivalent in the social world, bringing, as he does, 'a much more testing vision of details and relations into this pathological study than he ever thought it necessary to apply to the complexities of love and marriage' (162). The story of his enmeshment in personal and professional compromise, and his remorseless progress towards mediocrity and failure is a common one: 'For in the multitude of middle-aged men who go about their vocations in a daily course determined for them much in the same way as the tie of their cravats, there is always a good number who once meant to shape their own deeds and alter the world a little. The story of their coming to be shapen after the average and fit to be packed by the gross, is hardly ever told even in their consciousness' (143). Nevertheless, in her renewed commitment to the ordinary rather than the exceptional, Eliot challenges conventional notions of the tragic, characterising immunity to common suffering as a form of moral stupidity, and urging a reorientation of perspective in the reader:

> we do not expect people to be deeply moved by what is not unusual. That element of tragedy which lies in the very fact of frequency, has not yet wrought itself into the coarse emotion of mankind; and per- haps our frames could hardly bear much of it. If we had a keen vision and feeling of all ordinary human life, it would be like hearing the grass grow and the squirrel's heart beat, and we should die of that roar which lies on the other side of silence. As it is, the quickest of us walk about well wadded with stupidity.   (192)

As a woman in Middemarch society, Dorothea Brooke faces a 'meanness of opportunity' (3) and 'intolerable narrowness' (36) which ensure that she is never tempted in quite the same way as Lydgate by hubristic fantasies of self-determination. She recognises from the outset that any grand plan that she might formulate will need to be played out through the intervention and indulgence of men – through Sir James, for example, as the builder of her cottages for the poor, or Casaubon as the guide to knowledge, who 'will take her along the grandest path' (28). Spared the professional pressures that Lydgate suffers – by grim virtue of having all professions closed to her – Dorothea is subjected to a more personal assault from the society's demands for conformity. Compliance for her is represented not as an option, but as a necessity; not just as a matter of virtue but, more starkly, as an issue of sanity: 'Women were expected to have weak opinions; but the great safeguard of society and of domestic life was, that opinions were not acted on. Sane people did what their neighbours did, so that if any lunatics were at large, one might know and avoid them' (9). Similarly, Mrs Cadwallader counsels Dorothea against isolating herself from the community, arguing that if she insists on living alone: 'You will certainly go mad . . . You will see visions. We have all got to exert ourselves a little to keep sane, and call things by the same names as other people call them by' (529). In so far as Dorothea is inclined to resist social expectations, she is seen as the 'dangerous part of the family machinery' (800).

Yet whatever the differences between Dorothea and Lydgate, the sense of defeat by society – the thwarting of intent – is shared by both protagonists. Lydgate regards himself as a failure, despite the eventual establishment of a lucrative practice at a fashionable watering-place, and as a victim of the Middlemarch community: 'He had meant everything to turn out differently; and others had thrust themselves into his life and thwarted his purposes' (727). Dorothea sees herself as similarly frustrated, protesting to Celia: 'I never could do anything that I liked. I never carried out any plan yet' (806).

III

Significantly, though, while the twin narratives of Dorothea and Lydgate explore the inescapable pressures of assimilation and conformity, and the inevitable engulfment of the individual within the social organism, they also paradoxically highlight the acute isolation of the individual within society. And it is this conjunction of interdependence and isolation which presents a new challenge to Eliot's investigation of ethics. We have already considered Eliot's contemplation of the mystery of otherness, especially in relation to *Silas Marner*. However, whereas that novel explored the possibility of attaining connection in human fellowship, despite incomprehension, it did so in a much more limited context than *Middlemarch* now attempts. Silas Marner is, and remains, a solitary figure on the margins of Raveloe society, whose capacity and impulse for communication and self-explanation are as limited as his possibilities of assimilation into that society. If in the figure of Marner Eliot creates the most alien of her characters – the most intractably other – who presents the most extreme challenge 'to *imagine* and to *feel* the pains and joys of those who differ from themselves' (III, 111), then in *Middlemarch* Eliot addresses a yet more disconcerting and difficult proposition – the intractable otherness of those who seem familiar, those with whom we live in close connection, those to whom we consciously and repeatedly offer ourselves for interpretation. While it is one thing to confront the mystery of a strange character like Marner, it is quite another to recognise the alienation at the heart of the closest relationships.

This is nowhere clearer than in the novel's various studies of marriage, which suggest that, while married life brings with it an 'awful . . . nearness' (784), the very facts of proximity and intimacy serve to heighten the pain of isolation within the bond. So, for example, having given himself up to the prospect of union with Dorothea, Casaubon finds himself 'utterly condemned to loneliness' (83), and driven further and further into disguise and self-insulating defensiveness by his conception of Dorothea as a 'spy', a 'cruel outward accuser ... in the shape of a wife' (198). Similarly, Lydgate and Rosamond each live in a world 'of which the other knew nothing' (163), the gulf between them so extreme that they seem like 'creatures of different species and opposing interests' (587).

A similar paradox underlies those scenes in the novel which ostensibly dramatise moments of connection between characters – moments in which self-transcendence seems to enable the achievement of almost heroic sympathy. The most famous example, perhaps, is the encounter between Dorothea and Rosamond in which Dorothea, overcoming the jealousy provoked by her discovery of Rosamond and Will Ladislaw in an intimate exchange, counsels Rosamond on the value of her marriage and the innocence of her husband. The other justly celebrated scene occurs between Mrs Bulstrode and her husband after Mrs Bulstrode has been acquainted with the details of her husband's nefarious past and the extent of his public disgrace. After locking herself in her room in order to brace herself for a new and shame-filled future, Mrs Bulstrode emerges in a gesture of supreme loyalty to take her place at her husband's side and share the 'merited dishonour' which is as bitter to her 'as it could be to any mortal' (739).

These scenes have been characterised by critics such as Elizabeth Ermarth as moments of 'crucial connection', when characters 'overcome some gap of difference between them', allowing the individual to 'find openings from self-enclosed circuits into wider possibility'.[8] Similarly, Penny Boumelha interprets these episodes as indicative of the 'momentary recognition of mutual worth'.[9] However, if one interrogates these encounters further, it is possible to read them not as instances of connection or mutuality, but rather as scenes of disconnection, which inscribe rather than eliminate the difference between characters. It is true that in acting against their own narrowest interests, Dorothea and Mrs Bulstrode both demonstrate a 'self-subduing act of fellowship' (789). But rather than transcendence, these acts actually represent a confirmation of the self. Both gestures are highly self-conscious. Dorothea is intent on holding back her tears, determined to 'master' and 'suppress' herself (782). Mrs Bulstrode's actions are even more markedly performative, as she costumes herself for the anticipated embrace of humiliation: 'She took off all her ornaments and put on her plain black gown, and instead of wearing her much-adorned cap and large bows of hair, she brushed her hair down and put on a plain bonnet-cap, which made her look suddenly like an early Methodist' (740). And both scenes culminate not in the articulation, and hence possible scrutiny, of mutual under-standing, but in a wordless gesture. Dorothea and Rosamund embrace with 'no words' (784), and Mrs Bulstrode touches her hus-band's shoulder, while his confession and her promise of faithfulness are, alike, 'silent' (740). The performative generosity of both ges-tures marks the protagonists out as more virtuous and worthy – as different, in fact – from the recipients, and the culminating silence of both scenes underscores the possibility for misunderstanding between characters rather than liberation from 'self-enclosed cir-cuits', as Elizabeth Ermath would have it.[10] So, Mrs Bulstrode can-not bring herself to ask how much of what she has heard is only slander and false suspicion, and her husband cannot say 'I am inno-cent' (740). Similarly, rather than finally achieving some genuine connection with Rosamond, Dorothea in fact misreads their exchange, overestimating Rosamond's kindness and misconstruing as 'generous effort' what is only 'a reflex of her own energy' (785). Rosamond's frank admission of her culpability for the inappropriate intimacy of her encounter with Will is an exercise in self-justifica-tion, born of hurt pride, rather than a responsiveness to another's pain, as her self-righteous note to Will subsequently makes clear: 'I have told Mrs Casaubon. She is not under any mistake about you. I told her because she came to see me and was very kind. You will have nothing to reproach me with now. I shall not have made any differ-ence to you' (790).

By underscoring the lack of mutuality within relationships and dramatising the incomprehension underlying moments of ostensible understanding, Eliot highlights the paradoxical loneliness of the individual at the heart of the societal 'web' – an isolation born of the 'difficult task of knowing another soul' (117). Repeatedly, the novel shows our capacity for understanding of the other chronically hampered by misinterpretation, misrepresentation and miscommu-nication.

Many critics have noted the centrality of hermeneutics to *Middlemarch*.[11] The impulse to interpret provides the impetus, for example, for Casaubon's and Lydgate's life work, the guiding preoc-cupation of Will Ladislaw's artistic endeavours, and even the essence of Mr Brooke's intellectual dilettantism. Yet it is in the reading – or, more properly, the misreading – of the other that the novel's principal drama is played out. Thus, for instance, the destinies of Dorothea and Lydgate are blighted by their disastrous failure to apprehend the signs that might have alerted them to the unsuitability of their respect-ive choice of partners. Dorothea's short-sightedness and her anx-ious bewilderment in the face of the necessity to decipher first the Greek alphabet, and then the art in Rome, are suggestive of a more general interpretative incapacity. In addition she is, by virtue both of her character and her gender, doubly vulnerable to the likelihood of misreading. Her idealising nature leads her to compensate for Casaubon's deficiencies by projection, finding in the 'ungauged reservoir' of Mr Casaubon's mind 'every quality she herself brought' (23). And, more generally, the constrictions of her life as a woman, compelled to struggle within 'the bonds of a narrow teaching, hemmed in by a social life which seemed nothing but a labyrinth of petty courses, a walled-in maze of small paths that led no whither' (28), leave her, like Maggie Tulliver, susceptible to an overestimation of the means of escape. As unlikely as Casaubon might seem in the role of white knight, he does function as a version of that fantasised passport to a 'fuller life' (43) to which women are especially vulner-able.[12] So, to her great cost, Dorothea fabricates an 'original romance for herself' out of the prospect of marriage to Casaubon (206). The narrowness of her feminine world renders her on the one hand liable to over-reading, and on the other unskilled in interpreting the clear signals provided by the 'frigid rhetoric' of Casaubon's proposal: 'How could it occur to her to examine the letter, to look at it critical-ly as a profession of love?' (43). The intellectual naïveté which allows her to misjudge Casaubon as a 'modern Augustine' (24) is com-pounded by a sexual innocence which leads her to censor all con-sideration of the corporeal from her view of her relationship with Casaubon. Whereas those around her take their clue from Casaubon's dessicated figure to extrapolate a more general sterility, Dorothea steadfastly refuses to contemplate the perspective offered by Celia's 'carnally-minded prose' and silences all 'observations of that kind' (47).

Lydgate's failure to interpret his partner correctly is no less disas-trous than Dorothea's, but the forms of his misreading function like the mirror reverse of hers. While she refuses to contemplate the phy-sical, Lydgate cannot see beyond it, judging beauty to be 'by its very nature virtuous' (162). And whereas Dorothea overesti-mates Casaubon's character, Lydgate patronisingly underestimates

Rosamond's, superimposing his own view of ideal feminine docility upon what is, in fact, a capacity for 'terrible tenacity' (576).

Misinterpretation of the other, then, is endemic in the novel. Some characters actively collaborate in that misunderstanding by careful misrepresentation. Bulstrode, for example, is secretive and hypocritical in his conduct and demeanour, and Rosamond, similarly, is so calculating in her self-representation that 'she even acted her own character' (115). Yet, sincerity and frankness are no more guaranteed to ensure understanding. Casaubon is innocent of duplicity in his dealing with Dorothea, having 'not actively assisted in creating any illusions about himself' (193), and Lydgate is almost antagonistic in his straightforwardness. Nevertheless, he is apprehended 'merely as a cluster of signs for his neighbours' false suppositions' (140).

This sense of isolation and misunderstanding provides a less frequently acknowledged counterbalance to the novel's more famous sense of connectedness.[13] Indeed, militating against the organicism of the recurring web metaphor is a sense of the 'stupendous fragmentariness' (190) against which both the author and the characters struggle. In the face of her fear in composition of having 'too much matter, too many "momenti" ' (V, 137), Eliot's 'crowning task' was, like Casaubon's, 'to condense' the accumulated fragments into a coherent whole (24). She addressed this challenge in characteristic ways. Stylistically, she stressed the association between potentially disparate elements through the extensive use of metaphor and generalisation. And, structurally, the pervasive use of doubling or parallelism within the narrative was used to create a sense of the ways in which human lots are 'woven and interwoven' (139).

The characters, too, long for some ordering principle to form a bulwark against a threatening sense of fragmentation and dispersal. For all its comic superficiality, Mr Brooke's sense of intellectual vertigo in the face of scientific theory – 'I saw it would not do. It leads to everything' (16) – is not entirely dissimilar to Dorothea's sense of awe and inadequacy before the alarming artistic profusion of Rome. And Lydgate's search for the primitive tissue which would show 'new connexions and hitherto hidden facts of structure' (146) is directly analogous to Casaubon's quest for the key to all mythologies, which might show 'that all the mythical systems or erratic mythical fragments in the world were corruptions of a tradition originally revealed' (23). Both represent a desire for a foundational knowledge, which might render the otherwise bewildering array of disparate parts comprehensible as a whole. Both are expressions of that 'eagerness for a binding theory' (84) which Dorothea shares, and which characterises the age more generally. The great taxonomic undertakings of Darwin, for example, or the grand narrative of Comte's three phases of civilisation, reflect at once a desire for, and a confidence in, the synthesising possibilities of theory. In an age 'helped by no coherent social faith and order' (3), the advancement of knowledge holds out the promise of certainty formerly provided by religious faith. As George Lewes observed, 'We are slowly coming to recognise that there may be a science of History, a science of Language, a science of Religion, and, in fact, that all knowledge may be systematised in a common method.'[14]

More than any grand narrative or project, however, the most pervasive and significant ordering principle in the novel emerges from the shaping force of egoism in the individual, as one of the text's most famous metaphors attests:

> An eminent philosopher among my friends, who can dignify even your ugly furniture by lifting it into the serene light of science, has shown me this pregnant little fact. Your pier-glass or extensive surface of polished steel made to be rubbed by a housemaid, will be minutely and multitudinously scratched in all directions; but place now against it a lighted candle as a centre of illumination, and lo! the scratches will seem to arrange themselves in a fine series of concentric circles round that little sun. It is demonstrable that the scratches are going everywhere impartially, and it is only your candle which produces the flattering illusion of a concentric arrangement, its light falling with an exclusive optical selection. These things are a parable. The scratches are events, and the candle is the egoism of any person now absent – of Miss Vincy, for example. (262)

Repeatedly, characters depend on that 'flattering illusion' to read and write their own narratives. The most striking example of this is provided by Rosamond. Just as she arranges 'all the objects around her with the same nicety as ever' (758) in her domestic environment, her monumental ego is the central reference point for all her understanding. She reads the world through the filter of her desires, always anticipating the favourable rather than the realistic outcome. Thus, for example, in convincing herself that Will Ladislaw's return to Middlemarch would somehow precipitate Lydgate's acquiescence to her plan to move to London, 'she felt assured that the coming would be a potent cause of the going, without at all seeing how. This way of establishing sequences is too common to be fairly regarded as a peculiar folly in Rosamond. And it is precisely this sort of sequence which causes the greatest shock when it is sundered' (758). So entrenched is Rosamond's vision within the rigid perimeters of self – so 'little used to imagining other people's states of mind except as a material cut into shape by her own wishes' (765) is she – that when she is brought to confront an alternative perspective through Will's aggressive criticism, she loses all points of reference, 'almost losing the sense of her identity' (767).

While manifestly less egregious, Dorothea's self-narration is also distorted by egoism. The 'romance' that she creates for herself out of the prospect of marriage to Casaubon depends on the priority she gives to her 'own dreams' over the 'realities of his lot' (207). Her conception of Casaubon's greatness, then, flies in the face of empirical fact and is founded rather on her desire to have a husband 'who was above me in judgment and in all knowledge' (40). And even as her fantasy is shattered, she finds it more palatable to recast the narrative, with herself still in the central role as martyr, than to see beyond her own perspective to confront Casaubon's reality:

> it had been easier to her to imagine how she would devote herself to Mr Casaubon, and become wise and strong in his strength and wisdom, than to conceive with that distinctness which is no longer reflection but feeling – an idea wrought back to the directness of sense, like the solidity of objects – that he had an equivalent centre of self, whence the lights and shadows must always fall with a certain difference. (208)

Casaubon meets Dorothea's 'flattering illusion' with a version on his own. He, for his part, is 'not surprised' (48) by Dorothea's admiration and is inclined to accept that 'others were providentially made for him' (83). However, any criticism of his complacency is challenged by Eliot's stress on the ubiquity of such 'unreflecting egoism' (345). If Casaubon is not surprised, 'what lover would have been?' (48). And if Casaubon's perspective depends on his being 'the centre of his own world', then it is a trait 'not quite alien' to any of us (83). Indeed, if he is guilty of solipsistic blindness, it is nothing more than 'society sanctions' (275) and sexual politics encourage: 'Society never made the preposterous demand that a man should think as much of his own qualifications for making a charming girl happy as he thinks of hers for making himself happy. As if a man could choose not only his wife but his wife's husband! Or as if he were bound to provide charms for his posterity in his own person!' (276).

For all that this inclination to order and make sense of the world through the prism of self is 'common' and 'quite ordinary' (413), however, Eliot's 'parable' of the pier-glass makes it abundantly clear that the desired, and desirable, patterning provided by the 'candle' of egoism is achieved only by means of distortion. The 'illusion' may be 'flattering', but it is achieved at great cost, as Eliot indicates more bluntly in a second metaphor which takes up the same theme: 'Will not a tiny speck very close to our vision blot out the glory of the world, and leave only the margin by which we see the blot? I know no speck so troublesome as self' (413).

Viewed in this way, the reassurance offered by the patterning of the ego is only ever superficial, covering a deeper blight. With such limitation of vision, characters like Casaubon are mired 'in small currents of self-preoccupation' (277), condemned to be 'present at this great spectacle of life' and yet never 'liberated from a small hungry shivering self' (277). And even more generous characters are isolated by their incomprehension of the other, with Farebrother, for example, unable to understand Lydgate's proud reticence, 'having very little corresponding fibre in himself' (631), and Fred Vincy confident that he sees to the bottom of his uncle's soul, 'though in reality half what he saw there was no more than the reflex of his own inclinations' (117). Paradoxically, then, rather than providing a bulwark against the 'stupendous fragmentariness' of the world, the narrative of self in the end reaffirms that fragmentation.

How, then, can we transcend the isolation and solipsistic blindness of the individual narrative to relate in any meaningful way to the other? Or, in the novel's terms, how can we escape the 'moral stupidity' (208) of self-absorption and access the 'rapturous consciousness of life beyond the self' (3)? The ultimate ethical challenge, *Middlemarch* suggests, is to live vigilantly conscious of the fact that the other has 'an equivalent centre of self' (208). That recognition is not contingent upon familiarity or understanding, in the usual way of empathy, and even less upon the suppositions of sameness which, as we have seen, arise from the ego. Although one seeks the 'fullest knowledge and the fullest sympathy', such a goal is aspirational rather then achievable, for even 'the quickest of us walk about well wadded with stupidity' (192). In this, Eliot's penultimate novel, then, the non-self remains just as intractably alien as the earlier *Silas Marner* had suggested. Indeed, as we have been arguing, in *Middlemarch* the alienation is all the more striking because it occurs in circumstances of great intimacy, which reveal 'that total missing of each other's mental track, which is too evidently possible even between persons who are continually thinking of each other' (577).

Nevertheless, there is a way forward, Eliot suggests, in the apprehension not of sameness, but of correspondence, of the other's *equivalent* centre. A willingness to assume, and to credit, that possibility of correspondence entails a preparedness to unsettle one's conception of the world – to allow for the existence of a competing narrative. Mary Garth achieves this ethical manoeuvre very simply when Rosamond dismisses the inconsequential Miss Morgan as 'so uninteresting', and Mary replies, ' "She is interesting to herself, I suppose" ' (111). For Dorothea, the achievement is harder won. She has, of course, a disposition to look beyond the self, 'yearning to know what was far from her' and 'constantly wondering what sort of lives other people lead, and how they take things' (322). Yet in order to effect that extension of perspective, she has to allow both the reality of another's narrative and the partiality of her own. That ethical capacity for the reorientation of the ego is first suggested by Eliot in the character of Mr Irwine in *Adam Bede*, who shows himself able to entertain an unsettling view of himself offered by his critic, Will Maskery. Maggie Tulliver, similarly, glimpses in the teachings of Thomas à Kempis 'for the first time . . . the possibility of shifting the position from which she looked at the gratification of her own desires' (*Mill*, 290). For Dorothea the process begins on her honeymoon in Rome with the 'waking of a presentiment that there might be a sad consciousness in [Casaubon's] life which made as great a need on his side as on her own' (208). It is consolidated when, with the 'clearest perception', she can look steadily both from her perspective at 'her husband's failure' and from his 'at his possible consciousness of failure' (361). In this she achieves that '*ekstasis* or outside standing-ground' (*Mill*, 292) which promises the only hope for liberation from the ethical trap of egoism.[15]

Dorothea's capacity for 'self-subduing' fellowship (789) is highlighted in contrast with Rosamond, whose vision is never dislodged from the 'flattering illusion' of centrality. She, thus, consistently fails to engage with her husband 'as he was himself', and always privileges instead 'his relation to her' (164). Unlike Dorothea, Rosamond never allows herself to be vulnerable to another's competing narrative, regarding herself as the 'one person . . . whom she did not regard as blameworthy' (655). Rosamond's failure to negotiate the ethical challenge of self-transcendence is played out in her protracted marital conflict, and whereas she fantasises that Will Ladislaw would have made a better husband, Eliot is explicit in her attribution of blame to Rosamond's insurmountable egoism: 'No notion could have been falser than this, for Rosamond's discontent in her marriage was due to the conditions of marriage itself, to its demands for self-suppression and tolerance, and not to the nature of her husband' (742).

Ethical vision, then, depends on a capacity to shift perspective – to unsettle the 'flattering illusion' of one's own narrative by the habitual assumption of the possibility of another view. However, while a character like Dorothea can struggle to acknowledge the existence of the competing narrative, she cannot, despite all her efforts at self-forgetfulness, apprehend its details. She cannot, that is, 'turn from the outside estimates of a man, to wonder . . . what is the report of his own consciousness' (82). That capability is reserved in the end for art and the artist. It takes place at the level of the diegesis, beyond the drama played out between the characters. So, the necessity for 'quick alternative vision' (151) is stressed at a structural level both in the parallelism which makes 'the mind flexible with constant comparison' (209) and in the consistent narrative stress on shifting perspectives, which mirrors Lydgate's prescription for successful analysis: 'there must be a systole and diastole in all inquiry . . . a man's mind must be continually expanding and shrinking between the whole human horizon and the horizon of an object-glass' (630). The role of the artist in redirecting the focus, and hence in extending the ethical scope, is never more clearly felt in Eliot's work than in the highly self-conscious reorientation at the beginning of Chapter XXIX:

> One morning some weeks after her arrival at Lowick, Dorothea – but why always Dorothea? Was her point of view the only one possible with regard to this marriage? I protest against all our interest, all our effort at understanding being given to the young skins that look blooming in spite of trouble; for these too will get faded, and will know the older and more eating griefs which we are helping to neglect. In spite of the blinking eyes and white moles objectionable to Celia, and the want of muscular curve which was morally painful to Sir James, Mr Casaubon had an intense consciousness within him, and was spiritually a-hungered like the rest of us. He had done nothing exceptional in marrying – nothing but what society sanctions, and considers an occasion for wreaths and bouquets. (275)

In this respect, *Middlemarch* represents the pinnacle of achievement for one who began her novel-writing career with the conviction that 'the extension of sympathy' represented greatest benefit and the highest duty of art.

10

'The transmutation of the self': *Daniel Deronda*

I

While *Middlemarch* depicts its protagonist as defeated by the constrictions of 'an imperfect social state' (821) and ends with the regretful recognition that, given Dorothea's inevitable struggle with 'prosaic conditions', the 'determining acts' of her life could never be 'ideally beautiful' (821), Eliot's final novel, *Daniel Deronda*, reserves a grander fate for its hero. Eliot was keenly aware of the dissatisfaction generated by the unheroic future ascribed to her 'new Theresa' (821) in *Middlemarch*, 'perfectly sure that everybody will be disappointed' (V, 333). Even within the novel she explicitly acknowledged that many would think it 'a pity that so substantive and rare a creature should have been absorbed into the life of another, and be only known in a certain circle as a wife and mother' (819), and though she deleted it from later editions, she gave vent to her own frustration in the first edition:

> Among the many remarks passed on her mistakes, it was never said in the neighbourhood of Middlemarch that such mistakes could not have happened if the society into which she was born had not smiled on propositions of marriage from a sickly man to a girl less than half his own age – on modes of education which make a woman's knowledge another name for motley ignorance – on rules of conduct which are in flat contradiction with its own loudly-asserted beliefs. While this is the social air in which morals begin to breathe, there will be collisions such as those in Dorothy's life.[1]

However, as we have seen with Eliot's anticipation of the disappointment likely to be caused by her ending to *The Mill on the Floss*, her commitment to scrupulous realism once more gave her little room to move in shaping the novel's ending. And, as with the earlier novel, if realism enabled *Middlemarch*'s penetrating diagnosis of Dorothea's predicament, it also prohibited fantastical reversals in the conclusion. Eliot had previously explained to her publisher that she was neither interested nor capable of exhibiting things as they 'should be'; rather she strove to show things 'as they have been or are' (II, 362). Hence, she justified the contracted future imagined for Dorothea with the impatient observation that no alternative realistically presented itself: 'no one stated exactly what else that was in her power she ought rather to have done' (819).

Eliot had, of course, signalled her intentions for Dorothea at the novel's outset, and she warned John Blackwood 'to look back to the Prelude' (V, 330), to prepare himself for the ending. Yet if the Prelude warned the reader what to expect in *Middlemarch*, it also curiously foreshadowed the trajectory of Eliot's next novel. As though a reversed template, all that was denied *Middlemarch*'s female protagonist – the inspiring 'national idea', 'the epic life . . . of far-resonant action', the 'spiritual grandeur' matched by enabling opportunity, 'the coherent social faith and order which could perform the function of knowledge for the ardently willing soul' (*M*, 3) – was bestowed upon the male hero of *Daniel Deronda*, who, like a new Moses, is called through the workings of 'a mysterious Fate' to the 'ideal task', the 'social captainship', for which he longs (*DD*, 536, 642).

That reversal in the fate of her protagonists is enabled by a shift in mode from determinism in *Middlemarch* to prophecy in *Daniel Deronda*. Throughout her career, Eliot's realism had always been fundamentally informed by her sense of determinism. So, Dorothea could not triumph over her circumstances because, Eliot insisted, 'there is no creature whose inward being is so strong that it is not greatly determined by what lies outside it' (821). Dorothea's achievement of heroic fulfilment would constitute a breach of 'that invariability of sequence' which, Eliot believed, formed the basis not only of physical science but of 'our social organization, our ethics and our religion' (*SCW*, 21). Until her final novel Eliot held true to her conviction that the 'law of consequences' was 'inexorable' (*SCW*, 21). Characters like Tertius Lydgate, who confidently expect to shape their own fate, are guaranteed a hard lesson, for the fantasy of self-determination is shown to be but one version of those 'false and enfeebling' consolations through which men seek to 'get rid of this need for *absolute* resignation' (IV, 499).

However, the possibility of self-determination is precisely what prophecy offers, and under its auspices in *Daniel Deronda*, a new logic obtains in one part of the narrative. In fact, prophecy and determinism have much in common. Both are based on a sense of the inevitable and rely on an unfolding to reveal their potency. However, whereas determinism is spoken by the past, prophecy speaks the future. Determinism is completely enmeshed in sequence, as the sum of the past, in contrast to prophecy which has a capacity to rupture the 'invariability of sequence'. It can effect an intervention, instituting a new beginning, and in that sense prophecy implies a capacity for construction or authorship. Thus, it is possible, for example, for Deronda 'to receive from Mordecai's mind the complete ideal shape of that personal duty and citizenship which lay in his own thought like sculptured fragments' (437), and with this new 'shape' radically alter the predicted and predictable course of his history.

This contrast between prophecy and determinism can be traced not just in the difference between Eliot's final two novels. It is equally clear within *Daniel Deronda* in the split between the English and Jewish sub-plots. At its simplest, Gwendolen Harleth inhabits a realm of realism and determinism, while Daniel Deronda dwells in a space of epic and prophecy. While Deronda can satisfy the yearning of a hero, fulfilling the desire of all 'fuller nature[s] . . . to be an agent' (407), Gwendolen is the victim in a drama that is beyond her control. Ironically, it is Gwendolen who repeatedly recurs to a rhetoric of agency: 'I am determined to be happy. . . . I have made up my mind not to let other people interfere with me' (22). She means 'to lead' and to 'conquer circumstance by her exceptional cleverness' (31). However, such talk only provides a cruel parody of her profound lack of control – her vulnerability to chance, her subjection to others and, no less, her subjugation to her own unconscious impulses, which constitute 'a possible self, a self not to be absolutely predicted about, [that] caused her some astonishment and terror' (114). Thus, she can no more will a successful outcome at the gambling table in Leubronn, or stave off her family's financial ruin at the hands of colonial speculators, than she can engineer a satisfactory result in the greatest of all her 'gambles', marriage to Grandcourt.

This irony is compounded by the fact that Gwendolen also claims some power of prophecy, but despite her 'belief in her star' (201) and her confidence in her capacity to 'foresee' the future (123), she is impotent in the face of the future. Her powers of prediction amount to nothing more than 'the reflex of a wish' (82). In contrast, Daniel is liberated from uncertainty and contingency once he is drawn into the orbit of Mordecai's prophecy. When Mordecai refuses to believe that Deronda is not Jewish, he does so with the authority of 'vision', not the projection of wish-fulfilment. When he responds to Deronda's assertion that he is a Gentile with the bald assertion, 'It can't be true' (429), the reader is alerted to the transition of Daniel's narrative from the realist parameters in which it began, to the epic dimension in which it will conclude. Whereas Deronda's advice to Gwendolen that she look at her life 'as a debt' (658) locks her into a past, with dread and remorse as her guides, Deronda is freed into a future by virtue of 'visionary selection' (466). While Gwendolen comes full circle with her return to a 'small life' of 'penitential' purpose at Offendene (689), in perhaps the most melancholy contraction meted out by Eliot's realism to any of her heroines, Deronda moves forward to embrace a future in the East, as heroic in its grandeur as it is unconvincing in its vagueness.

II

This split in the text has been a source of critical focus and controversy since the novel first appeared in 1876. Eliot knew she was taking a risk with her Jewish plot, which she recognised from the outset was 'likely to satisfy nobody'.[2] Her apprehension was justified – but as she became 'aware of much repugnance or else indifference towards the Jewish part of Deronda, and of some hostile as well as adverse reviewing', she consoled herself with the fact that 'Words of gratitude have come from Jews and Jewesses, and there are certain signs that I may have contributed my mite to a good result.'[3] To Eliot's mind, the problem was simply one of anti-Semitism, in which she saw herself paying a price for creating a challengingly sympathetic portrait of Jews.[4] For later critics, the issue has been more properly identified as an aesthetic one, centring on the irreconcilability of the novel's two halves with their tension between realism and epic, or empiricism and idealism, and for the greater part of its history, readers and critics alike have tended variously to regret or ignore the Jewish sub-plot. At its most extreme, F. R. Leavis proposed in *The Great Tradition* that the 'fervid and wordy unreality' of the Jewish section should be discarded entirely and the impressive English section should be preserved under the title *Gwendolen Harleth*.[5]

Recent critical preoccupations with race and imperialism have, however, revived interest in the Jewish section of the novel,[6] and a range of other studies have argued that the novel is not as irrevocably split as the critical debate has often implied. Cynthia Chase, for example, has suggested that the two halves of the novel operate in self-conscious dialogue. She focuses particularly on Hans Meyrick's letter to Deronda in Chapter 52, arguing that it represents a crucial intersection of the two plots and functions as deconstruction of the novel. [7] Certainly, following as it does immediately upon the revelation of Deronda's parentage, Meyrick's letter spoofs the inevitability, within the terms of the Mordecai plot, of Daniel's Jewishness: 'I never held it my *forte* to be a severe reasoner, but I can see that if whatever is best is A and B happens to be best, B must be A, however little you might have expected it beforehand' (549).

A similar dialogue between the two narrative modes of the respective plots can be found in the episode when Mordecai tells the story of the Jewish maiden, who loved the Gentile king so well, she entered prison and changed clothes with the woman whom the king loved, thus sacrificing herself for the sake of the king's happiness. Mordecai interprets the tale in the terms of the grand rhetoric of his messianic obsession: 'This is the surpassing love, that loses self in the object of love' (629). Mirah contests the validity of his reading, however, insisting, in the more familiar language of psychological realism, that 'that was not it. She wanted the king when she was dead to know what she had done, and feel that she was better than the other. It was her strong self, wanting to conquer, that made her die' (629).

The pivotal figure in the dialogue is Deronda, who feels 'on the one side the grasp of Mordecai's dying hand on him' and 'on the other [Gwendolen] this fair creature in silk and gems, with her hidden wound and her self-dread, making a trustful effort to lean and find herself sustained' (482). Deronda is kept within the orbit of the English plot by the suggestion of romance with Gwendolen. Their relationship has the potential, in Sir Hugo's terms, to be 'as pretty a story as need be that this fine creature and his favourite Dan should have turned out to be formed for each other' (654). And yet he is extricated from the romance, and preserved for the epic, by the timely intervention of Mordecai's prophecy: 'if all this had happened little more than a year ago, he would hardly have asked himself whether he loved her: the impetuous determining impulse which would have moved him would have been to save her from sorrow. . . . But now, love and duty had thrown other bonds around him, and that impulse could no longer determine his life' (655). It is, of course, no contest: the possibilities of romance cannot compete with the imperatives of epic – 'poor Gwendolen' is no match for Mirah, who 'had taken her place in his soul as a beloved type – reducing the power of other fascination and making a difference in it that became deficiency' (637). With the expectations of a 'pretty story' thwarted for the reader and Sir Hugo alike, the tension between narrative modes is articulated by Lady Mallinger, who, as spokesperson for the English plot, offers her own trenchant assessment of the conclusion: 'although she herself was not fond of widows she could not help thinking that such a marriage would have been better than his going altogether with the Jews' (681).

Rosemary Ashton has argued that the two parts of the novel are united by a metaphorical vocabulary of 'loss and gain, of gambling and redemption' and by a series of 'ironic and inverted parallels'[8] – both formal devices characteristic of Eliot. Sally Shuttleworth maintains, similarly, that it is only when the novel is viewed in purely thematic terms that the 'simplistic division attributed to it by critics' adheres. Rather, she reads the disparate elements as all part of a search for an adequate form in which to express a 'radical social vision'.[9] Tracing a shift in Eliot's methodology from the empiricism of the natural historian to the idealism of the experimental scientist, Shuttleworth contends that in *Daniel Deronda* Eliot's goal as a novelist is 'no longer to represent a fixed "reality" but to challenge the social assumptions, values and practices that she saw operating in society'.[10] Catherine Belsey likewise argues that when read as radical critique – or, in her terms, as 'the history of an impossible resistance'– all aspects of the novel are equally relevant as the exploration of 'domination and subordination'.[11]

There is much in the novel to support a view of it as radical critique. The moral indolence of the English upper classes is exposed, for example, in scenes of mindless pursuit of pleasure and diversion. Extended parallels are also drawn between colonial and sexual domination, with Grandcourt's sadistic mastery of women explicitly linked to the brutality of England as an imperial power: 'If this white-handed man with the perpendicular profile had been sent to govern a difficult colony, he might have won reputation among his contemporaries. He had certainly ability, would have understood that it was safer to exterminate than to cajole superseded proprietors, and would not have flinched from making things safe in that way' (507). Gwendolen is repeatedly objectified by the male gaze, scrutinised by Deronda no less than by Grandcourt, and in her preoccupation with her own reflection, she shows that she has learned to identify herself as male onlookers have constructed her.

Furthermore, Gwendolen's naïve egoism in entering that marriage to Grandcourt with her own determination to dominate neither masks nor diminishes the culpability of her society in yielding her up to the arrangement. Her uncle, the Reverend Gascoigne, looks on his niece as a speculation, 'worth some expense' in the effort to orchestrate a 'first-rate marriage' (28). He willingly turns a blind eye to the existence of Grandcourt's mistress and four illegitimate children, and in this he reflects a broadly accepted double standard: 'No one talked of Mrs Glasher now, any more than they talked of the victim in a trial for manslaughter ten years before' (287). Even the devoted Mrs Davilow, Gwendolen's mother, acquiesces to the sacrifice of her daughter, consoling herself with the thought that marriage would make Gwendolen 'as happy as she would be with any one else – or as most other women are' (110).

The radicalism of the novel, however, should not be overstated. For all that it is incisive in its analysis of sexual politics in relation to Gwendolen's marriage to Grandcourt, it also offers the self-effacing Mirah as a type of perfect womanhood. Mrs Meyrick reports to Deronda that it is in Mirah's nature 'only to submit' (191), and in the scheme of the novel, Mirah's passivity is construed as a virtue. Her disposition is held up as a salutary example to Gwendolen, who recognises that 'her own submission was something very different' (475), the consequence of defeat, not duty. Even more pointedly, Mirah is represented as the obverse of Deronda's unsatisfactory mother, the Princess Halm-Eberstein. Whereas the Princess repudiates her faith and rebels against her upright father, Mirah clings to Judaism and remains dutiful to her exploitative parent, believing it wrong to abandon him and living piously in dread of transgression: 'for I thought I might get wicked and hateful to myself, in the same way that many others seemed hateful to me. For so long, so long I had never felt my outside world happy; and if I got wicked I should lose my world of happy thoughts where my mother lived with me' (182). The Princess abandons her family in her self-glorifying pursuit of her operatic career, while Mirah has to be compelled by her ambitious father into the exhibitionism of the stage. Demure and humble, her singing voice is appropriately domestic, more suited to parlours than to concert halls.

Certainly the Princess is afforded her moment of self-justification, as she forcefully outlines the repression of her Jewish upbringing:

To have a pattern cut out – 'this is the Jewish woman; this is what you must be; this is what you are wanted for; a woman's heart must be of such a size and no larger, else it must be pressed small, like Chinese feet; her happiness is to be made as cakes are, by a fixed receipt.' That was what my father wanted. He wished I had been a son; he cared for me as a makeshift link. (541)

However, the validity of her protest against patriarchal restraint and stifling conformism is obscured by the selfishness and vehemence with which it is articulated. Though it is Deronda who invites her exposition, he seems uncharacteristically deaf to it. He responds not with sympathy, but with an immediate inquiry about his grandfather, the offending patriarch, and in this he mirrors the more general deflection of the Princess's story in the novel.[12] Her outburst functions principally not to diagnose the cruel sexism of her milieu, but to exonerate Deronda of any ties, freeing him to embrace his new ideal family with Mordecai and Mirah: 'you owe me no duties. I did not wish you to be born. I parted with you willingly' (543). In the end, she is judged for her dereliction as a mother, rather than for her dedication as an artist.

The tendency in the novel to privilege female submission over assertion is reflected in the tenor of Deronda's advice to Gwendolen, which consistently advocates self-effacement and acquiescence, and is compounded by the way in which the role of the male guide is sacralised. So, Gwendolen's dependence on Deronda's advice turns him 'into a priest' (369), and he comes to occupy the position of Gwendolen's 'outer conscience' serving her 'in the stead of God' (653). In some ways, it is true, Eliot does seem to undercut this construction of Deronda, ascribing it to the exaggeration born of Gwendolen's desperation. Deronda, for example, reflects ruefully at one point on his foolishness in 'falling into an exaggeration of his own importance, and a ridiculous readiness to accept Gwendolen's view of himself' (482). Nevertheless, however much Gwendolen is inclined towards exaggeration, his role as saviour is enhanced in the plot by his enigmatic appearance at times of crisis – to Gwendolen in the gaming room at Leubronn, to Mirah as she is about to drown herself in the river, and, like a vision as the 'prefigured friend . . . from the golden background' (422), to Mordecai on the bridge. And there is an element of the self-styled saviour in Deronda: 'Persons attracted him, as Hans Meyrick had done, in proportion to the possibility of his defending them, rescuing them, telling upon their lives with some sort of redeeming influence' (273).

III

This ambivalence on sexual politics is not new in Eliot: we have seen it, for example, in *Felix Holt*. However, there is a more fundamental conservatism in this novel, which distinguishes it from all Eliot's previous work. In its exploration of the ethical challenge of negotiating difference, *Daniel Deronda* moves away from the more complex understandings of the earlier novels towards an evasion of the challenge of otherness through the appropriation of difference into a fantastical sense of wholeness.

In many ways the character of Daniel Deronda seems to represent the culmination of Eliot's ethical heroes. He has in abundance all the qualities that distinguish the ethical figures of her earlier work – empathy, imagination, humility, receptivity and flexibility of perspective. He has none of the egoism that gives rise to a 'want of sympathy' (510) and its concomitant 'moral stupidity' (148). He is free of that 'dullness towards what might be going on in other minds . . . which is among the commonest deficiencies even in good-natured men' (147). He has the mental and moral flexibility that allows him to shift his sympathy 'from the near to the distant, and back again from the distant to the near' (175), recalling that 'quick alternative vision' (*M*, 151) – that re-directing of focus – which allows for ethical extension in *Middlemarch* and which, Eliot contends, constitutes 'the chief elements of greatness: a mind consciously, energetically moving with the larger march of human destinies, but not less full of conscience and tender heart for the footsteps that tread near and need a leaning place' (465). Like the most virtuous characters in *Middlemarch*, Deronda has the capacity to de-centre himself and see his own narrative as 'one among a myriad' (149). And unlike the egoist Rosamond Vincy, whose very identity depends on her sense of centrality, Deronda feels an 'habitual shame at the acceptance of events as if they were his only' (538) and can contemplate as a meditative exercise 'how far it might be possible habitually to shift his centre till his own personality would be no less outside him than the landscape' (160). From an early age, he distinguishes himself from his peers by 'an activity of imagination on behalf of others' (151).

In addition, he manifests that impulse towards exogamy which marks characters like Maggie Tulliver and Silas Marner as ethically enlightened. Even as a boy, Deronda is drawn to the study of 'universal history, which made him want to be at home in foreign countries' (153). Without wishing to forswear his Englishness, he wants 'to understand other points of view' and 'to get rid of a merely English attitude in his studies' (155). It is, of course, this receptivity to otherness that prepares him for his moment of grace and enables the embrace of Mordecai and his prophecy. In all, it almost seems as if Deronda is articulating Eliot's own novelistic project when he announces to his mother that what he has 'been most trying to do for fifteen years is to have some understanding of those who differ from myself' (540).

However, in earlier works we have seen Eliot confront the limits of such sympathy in the face of the intractably alien nature of the other. Those limits are touched upon in this novel in the scene between Deronda and his mother. Confident of his empathetic skill, Daniel claims the insight of his sympathetic nature: 'Though my own experience has been quite different, I enter into the painfulness of your struggle. I can imagine the hardship of an enforced renunciation' (541). His mother, however, is implacable in her insistence that there is a point beyond which he cannot imaginatively enter her reality: ' "No," said the Princess, shaking her head and folding her arms with an air of decision. "You are not a woman. You may try – but you can never imagine what it is to have a man's force of genius in you, and yet to suffer the slavery of being a girl" ' (541).

In *Daniel Deronda*, though, the ethical challenge presented by this impasse is for the first time evaded. There is, in fact, a certain irony in this evasion because in her choice to treat the Jewish question, Eliot had made a deliberate and principled decision to engage with an important and problematic area of contemporary difference:

> precisely because I felt that the usual attitude of Christians towards Jews is – I hardly know whether to say more impious or more stupid when viewed in the light of their professed principles, I therefore felt urged to treat Jews with such sympathy and understanding as my nature and knowledge could attain to. Moreover, not only towards the Jews, but towards all oriental peoples with whom we English come in contact, a spirit of arrogance and contemptuous dictatorialness is observable which has become a national disgrace to us. There is nothing I should care more to do, if it were possible, than to rouse the imagination of men and women to a vision of human claims in those races of their fellow-men who most differ from them in customs and beliefs. (VI, 301)

True to her initial intention, she begins the process of tackling anti-Semitism by showing its taint even in the hero: 'Deronda could not escape (who can?) knowing ugly stories of Jewish characteristics and occupations' (176). She dramatises the process of his gradual enlightenment through his relationship with the saintly Mirah and Mordecai and the sturdy Cohens to the point where he greets the revelation of his own Jewishness with spontaneous gladness. Daniel's moments of self-scrutiny serve an educative, perhaps even morally coercive, function for the reader, as he becomes aware that his prejudice is born of 'unfairness and ridiculous exaggeration' (310) and, on revisiting the Cohens finds himself 'almost ashamed of the supercilious dislike these happy-looking creatures had raised in him by daylight. Nothing could be more cordial than the greeting he received, and both mother and grandmother seemed to gather more dignity from being seen on the private hearth, showing hospitality' (334).

This drama of otherness, by now very familiar in Eliot's fiction, is, however, transformed in *Daniel Deronda*, as the fundamental difference between self and other is collapsed through Deronda's discovery of his Jewishness. By prophetic fiat, the other becomes the self. Indeed, the sense of Daniel's epic destiny depends not only on a repudiation of difference, but it also comes to rely on its concomitant, the psychological fantasy of wholeness, in which there is no lack. This fantasy is played out particularly in the vocabulary of Deronda and Mordecai's relationship. So, Daniel is imaged as Modecai's 'new self' (423), and he comes to speak 'from Mordecai's mind as much as from his own' (640). Their separate identities are fused as Mordecai demands that Daniel be 'not only a hand to me, but a soul – believing my beliefs – being moved by my reasons – hoping my hopes – seeing the vision I point to – beholding a glory where I behold it!' (428). That fusion is further stressed by images of gestation. Mordecai claims that Daniel has 'risen within him' (430) and Eliot declares that in order to understand 'the sense of spiritual perpetuation' between the two men, one needs to think in terms of 'that maternal transference of self': 'Imagine – we all of us can . . . the face of a man little above thirty . . . then give to the yearning consumptive glance something of the slowly dying mother's look when her one loved son visits her bedside, and the flickering power of gladness leaps out as she says, "My boy!" ' (425). Similarly, through Mordecai Deronda finds in Hebrew his mother-tongue, whereas when he visits his biological mother for the first time, he 'could not even conjecture in what language she would speak to him' (535).

When Mordecai first looks for Daniel, he longs 'to find a man who differed from himself' (405); but the nature of the difference he seeks is superficial. It extends only to the incorporation of the features of the 'refined Jew', the characteristics which will make for success: 'he must be a Jew, intellectually cultured, morally fervid . . . his face and frame must be beautiful and strong, he must have been used to all the refinements of social life, his voice must flow with a full and easy current, his circumstances be free from sordid need' (405). In short, he must dissipate difference by incorporation: he must be at once an English gentleman *and* a Jew. In this sense, the secret of his birth has allowed Daniel the 'benefit' of 'as wide an instruction and sympathy as possible' (567). He has missed out on nothing, garnering all that comes of being the son of Sir Hugo Mallinger, including an Oxford education, while his Jewishness remains latent and intact, protected by a genetic essentialism. Daniel's fate, then, defies the alternatives of the binary logic of difference – a *or* b, a *or* not-a – and recalls instead the crazy reasoning of Hans's letter: 'B must be A' (549). So, too, Deronda defends the myth of the 'Bouddha' who gives himself to the famished tigress in order to save her and her little ones from starving – a startling image of incorporation, if ever there was one – as 'an extreme image of what is happening everyday – the transmutation of the self' (400). In this way Daniel becomes Mordecai's fantastic supplement, the product of his desire and imagination, which had constructed:

> another man who would be something more ample than the second soul bestowed, according to the notion of the Cabbalists, to help out the insufficient first – who would be a blooming human life, ready to incorporate all that was worthiest in an existence whose visible, palpable part was burning itself fast away. His inward need for the conception of this expanded, prolonged self was reflected as an outward necessity. . . . And as the more beautiful, the stronger, the more-executive self took shape in his mind, he loved it beforehand with an affection half identifying, half contemplative and grateful. (406)

In this 'willing marriage' between Daniel and Mordecai, which 'melts soul into soul' (643), a completeness is achieved: they are 'perfected together' (461). Yet the point is that such symbiosis represents an impossible union. It belongs in the realm of the psychoanalytic Imaginary, with its fantasy of dyadic relationship, where the disturbing divisions of self and other, sameness and difference, are obliterated.

Deronda's relationship with Mordecai is fundamentally an engagement with sameness, fulfilling his longing for a companion: 'a young man like himself who sustained a private grief and was not too confident of his own career; speculative enough to understand every moral difficulty, yet socially susceptible, as he himself was, and having every outward sign of equality either in bodily or in spiritual wrestling' (403). In this love of the same, they are like 'two undeclared lovers' (424), leaving little room for the most conventional engagement with difference or otherness which is most usually represented by heterosexual relationship. Accordingly, Daniel's relationship with Mirah always seems subsidiary to the bond with Mordecai. For the greater part of the novel Daniel feels 'no likelihood' that he should ever woo Mirah 'who had become dear to him amid associations that forbade wooing' (637). When he finally does declare his love to Mirah, his first words are 'Let us go and comfort Ezra' (679), and the brother remains quite literally central as the novel ends, not with any marital embrace, but with Daniel and Mirah on either side of the dying Ezra, their 'arms around him' (695).

The same suggestion of fantastic, or Imaginary, wholeness can be found in the way in which Daniel seems to incorporate the feminine into himself. In some respects this can be read as little more than one aspect of his empathetic nature. Having 'not lived with other boys' (141) in his youth, and, like Will Ladislaw, shared with women the outsider's position by virtue of his foreignness and dispossession, Deronda possesses a 'deeply-laid care for womanhood which had begun when his own lip was like a girl's' (637). However, the novel insists on something more far-reaching than mere sympathy. Just as Deronda absorbs the otherness of the Jew into himself, so the imagery suggests an incorporation of femaleness, which diffuses that opposition of male and female which his mother has so bitterly described. Hence, in the confrontation with the Princess, it 'seemed all the woman lacking in her was present in him' (566), and when he allows himself to sob in solitude for Gwendolen, he does so with 'more than a woman's acuteness of compassion' (585).

This fantasy of wholeness is replicated and amplified in the novel's depiction of the Zionist project. On the one hand, as one would expect of the notion of a discrete homeland, there is a stress on the importance of separateness. In the discussion at the working-men's club, for example, Mordecai refutes Gideon's argument for the inevitable assimilation of the Jews, calling instead for a revival of an 'organic centre' – a home state which would give 'outward reality' to the unity and difference of Judaism, which has been heroically preserved in the face of hardship and persecution:

'I say that the effect of our separateness will not be completed and
have its highest transformation unless our race takes on again the
character of a nationality. That is the fulfilment of the religious trust
that moulded them into a people, whose life has made half the inspiration of the world. What is it to me that the ten tribes are lost untrace-
ably, or that multitudes of the children of Judah have mixed
themselves with the Gentile populations as a river with rivers? Behold
our people still!'   (456)

Similarly, Deronda's grandfather advocates 'separateness with communication' (619), adamant that the Jewish people should not lose
themselves amongst Gentiles: ' "It's no better," said he, "than the
many sorts of grain going back from their variety into sameness" '
(619).

However, as with the question of Daniel's Jewishness, this is separateness represented as achievable without loss – fantastically, suggesting difference without lack. And, with the same principle of
incorporation or supplementation, this 'new Judaea' will carry 'the
culture and sympathies of every great nation in its bosom' (456). It
will be poised between East and West, between past and future – like
Daniel and Mordecai, all elements 'perfected together' (461). It will
take all that has been known in 'the memories of the East and West'
and correct them with 'the full vision of a better' (458). In this myth-
ic conclusion – to Mordecai's quest and to the novel – separateness
has none of the cost of difference, and none of the deficiency of partialness:

> the *Shemah*, wherein we briefly confess the divine Unity, is the chief
> devotional exercise of the Hebrew; and this made our religion the fun-
> damental religion for the whole world; for the divine Unity embraced
> as its consequence the ultimate unity of mankind. See, then – the
> nation which has been scoffed at for its separateness, has given a bind-
> ing theory to the human race. Now, in complete unity a part possesses
> the whole as the whole possesses every part: and this is the way human
> life is tending toward the image of the Supreme Unity.   (628)

IV

Thus, Eliot's conclusion to her final novel amounts to wish-fulfilment. It offers both the resolution to difference and, for the first time,
an ideal fate for her hero, a fate which incorporates all that she
regarded as worthy in life: an 'enlarging belief' (308), 'a definite line

of action' (308), 'social captainship' (642), the merging of love and duty, and an opportunity to be 'an organic part of social life' (308). Yet, the ending is shadowed by the sad and diminished figure of Gwendolen, whose incomprehension at Deronda's 'mysteriously-shadowed particular ideas' (688) seems fair commentary on the vagueness of his 'purposes which will take me to the East' (688). Within the realm of realism, Gwendolen's plan to sail away 'into a world where people were not forced to live with any one they did not like' (596) has the status of a childish fancy; within the epic narrative Deronda's curiously similar project to journey to the East to lead his kind constitutes heroic fulfilment.

The resolution turns, of course, on Deronda's Jewishness – and here, too, Eliot makes a significant shift from her earlier fiction. In *Silas Marner* and *Felix Holt* the issue of fostering and identity have been treated quite differently. Eppie and Esther both choose nurture over nature, and those characters who argue the case for nature as 'the strongest claim of all' (*SM*, 164) – of 'breed [as] stronger than pasture' (*SM*, 96) – are shown to belong to closed and withering societies, where the pursuit of sameness is absurd and damaging. They lack the moral generosity and openness to the stranger, which allows for a more expansive conception of kinship.

Daniel Deronda, however, reverses the ethical choice of exogamy over endogamy, with its insistence on a racial essentialism. Hans Meyrick's quest for Mirah's hand is doomed to failure, for example, because she will not marry a non-Jew. Conversion is impossible: she sees her Jewishness as 'what I am really. I am not pretending anything. I shall never be anything else' (418). Similarly, Deronda's worthiness of character is incidental to his suitability; it is the discovery of his Jewishness that makes the marriage possible.

The primacy of nature over nurture is affirmed throughout the novel through a vocabulary of biology. So, for example, Mrs Meyrick concludes that Mirah's mother must have been good according to the logic of genetics: 'A good woman, you may depend: you may know it by the scoundrel the father is. Where did the child get her goodness from? Wheaten flour has to be accounted for' (190). Similarly, Deronda's relationship to his grandfather is represented by the Princess as the 'young growth from the old root' (571), just as Mordecai sees their connection as 'leaves from a common stem with stirrings from a common root' (489). In fact, the novel does more than simply give priority to biological connection – more strikingly, it suggests that genes confer fundamental identity. Thus, at the very moment of the revelation of Deronda's parentage, when the fact of his Jewishness has no history, his mother perceives in him 'a latent obstinacy of race' (544). Similarly, with a kind of genetic revisionism, Deronda ascribes a lifetime's restlessness to 'an inherited yearning – the effect of brooding, passionate thoughts in many ancestors' (642). And that view is authorised by Mordecai's conception of an inherent and inherited race memory: 'The heritage of Israel is beating in the pulse of millions; it lives in their veins as a power without understanding, like the morning exultation of herds; it is the inborn half of memory, moving as in a dream among writings on the wall, which it sees dimly but cannot divide into speech' (457).

If the conclusion of Deronda's epic, then, offers an affirmation of sameness, it is sameness fantastically supplemented by the absorption of difference. That point is clear when Deronda's story is contrasted with that of Fedalma in *The Spanish Gypsy*. On the one hand, when Fedalma, after a lifetime of Christian privilege, discovers her true Gypsy ancestry, the tragedy of her life is activated by difference – by what she must forfeit in terms of the love and community of her betrothed, the Christian Duke Silva. Deronda, on the other hand, loses nothing worth having, and gains a culture, a history, a purpose and a wife. Whereas Eliot's previous fiction consistently tested the limits of that most fundamental ethical problem – the negotiation of difference – *Daniel Deronda* ends with the evasion of that problem and the justification for an embrace of likeness:

> It was as if he had found an added soul in finding his ancestry – his judgment no longer wandering in the mazes of impartial sympathy, but choosing, with that noble partiality which is man's best strength, the closer fellowship that makes sympathy practical – exchanging the bird's eye reasonableness which soars to avoid preference and loses all sense of quality, for the generous reasonableness of drawing shoulder to shoulder with men of like inheritance.   (638)

11

Conclusion

I

At the time of Eliot's death in December 1880, she was generally regarded as the greatest living writer of fiction. Leslie Stephen declared that such a view was unanimous: 'No one – whatever might be his special personal predilections – would have refused that title to George Eliot.'[1] Yet even as he offered his eulogy in *The Cornhill Magazine*, Stephen's laudatory assessment anticipated some of the concerns which would soon overturn Eliot's high reputation. He addressed a prevailing suspicion that she was overly intellectual; he suggested that there had been a dropping off of talent in her last two novels; and, only two months after she died, he placed her firmly in the past as 'the termination of the great period of English fiction that began with Scott . . . the last great sovereign of a literary dynasty'.[2] Anthony Trollope took up the theme in 1883, objecting to the analytical rather than creative bias of her mind, which led Eliot to write 'like a philosopher',[3] although it was probably Henry James who guaranteed that this estimate would prevail for more than fifty years. In a series of articles, beginning in the mid-1860s, James acknowledged genuine admiration for Eliot, while at the same time making a case for the deficiency of her imagination. He was offended by what he took to be the 'diffuseness' of Eliot's fiction, its absence of 'design and construction', and its lack of 'organized, moulded, balanced composition'.[4] Thus, within ten years of her death Eliot stood reproved for her seriousness,[5] and condemned for her lack of form and imagination.

The air of respect which had accompanied these criticisms was dissipated by George Saintsbury in 1895 with his essay on Eliot in

Corrected Impressions: Essays on Victorian Writers. As the title of his book suggested, Saintsbury was intent on declaring that the emperor had no clothes on: 'Twenty years ago it required, if not a genuine strength of mind, at any rate a certain amount of "cussedness" not to be a George-Eliotite.'[6] Now he felt sufficiently confident to assert that neither Eliot nor Charlotte Brontë had in any degree 'the male faculties of creation and judgment'.[7] In an ironic anticipation of John Bayley's late-twentieth-century dismissal of Eliot, which we considered in the Introduction, Saintsbury declared the demise of Eliot's relevance and reputation at the end of the nineteenth:

> what many independent critics had been saying for years became the public voice on the appearance of *Daniel Deronda*. Coterie admiration lasted a little longer; and that popular reflex which a well-engineered fame always brings with it, a little longer still. And then it all broke down, and for some years past George Eliot, though she may still be read, has more or less passed out of contemporary critical appreciation.[8]

This critical eclipse was to last for another fifty years. In 1934, for example, Lord David Cecil's influential *Early Victorian Novelists: Essays in Revaluation* reaffirmed every reservation expressed by Eliot's late nineteenth-century detractors. To his mind, Eliot's 'exclusively moral point of view' was 'alien . . . bleak and unsatisfying'. Her work was deficient in form, lacking 'orderly imagination', and there was a 'congenital disproportion' in Eliot's talent, with the intellect overwhelming imagination. Once again, she was consigned to a past epoch, 'at the gateway between the old and new'.[9]

The one notable exception to this generally negative critical estimate was Virginia Woolf's essay in *The Times Literary Supplement* in 1919, which was as sympathetic in tone as George Saintsbury had been hostile. While Saintsbury prided himself on his act of unmasking, Woolf uncovered a truth of a different kind – the strangely personal and decidedly sexist animus which inflected a good deal of Eliot criticism. Woolf begins her essay with a confession of her own complicity in the underestimation of Eliot's achievement:

> To read George Eliot attentively is to become aware how little one knows about her. It is also to become aware of the credulity, not very creditable to one's insight, with which, half consciously and partly maliciously, one had accepted the late Victorian version of a deluded woman who held phantom sway over subjects even more deluded than herself.[10]

Yet as she interrogates that 'late Victorian version', she comes to recognise the fact that it was Eliot's gender as much as her art that was frequently and freely found wanting: 'In fiction, where so much of personality is revealed, the absence of charm is a great lack; and her critics, who have been, of course, mostly of the opposite sex, have resented, half consciously perhaps, her deficiency in a quality which is held to be supremely desirable in women.'[11] In her reassertion of Eliot's greatness, Woolf reversed her father, Leslie Stephen's deprecation of the later fiction: 'It is not that her power diminishes, for, to our thinking, it is at its highest in the mature *Middlemarch*, the magnificent book which with all its imperfections is one of the few English novels written for grown-up people.'[12]

The momentum of the critical pendulum which had swung steadily against Eliot since her death was halted by two books in 1948, F. R. Leavis's *The Great Tradition* and Joan Bennett's *George Eliot: Her Mind and Her Art*, which, taken together, refuted the principal critical charges against her. Leavis challenged above all the negative estimate of Eliot's moral intelligence, refusing the Jamesian distinction between the aesthetic and the moral: 'Is there any great novelist whose preoccupation with "form" is not a matter of his responsibility towards a rich human interest, or complexity of interests, profoundly realized? – a responsibility involving of its very nature, imaginative sympathy, moral discrimination and judgment of relative human values?'[13] And Bennett began the reassessment of Eliot's mastery of form, stressing the 'organic form of her novels' as innovation rather than absence.[14] The rehabilitation of Eliot's reputation thus begun, culminated in Barbara Hardy's influential *The Novels of George Eliot: A Study in Form* (1959) and W. J. Harvey's *The Art of George Eliot* (1962).

The other decisive aspect of this mid-century sea change in Eliot's critical reputation was the revaluation of the intellectual richness of Eliot's fiction, with critics like Basil Willey, George Levine and U. C. Knoepflmacher re-examining her contributions and debts to the wider philosophical debates of her time.[15] This enterprise was underpinned, of course, by the massive contribution to Eliot scholarship provided by Gordon Haight with the 1955 publication of *The George Eliot Letters* in seven volumes and his authoritative biography of Eliot in 1968.

II

The emergence of critical theory as a powerful force in literary studies in the 1970s proved another watershed for Eliot's reputation as a novelist. In particular, her adherence to realism and her relationship to feminism became the two areas of contention around which debate centred. The attacks on Eliot's realism took a variety of forms, but all turned on a basic objection to its deceptiveness. Influenced by the work of Roland Barthes, poststructuralist critics criticised Eliot's novels for the ways in which they sought to disguise their constructedness and offer themselves as a transparent and unproblematic window on reality.[16] Some objected to the inconsistency of the form, drawing attention to the ways in which the principles of realism were at odds with the didactic purpose and providential reversals of Eliot's fiction.[17] Others raised more fundamental ideological objections to realism's complicity with, and confirmation of, the bourgeois liberal status quo. Leo Bersani's *A Future for Asyntax*, for example, highlighted the way in which realism offered the reader the illusion of coherence and significance. So, psychological complexity was tolerated, he argued, 'as long as it doesn't threaten the ideology of self as a fundamentally intelligible structure unaffected by a history of fragmented, discontinuous desires'.[18] Its allegiance to the myth of the unified individual human subject was matched by its service to nineteenth-century society 'providing it with strategies for containing (and repressing) its disorder within significantly structured stories about itself'.[19] For Marxist critics like Terry Eagleton, this complicity with the status quo represented a denial of the contradictions underlying capitalism itself.[20]

These attacks on Eliot prompted a host of persuasive replies. David Lodge's essay '*Middlemarch* and the Idea of the Classic Realist Text', for example, in refuting Colin MacCabe, provides a useful summary of the poststructuralist case against Eliot, while arguing convincingly that it is based on the notion of a naïve realism, or mimetic illusion, which never applied to Eliot's fiction.[21] Penny Boumelha, in a similar vein, argues that the concept of classic realism is too simple and is 'useful at best to identify an aspiration of texts, a self-image which the inevitably less coherent, less unified, more contradictory texts themselves only fitfully achieve as a practice'.[22] George Levine makes a convincing case for the fact that both George Lewes and George Eliot were fully aware of the inevitably limited nature of that aspiration. Both, he argued, sustain a position, that to contemporary criticism may seem self-divided:

but that they did hold the position is self-evident. Beginning with the recognition of fictionality, they proceed to argue for representation. Here is a crucial statement of Lewes: 'A distinction is drawn between Art and Reality, and an antithesis between Realism and Idealism which would never have gained acceptance had not men in general lost sight of the fact that Art is a Representation of Reality – a Representation which, inasmuch as it is not the thing itself, but only represents it, must necessarily be limited by the nature of its medium' ('Realism in Art: Recent German Fiction', *Westminster Review*, 70 (1858), 273).[23]

And Felicia Bonaparte has similarly pointed out that Eliot's realism makes only 'a tentative and partial claim to accuracy in relation to fact' because Eliot recognised that all empirical observation, whether scientific or not, could 'never be known to be knowledge of what is but only of what is perceived'.[24]

Deconstructive critics have further challenged both the aspiration to, and the fact of, any simple transparency in Eliot's fiction, highlighting the ways in which her works 'subversively undermine traditions of narrative, history and meaning that her culture had apparently taken for granted'.[25] K. M. Newton, for example, draws an important distinction between Eliot's realism 'at the level of "story" ' and her 'continual experimentation at the level of "discourse" '.[26] And critics such as J. Hillis Miller and Cynthia Chase have analysed the ways in which Eliot's novels actually destabilise realist narrative conventions, affirming George Levine's claim that Eliot 'seems to be easily assimilable to our contemporary fascination with deconstruction'.[27]

III

The rise of feminist criticism in the 1970s inevitably sparked a resurgence of interest in Eliot. As works such as Ellen Moers's *Literary Women* and Elaine Showalter's *A Literature of their Own* sought to trace a female literary tradition, Eliot's stature and importance as a writer made it imperative to accommodate her in any new canon or pantheon. Her extraordinary success led feminists to expect more from her, according to Deirdre David, than 'from other Victorian women intellectuals'.[28] At the same time, though, the more conservative aspects of Eliot's thinking were difficult to reconcile with feminist tenets, leading to a sense of disappointment and vexation which Elaine Showalter documented in her article 'The Greening of Sister

George'.[29] Zelda Austen gave voice to that disappointment at its simplest – and most simplistic: 'Feminist critics are angry with George Eliot because she did not permit Dorothea Brooke in *Middlemarch* to do what George Eliot did in real life.'[30]

A similar ambivalence was evident in a variety of studies which traced Eliot's relation to mid-Victorian feminism, both in her life and her fiction. Eliot's refusal to endorse moves to extend the franchise to women and her scornful analysis of her sister authors were balanced, on the one hand, against her support for the Married Women's Property Bill and for women's education, on the other. And a variety of works examined the novels for their representation of women, implicitly or explicitly measuring them against a notional feminist ideal.[31] There was a certain theoretical naïveté in these early feminist engagements with Eliot. As Penny Boumelha has argued, the twin demand implicit in such criticism – both for depiction of injustice and abuses suffered by women and for positive role models – led to the 'requirement of, in effect, fantasy heroines within realist textual environments [which] places unanswerable and anachronistic demands upon the possibilities of writing within mid-nineteenth century realism'.[32]

The ideological zeal of the first-wave feminist analyses has given way to more measured assessments of the kind exemplified by Gillian Beer's influential 1986 study, *George Eliot*:

> George Eliot, then, did engage with issues vital in the life of the women's movement. The kind of comment we often encounter that 'she always sought to be free of any close involvement with the feminist movement of her time either in life or in literature' (Miles, 1974; p. 52) is simply not true. Nor is Ellen Moers's flat assertion that George Eliot was 'no feminist' to be accepted. We do not need to convert her into a radical feminist: it would be pointless to pretend to do so. What is demonstrable is that she was intimately familiar with the current writing and actions of the women's movement and that in *Middlemarch* particularly, she brooded on the curtailment of women's lives in terms drawn from that movement and in sympathy with it.[33]

More generally, feminism's increasing engagement with poststructuralism, deconstruction and psychoanalysis has led to a more sophisticated apprehension of the complex, unstable and frequently contradictory aspects of Eliot's texts, and of their susceptibility to feminist appropriation.[34]

Some of the most impressive recent work on Eliot has been done by New Historicist critics, who while relocating Eliot's work within its historical context, have brought to their analyses a new capacity to interrogate the novels, in all their contradictoriness, not merely as reflective, but as symptomatic, of their period.[35] It is work of this kind, alert to the ways in which Eliot was produced by, and product-ive of, her historical context, and to the ways in which her work might be read today in fruitful dialogue with philosophers, histor-ians, scientists, psychoanalysts and the like, that promises to do jus-tice both to her massive intellect and to her prodigious talent.

Notes

CHAPTER 1: INTRODUCTION

1. Quoted in *The George Eliot Letters*, ed. Gordon Haight (New Haven, CT: Yale University Press, 1955), vol. V, p. 353. All further references to this work will be incorporated in the text, abbreviated to volume and page numbers.

2. Dinah Mulock, 'To Novelists – and a Novelist', *Macmillan's Magazine*, April 1861, 442.

3. Gordon Haight, 'George Eliot and Her Correspondents', *The George Eliot Letters*, vol. I, p. xliv.

4. George Eliot, *The Journals of George Eliot*, ed. Margaret Harris and Judith Johnston (Cambridge: Cambridge University Press, 1998), p. 61.

5. Charles Darwin, quoted in Gillian Beer, *Darwin's Plots: Evolutionary Narrative in Darwin, George Eliot and Nineteenth-Century Fiction* (Cambridge: Cambridge University Press, 2000), p. 156.

6. George Eliot, *The Mill on the Floss* (1860; rpt. Oxford: Oxford University Press, 1996), p. 273. All further references to this work will be incorporated in the text, abbreviated where necessary to *Mill*.

7. Less admiringly, George Saintsbury, reviewing Eliot's career in 1895, claimed that George Lewes's 'scientific phraseology . . . invaded his companion's writing like a positive contagion' (*Corrected Impressions: Essays on Victorian Writers*, quoted in *A Century of George Eliot Criticism*, ed. Gordon Haight (Boston, MA: Houghton Mifflin, 1965), p. 168).

8. George Eliot, review of John Ruskin's *Modern Painters*, vol. III, in *George Eliot: Selected Critical Writings*, ed. Rosemary Ashton (Oxford: Oxford University Press, 1992), p. 248. All further references to this work will be incorporated in the text, abbreviated to *SCW*.

9. Edmund Gosse, *Father and Son: A Study of Two Temperaments* (1907; rpt. Harmondsworth: Penguin, 1970), p. 75.

10. *Ibid.*, p. 74.

11. Lord Acton, review of John Cross, *George Eliot's Life*, quoted in David Carroll, *George Eliot and the Conflict of Interpretations: A Reading of the Novels* (Cambridge: Cambridge University Press, 1992), p. 3.

12. Basil Willey, *Nineteenth-Century Studies: Coleridge to Matthew Arnold* (London: Chatto and Windus, 1968), p. 205.

13. See Chapter 11, pp. 160–1.

14. John Bayley, review of Kathryn Hughes, *George Eliot: The Last Victorian,* in *The New York Review,* 21 October 1999, p. 60.

15. Simon Dentith, *Bakhtinian Thought* (London: Routledge, 1995), p. 99.

16. Even at the time of writing, Eliot was enthusiastically read by the young Sigmund Freud. In an article in *The American Journal of Psychoanalysis,* Carl T. Rosenberg reveals that *Middlemarch,* in particular, made a deep impression on Freud, and, according to his biographer Ernst Jones, it 'illuminated important aspects of his relation' with his fiancée. Rosenberg details the connections between the two figures, and speculates that Eliot 'may have influenced Freud in his thinking about character structure, love relationships, and identity, both personal and social' ('George Eliot – Proto-Psychoanalyst', *The American Journal of Psychoanalysis,* 59: 3 (1999), 258).

17. Emmanuel Levinas, 'Time and the Other', in *The Levinas Reader,* ed. Sean Hand (Oxford: Blackwell, 1994), p. 41.

18. J. Hillis Miller, *The Ethics of Reading: Kant, de Man, Eliot, Trollope, James, and Benjamin* (New York: Columbia University Press, 1987), p. 3.

19. Margot Waddell, 'On Ideas of "The Good" and "The Ideal" in George Eliot's Novels and Post-Kleinian Psychoanalytic Thought', *The American Journal of Psychoanalysis,* 59 (1999), 272.

20. George Eliot, review of Fredrika Bremer's *Hertha* in *Essays of George Eliot,* ed. Thomas Pinney (London: Routledge and Kegan Paul, 1963), p. 332.

21. Herbert Spencer, 'Progress: Its Laws and Cause', quoted in Haight, *The George Eliot Letters,* II, p. 341.

22. George Eliot, *Adam Bede* (1859; rpt. Oxford: Oxford University Press, 1966), p. 49. All further references to this work will be incorporated in the text, abbreviated where necessary to *AB.*

23. Willey, *Nineteenth-Century Studies,* p. 187. For commentaries on the influence of Positivism on Eliot see, for example, Willey, *ibid.*; J. B. Bullen, 'George Eliot's *Romola* as Positivist Allegory', *Review of English Studies,* 104 (1975), 425–35; T. R. Wright, 'George Eliot and Positivism', *Modern Language Review,* 76 (1981), 257–72; William Myers, *The Teaching of George Eliot* (Leicester: Leicester University Press, 1984); Martha Vogeler, 'George Eliot and the Positivists', *Nineteenth-Century Fiction,* 35 (1980), 405–31.

24. Quoted in Colin Davis, *Levinas* (Cambridge: Polity, 1996), p. 24.

25. Gillian Beer, *The Romance (The Critical Idiom)* (London: Methuen, 1970), p. 71.

26. Quoted in Davis, *Levinas*, p. 31.

27. George Eliot, *Romola* (1863: rpt. Oxford: Oxford University Press, 1994), p. 232. All further references to this work will be incorporated in the text, abbreviated where necessary to *R*.

28. George Eliot, *Middlemarch* (1872; rpt. Oxford: Oxford University Press, 1996), p. 139. All further references to this work will be incorporated in the text, abbreviated where necessary to *M*.

29. Raymond Williams, *The English Novel: From Dickens to Lawrence* (St Albans: Paladin, 1974), p. 11.

30. George Eliot, *Daniel Deronda* (1876; rpt. Oxford: Oxford University Press, 1988), p. 461. All further references to this work will be incorporated in the text, abbreviated where necessay to *DD*.

CHAPTER 2:   THE MAKING OF A NOVELIST

1. In 1855 and 1856, the two years prior to the commencement of her fiction-writing career, Eliot earned £119 and £140 respectively from her writing for periodicals. In the subsequent five-year period she earned £11,218 – £443 for *Scenes of Clerical Life*, £1745 for *Adam Bede*, £3685 for *The Mill on the Floss* and £5345 for *Silas Marner* (*The Journals of George Eliot*, ed. Margaret Harris and Judith Johnston (Cambridge: Cambridge University Press, 1998) pp. 58, 64–5, 72, 75, 88). By 1862, Eliot could command the highest price ever paid for a novel, £7000, from George Smith for *Romola* (VIII, 301).

2. Daniel Cottom, *Social Figures: George Eliot, Social History and Literary Representation* (Minneapolis: University of Minnesota Press, 1987), p. 11.

3. While Eliot claimed that she 'hardly ever read anything that is written about myself – indeed, never unless my husband expressly wishes me to do so by way of exception' (VI, 318), there was evidently a degree of pretence in this, since she spent her career engaging with criticism, and John Blackwood confirmed that 'she certainly hears plentifully all that is said or written in London on the subject of Deronda' (VI, 253).

4. Eliza Lynn Linton, *My Literary Life* (London: Hodder and Stoughton, 1899), p. 99.

5. Margaret Oliphant, *Autobiography and Letters of Mrs Oliphant*, ed. Mrs Harry Coghill (Edinburgh: Blackwood and Sons, 1899), p. 4.

6. John Cross, *George Eliot's Life as Related in Her Letters and Journals* (Leipzig: Tauchnitz, 1885), p. 283.

7. George Eliot, *Felix Holt* (1866; rpt. Oxford: Oxford University Press, 1988), p. 299; *Scenes of Clerical Life* (1858; rpt. Oxford: Oxford

University Press, 1988), p. 52. All further references to these works will be incorporated in the text, abbreviated where necessary to *FH* and *SC*.

8. George Eliot, *The Spanish Gypsy* (Edinburgh: Blackwood & Sons, 1868), p. 107. For a further discussion of this aspect of Eliot's fiction, see Pauline Nestor, *Female Friendships and Communities: Charlotte Brontë, George Eliot, Elizabeth Gaskell* (Oxford: Clarendon Press, 1985), pp. 189–204.

9. George Eliot, 'Armgart' in *Collected Poems* (London: Skoob, 1989), pp. 129, 131, 128.

10. *Ibid.*, p. 117.

11. For an extended discussion of the problematic and controversial aspects of Eliot's realism, see Chapter 11, pp. 159–60.

12. George Eliot, 'Worldliness and Other-Worldliness: the Poet Young', in *Essays of George Eliot*, ed. Thomas Pinney (London: Routledge and Kegan Paul, 1963), pp. 371 and 379.

13. *Ibid.*, pp. 366 and 371.

14. George Eliot, 'Leaves from a Note-Book' in *ibid.*, p. 440.

15. Eliot, 'Worldliness and Other-Worldliness', p. 363.

16. George Eliot, 'Three Novels', in Pinney, *Essays*, p. 327.

17. *Ibid.*, p. 327.

18. George Eliot, review of Charles Kingsley's *Westward Ho!* in *ibid.*, p. 123.

19. Eliot, 'Worldliness and Other-Worldliness', p. 379.

CHAPTER 3: *SCENES OF CLERICAL LIFE*

1. Quoted in David Carroll (ed.), *George Eliot: The Critical Heritage* (London: Routledge, 1971), p. 65.

2. *Ibid.*, p. 67.

3. David Lodge, Introduction, *Scenes of Clerical Life* (Harmondsworth: Penguin, 1973), p. 18.

4. Ludwig Feuerbach, *The Essence of Christianity*, trans. Marian Evans (1854; rpt. London: Trubner, 1881), p. 54.

5. Quoted in Colin Davis, *Levinas* (Cambridge: Polity, 1996), pp. 21 and 24.

6. Feuerbach, *The Essence of Christianity*, p. 54.

CHAPTER 4: *ADAM BEDE*

1. The clear echo of the Riehl review can be heard in *Adam Bede*. In the review, Eliot urges the reader to observe a company of haymakers:

> When you see them at a distance . . . you think these companions in labour must be as bright and cheerful as the picture to which they give animation. Approach nearer, and you will certainly find that hay-making time is a time for joking, especially if there are women among the labourers; but the coarse laughter that bursts out every now and then, and expresses the triumphant taunt, is as far as possible from your conception of idyllic merriment. (*SCW*, 262)

> In *Adam Bede* she makes the same point about perspective and realism through the same image: 'The jocose talk of haymakers is best at a distance; like those clumsy bells round the cows' necks, it has rather a coarse sound when it comes close, and may even grate on your ears painfully' (207).

2. Gillian Beer sees *Adam Bede* as a 'revision of *Ruth*', though it may also be influenced by Walter Scott's *The Heart of Midlothian*, which treats not only the illegitimate pregnancy but also child murder. See Gillian Beer, *George Eliot* (Brighton: Harvester, 1986), p. 59.

3. Quoted in Colin Davis, *Levinas* (Cambridge: Polity, 1996), p. 25.

4. Dorothy Atkins, *George Eliot and Spinoza* (Salzburg: University of Salzburg, 1978), pp. 77 and 82.

CHAPTER 5: *THE MILL ON THE FLOSS*

1. George Eliot, *The Journals of George Eliot*, ed. Margaret Harris and Judith Johnston (Cambridge: Cambridge University Press, 1998), p. 76.

2. *Ibid.*, p. 90.

3. *Ibid.*, p. 77.

4. George Eliot, 'The Lifted Veil', *The Works of George Eliot: Silas Marner, The Lifted Veil, Brother Jacob* (London: Virtue & Co., n.d.), p. 297.

5. Mary Wollstonecraft made much the same point more than sixty years earlier in her novella *Mary and the Wrongs of Woman* when she examined the 'treacherous fancy' which causes her heroine 'to sketch a character, congenial with her own, from these shadowy outlines . . . how difficult it was for women to avoid growing romantic, who have no active duties or pursuits' (*Mary and the Wrongs of Woman* (Oxford: Oxford University Press, 1980), pp. 78–9).

6. The sentence is added to the concluding paragraph of Book 3, Chapter V, 'Tom Applies His Knife to the Oyster' (Explanatory Notes, *Mill*, 527).

7. George Eliot, 'Worldliness and Other-Worldliness' in Thomas Pinney (ed.), *Essays of George Eliot* (London: Routledge and Kegan Paul, 1963), p. 374.

8. Eliot, *Journals*, p. 272.

9. Eliot's life-long interest in art was fuelled by the desire, like Maggie's, to enter into the mind of the other: 'in learning how to estimate the artistic products of a particular age according to the mental attitude and external life of that age, we are widening our sympathy and deepening the basis of our tolerance and charity' (*SCW*, 248).

10. Eliot, 'The Lifted Veil', p. 318.

11. Elaine Showalter, *A Literature of Their Own: Women Novelists from Brontë to Lessing* (London: Virago, 1982), p. 112.

12. Françoise Basch, *Relative Creatures: Victorian Women in Society and the Novel, 1837–67*, trans. A. Rudolf (London: Allen Lane, 1974), p. 97.

13. Pauline Nestor, *Female Friendships and Communities: Charlotte Brontë, George Eliot, Elizabeth Gaskell* (Oxford: Clarendon Press, 1985), p. 189.

14. Toril Moi, *Sexual/Textual Politics: Feminist Literary Theory* (London: Methuen, 1985), p. 8.

15. For a fuller discussion of the inadequacy of any simple reading of *Jane Eyre* as a feminist *Bildungsroman* see Pauline Nestor, *Charlotte Brontë's Jane Eyre* (London: Harvester Wheatsheaf, 1992).

16. Showalter, *A Literature of their Own*, p. 131.

17. Felicia Bonaparte, *Will and Destiny: Morality and Tragedy in George Eliot's Novels* (New York: New York University Press, 1975), p. 203.

18. Eliot's struggle with endings is well documented. At the beginning of her career, for example, she wrote to John Blackwood: 'Conclusions are the weak point of most authors, but some of the fault lies in the very nature of a conclusion, which is at best a negation' (II, 324); and, again, at the end, she noted: 'endings are inevitably the least satisfactory part of any work in which there is any merit of development' (VI, 242). Penny Boumelha, in her article 'George Eliot and the End of Realism', contends that Eliot's endings 'bring into fiction the collision of the unsatisfied, perhaps even illimitable, desire of her heroines with the restricted possibilities of the world as it could be imagined by realism' (in *Women Reading Women's Writing*, ed. Sue Roe (Brighton: Harvester, 1987), p. 33).

19. Removed from emotional investment in her characters, Eliot was capable of recognising the unreality of such nostalgia: 'Childhood is only the beautiful and happy time in contemplation and retrospect – to the child it is full of deep sorrows, the meaning of which is unknown' (I, 173).

CHAPTER 6: *SILAS MARNER*

1. George Eliot, *The Journals of George Eliot*, ed. Margaret Harris and Judith Johnstone (Cambridge: Cambridge University Press, 1998) p. 336.

2. *Ibid.*, p. 86.

3. *Ibid.*, p. 87.

4. George Eliot, *The Works of George Eliot: Silas Marner, The Lifted Veil, Brother Jacob* (London: Virtue & Co., n.d.), p. 408.

5. Terence Cave, 'Introduction', *Silas Marner: The Weaver of Raveloe* (1861; rpt. Oxford: Oxford University Press, 1996), p. vii. All further references to this work will be incorporated in the text, abbreviated where necessary to *SM*; Joseph Wiesenfarth, *George Eliot's Mythmaking* (Heidelberg: Carol Winter, 1977), p. 124.

6. Gillian Beer, *The Romance* (*The Critical Idiom*) (London: Methuen, 1970) p. 71.

7. Eliot, *Journals*, p. 87.

8. Pam Hirsch, *Barbara Leigh Smith Bodichon: Feminist, Artist and Rebel* (London: Chatto and Windus, 1998), p. 65.

9. Eliot, *Journals*, p. 87.

10. *Ibid.*

11. There is perhaps the suggestion of guilt evident in Eliot's self-justificatory response to the death of Herbert in 1875, six years after the demise of Thornton:

> From having been splendidly muscular and altogether vigorous he had become reduced by what he reported to be neuralgic pains. It now appears that a tendency to glandular disease which had shown itself in his early boyhood had returned and rapidly developed itself, so that every one of his glands was enlarged. He went to Durban for the sake of sea air and medical advice, but while there an attack of bronchitis hastened his death. He left a widow and two children, one of them an infant boy born in May last. He was a sweet-natured creature – not clever, but diligent and well-judging about the things of daily life, and we felt ten years ago that a colony with a fine climate, like Natal, offered him the only fair prospect within his reach. What

can we do more than try to arrive at the best conclusion from the conditions as they are known to us? The issue, which one could not foresee, must be borne with resignation – is in no case a ground for self-reproach, and in this case, I imagine, would hardly have been favourably altered by a choice of life in the old country.   (VI, 165)

12. Sally Shuttleworth, *George Eliot and Nineteenth-Century Science: The Make-Believe of a Beginning* (Cambridge: Cambridge University Press, 1984), p. ix.

13. Gillian Beer, *George Eliot* (Brighton: Harvester, 1986) pp. 54 and 116.

14. *Ibid.*, p. 116.

15. Cave, Introduction, p. xxviii.

16. *Ibid.*

17. *Ibid.*

18. Beer, *George Eliot*, p. 110.

19. Colin Davis, *Levinas* (Cambridge: Polity, 1996), p. 25.

20. Quoted in David Carroll (ed.), *George Eliot: The Critical Heritage* (London: Routledge, 1971), p.131.

21. Eliot clearly had Wordsworth in mind while writing *Silas Marner*. She takes lines from his poem 'Michael' as the epigraph for the novel, and she ventured the doubt to her publisher during composition that 'I should not have believed that any one would have been interested in it but myself (since William Wordsworth is dead) if Mr. Lewes had not been strongly arrested by it' (III, 382).

22. In this there are echoes of Eliot's observations on the 'spirit of communal exclusiveness' in her review of Riehl: 'the resistance to the indiscriminate establishment of strangers, is an intense traditional feeling in the peasant. "This gallows is for us and our children" is the typical motto of this spirit' (*SCW*, 276).

23. James McLaverty, 'Comtean Fetishism in *Silas Marner*', *Nineteenth-Century Fiction*, 36 (1982), 318. As McLaverty goes on to explain, 'Fetishism was for Comte the very first stage in man's progress, and it fulfilled man's needs and contributed to his dignity in special ways: the period saw the settlement of land, the discovery of fire, the establishment of the family, and the institution of adoption; it was the stage of human history at which men were most dependent on their feelings, even relying on them for simple explanations when they were otherwise unable to understand the world around them. The achievements of fetishism were so important that Comte thought it vital to incorporate them into his own Religion of Humanity, which was to be the final stage of human development' (p. 318).

24. Quoted in William Myers, *The Teaching of George Eliot* (Leicester, Leicester University Press, 1984), p. 34; Ludwig Feuerbach, *The Essence of Christianity*, trans. Marian Evans (1854; rpt. London: Trubner and Company, 1881), p. 11.

25. Davis, *Levinas*, p. 31.

26. T. S. Eliot, *Four Quartets* (London: Faber, 1976), p. 44.

27. It is precisely Dolly's non-cerebral approach which allows her access to a more fundamental understanding and goodness, and such a character gives the lie to the charge of intellectual elitism levelled by Daniel Cottom in *Social Figures: George Eliot – Social History and Literary Representation* (Minneapolis: University of Minnesota Press, 1987): 'No sooner did literacy and education become assumptions of social life than they were used to dismiss from the realm of discourse the language of any person or group that did not display their standards . . . it was her sense of her own intellectual condition [Eliot] was holding out for their pursuit and eventual delectation' (p. 12).

28. Feuerbach, *The Essence of Christianity*, p. 187.

CHAPTER 7: *ROMOLA*

1. In the event, of course, her novel was poached by the rival publisher, George Smith, who paid a record price of £7000 to attract the name of George Eliot as a drawcard to his flagging *Cornhill Magazine*.

2. George Eliot, *The Journals of George Eliot*, ed. Margaret Harris and Judith Johnston (Cambridge: Cambridge University Press, 1998), p. 118.

3. *Ibid.*, p. 104.

4. *Ibid.*, pp. 108 and 109.

5. John Cross, *George Eliot's Life as Related in Her Letters and Journals* (Leipzig: Tauchnitz, 1885) vol. II, p. 352.

6. Eliot, *Journals*, p. 105.

7. *Ibid.*, p. 112.

8. Quoted in David Carroll (ed.), *George Eliot: The Critical Heritage* (London: Routledge, 1971) p. 215.

9. Henry James, 'George Eliot's Life', *Atlantic Monthly*, LV (May, 1885), 672.

10. Andrew Brown, Introduction, *Romola*, p. xix.

11. Felicia Bonaparte painstakingly elucidates this poetic and symbolic dimension of the novel in *The Triptych and the Cross: The Central*

Myths of George Eliot's Poetic Imagination (New York: New York University Press, 1979).

12. James, 'George Eliot's Life', pp. 668–78.

13. George Levine, '*Romola* as Fable', in *Critical Essays on George Eliot*, ed. Barbara Hardy (London: Routledge and Kegan Paul, 1970), p. 79.

14. *Ibid.*, p. 78.

15. Ironically, as Eliot braced herself for the popular disappointment that would follow on the change of locale, *The Saturday Review* criticised the novel for being more of the same:

> The authoress of *Romola* has already published four tales of English life, and four tales of English life are quite enough to use up the experience and exhaust the reflections even of a mind so acute, so observant, and so meditative ... The minds of men gifted with great creative power can, indeed, turn from one set of subjects and one set of characters to another. Shakespeare, and Scott, and Goethe are, within certain limits, inexhaustible. But there is another order of minds, which is really creative and original, but which is always driven into the same groove, and which works within bounds which have been probably assigned by the actual experience of life. The authoress of *Adam Bede* has a mind of this sort. With all its humour, and feeling, and philosophical and pictorial power, it is centred upon a few elements of character, and is controlled as if by the inevitable presence of certain familiar incidents. Stripped of their Florentine covering, and divested of those touches of variety which the genius of the writer imparts to them, several of the characters of *Romola*, and some of the chief events, are old – not in the sense that they are mere repetitions, or that the authoress ever shows poverty of invention, but that they involve the same moral problems, and cause or encounter the same difficulties in life. (Quoted in Carroll, *George Eliot: The Critical Heritage*, p. 209)

16. Bonaparte, *The Triptych and the Cross*, p. 127.

17. *Ibid.*, p. 238.

18. Even as he boldly announces that he has 'locked all sadness away' (194) in a new-made 'tomb of joy' (191), the disturbing ambiguity of that designation betrays the impossibility of such control. Romola, too, senses the vulnerability of such arbitrary repression, when she insists that the buried sadness 'is still there – it is only hidden away' (194). And in keeping with these darker suggestions, the scene of ceremoniously locking away Romola's sadness is grimly echoed within two years of her marriage when Tito feels compelled to assert his 'masculine predominance' by locking Romola into the library and, once more, ostentatiously depositing the key in his pouch. Now, however, there is neither hope nor

ambiguity: 'He had locked-in his wife's anger and scorn, but he had been obliged to lock himself in with it' (273).

19. Levine, '*Romola* as Fable', p. 86.

CHAPTER 8: *FELIX HOLT*

1. George Eliot, *The Journals of George Eliot*, ed. Margaret Harris and Judith Johnston (Cambridge: Cambridge University Press, 1998), p. 122.

2. *Ibid.*, p. 123.

3. Peter Coveney, Introduction to *Felix Holt* (Harmondsworth: Penguin, 1972), p. 8.

4. Subsequently, of course, John Blackwood prevailed upon Eliot to elaborate on her particular brand of 'radicalism'. After the passage of the second Reform Bill in 1867, he wrote asking, 'Do you never think of writing any miscellaneous papers for the Magazine? It strikes me that you could do a first rate address to the Working Men on their new responsibilities. It might be signed Felix Holt' (IV, 395). The resulting 'Address to Working Men, by Felix Holt' was published in *Blackwood's Magazine* in January, 1868.

5. Coveney, 'Introduction', p. 64.

6. See, for example, Linda Bamber, 'Self-Defeating Politics in George Eliot's *Felix Holt*', *Victorian Studies*, 18 (1975), 419–35; David Carroll, '*Felix Holt*: Society as Protagonist', *Nineteenth-Century Fiction*, 17 (1962), 237–52; Coveney, 'Introduction'; Arnold Kettle, 'Felix Holt the Radical', in *Critical Essays on George Eliot*, ed. Barbara Hardy (London: Routledge & Kegan Paul, 1970); W. F. T. Myers, 'George Eliot: Politics and Personality', in *Literature and Politics in the Nineteenth Century*, ed. John Lucas (London: Methuen, 1971).

7. Coveney, 'Introduction', p. 63.

8. For an excellent discussion of this aspect of the novel, see Bamber, 'Self-Defeating Politics in George Eliot's *Felix Holt*'.

9. In the light of this political vacancy in the novel, it seems emblematic that the fullest exposition of Felix's position takes place outside the novel in the form of an addendum provided by the subsequent publication of the 'Address to Working Men, By Felix Holt' in *Blackwood's Magazine*.

10. Coveney, 'Introduction', p. 15.

11. For an extended exploration of the growth of knowledge and communications in England, see Alexander Welsh, *George Eliot and Blackmail* (Cambridge, MA: Harvard University Press, 1985).

12. Coveney, 'Introduction', p. 15.

13. For a discussion of this feature of women's literature, see Sandra Gilbert and Susan Gubar, *The Madwoman in the Attic: The Woman Writer and the Nineteenth-Century Literary Imagination* (New Haven, CT: Yale University Press, 1979).

CHAPTER 9: *MIDDLEMARCH*

1. John Cross, *George Eliot's Life as Related in Her Letters and Journals* (Leipzig: Tauchnitz, 1885), vol. III, p. 42.

2. *Ibid.*, p. 43.

3. Richard Holt Hutton, 'George Eliot as Author', *Essays on Some of the Modern Guides of English Thought in Matters of Faith* (London: George Smith, 1887), p. 238. Eliot's publisher, John Blackwood, was similarly unenthusiastic about her poetry, his cautious and diplomatic response betraying a concern about the ponderousness of her verse:

> I have had a copy of the proofs lying in my dressing room and have been reading and rereading the Poems at night. They are very beautiful. There is a solemn cadence and power, almost a warning voice about them all, which becomes very impressive when thought over. You must have been thinking if not writing Poetry all your life, and if you have any lighter pieces written before the sense of what a great author should do for mankind came so strongly upon you, I should like much to look at them.   (VI, 37)

4. After the shift away from 'the faithful representation of commonplace things' (*AB*, 178) in her poetry, *Middlemarch* marked a return to Eliot's original purpose with a design 'to show the gradual action of ordinary causes rather than exceptional' (V, 168). In the Prelude to the novel, Eliot specifically forsakes the realm of the 'epic life' and 'national idea' (3) in order to take up once more the common life of those who are 'foundress[es] of nothing' (4), for whom 'far-resonant action' (3) is an impossibility, and whose tragedy is no grander than that which arises from the discrepancy between lofty ideals and 'meanness of opportunity' (3).

5. Virginia Woolf, 'George Eliot', *Collected Essays* (London: Hogarth Press, 1968), vol. 1, p. 201.

6. Raymond Williams, *The English Novel from Dickens to Lawrence* (St Albans: Paladin, 1974), p. 11.

7. Quoted in Gillian Beer, *Darwin's Plots: Evolutionary Narrative in Darwin, George Eliot and Nineteenth-Century Fiction* (Cambridge: Cambridge University Press, 2000), p. 156.

8. Elizabeth Ermarth, *Realism and Consensus in the English Novel* (Princeton: Princeton University Press, 1983), p. 242.

9. Penny Boumelha, 'George Eliot and the End of Realism', in *Women Reading Women's Writing*, ed. Sue Roe (Brighton: Harvester, 1987), p. 22.

10. Ermarth, *Realism and Consensus in the English Novel*, p. 242.

11. Peter Garrett, for example, contends that *Middlemarch* is ' "about" interpretation' (*The Victorian Multiplot Novel: Studies in Dialogical Form* (New Haven, CT: Yale University Press, 1980), p. 151); David Carroll argues that 'the problem of interpretation' is fundamental to Eliot's concerns in the novel (*George Eliot and the Conflict of Interpretations: A Reading of the Novels* (Cambridge: Cambridge University Press, 1992), p. 3); and Felicia Bonaparte regards the question of interpretation 'as crucial to everything in the novel' (Introduction, *M*, p. xxii).

12. Captain Wybrow, Arthur Donnithorne, Stephen Guest and Henleigh Grandcourt all provide more immediately recognisable versions of the type in Eliot's fiction.

13. A notable exception to the arguments for the novel's sense of connectedness is provided by J. Hillis Miller, 'Optic and Semiotic in *Middlemarch*', in *The Worlds of Victorian Fiction*, ed. J. H. Buckley (Cambridge, MA: Harvard University Press, 1975), pp. 125–45.

14. Quoted in Alice Kaminsky, *George Henry Lewes as Literary Critic* (New York: Syracuse University Press, 1968), p. 18.

15. Eliot reaffirms this conviction that the achievement of this detached perspective, or 'alteration in my point of view', is the only protection against the 'slavish subjection' and 'stupidity' of egoism in the first chapter, 'Looking Inward', of *The Impressions of Theophrastus Such*:

> The standing-ground worth striving after seemed to be some Delectable Mountain, whence I could see things in proportions as little as possible determined by that self-partiality which certainly plays a necessary part in our bodily sustenance, but has a starving effect on the mind ... Examining the world in order to find consolation is very much like looking carefully over the pages of a great book in order to find our own name, if not in the text, at least in a laudatory note: whether we find what we want or not, our preoccupation has hindered us from a true knowledge of the contents. But an attention fixed on the main theme or various matter of the book would deliver us from that slavish subjection to our own self-importance. And I had the mighty volume of the world before me. Nay, I had the struggling action of a myriad lives around me, each single life as dear to itself as mine to me. Was there no escape here from the stupidity of a murmuring self-occupation. (*The Impressions of Theophrastus Such* (1879; rpt. London: Dent, 1995), p. 9)

CHAPTER 10: *DANIEL DERONDA*

1. Explanatory Notes, *M*, 849.

2. George Eliot, *The Journals of George Eliot*, ed. Margaret Harris and Judith Johnston (Cambridge: Cambridge University Press, 1998), p. 145.

3. *Ibid.*, p. 146.

4. The irony, of course, is that in recent studies Eliot has been criticised for the residual racism of her portrayal of the Jews. The depiction of the Cohen family, for example, recurs to the conventional anti-Semitic stereotype of the greedy, cunning Jew. Even the infant Jacob Cohen drives a hard bargain like an 'aged commercial soul' (329) and his father, Ezra, is 'the most unpoetic Jew' who shows 'no shadow of a Suffering Race distinguish[ing] his vulgarity of soul from that of a prosperous pink-and-white huckster of the purest English lineage' (331). As Susan Meyer points out, the novel 'by no means idealises Jews. Instead, what it idealises is the "refined Jew" ' (*Imperialism at Home: Race and Victorian Women's Fiction* (Ithaca, NY: Cornell University Press, 1996), p. 181). Meyer also argues that the novel's proto-Zionism should not be read simply as the expression of unqualified sympathy with the Jews. She maintains that it was English Gentiles in this period, and not Jews, who were fascinated with the idea of the Jewish return, and that their enthusiasm for the concept was born of a desire to further British imperialist self-interest in the Levant and to remedy the 'problem' of significant Jewish migration to England. While Eliot could not be accused of the first motive, given her anti-imperialist sentiments, she was, despite her sympathy, at least prepared to appeal to the logic of the second motive in Theophrastus Such's discussion of a Jewish homeland in 'The Modern Hep! Hep! Hep!':

> They are among us everywhere: it is useless to say we are not fond of them. Perhaps we are not fond of proletaries and their tendency to form Unions, but the world is not therefore to be rid of them. If we wish to free ourselves from the inconveniences that we have to complain of, whether in proletaries or in Jews, our best course is to encourage all means of improving these neighbours who elbow us in a thickening crowd, and of sending their incommodious energies into beneficent channels. (*The Impressions of Theophrastus Such*, (1879; rpt. London: Dent, 1995) p. 153)

For a further discussion of the novel's residual racism, see also Katherine Bailey Lineham, 'Mixed Politics: the Critique of Imperialism in *Daniel Deronda*', *Texas Studies in Literature and Language*, 34 (1992), 323–46.

5. F. R. Leavis, *The Great Tradition: George Eliot, Henry James and Joseph Conrad* (London: George Stewart, 1948), p. 113.

6. See, for example, Lineham, 'Mixed Politics' and Meyer, *Imperialism at Home*; Edward Said, 'Zionism from the Standpoint of its Victims', *Social Text*, 1 (1979), 7–58.

7. Cynthia Chase, 'The Decomposition of the Elephants: Double-Reading *Daniel Deronda*', *MLA*, 93 (1978), 215–27.

8. Rosemary Ashton, *George Eliot: A Life* (London: Hamish Hamilton, 1996), p. 350.

9. Sally Shuttleworth, 'The Language of Science and Psychology in George Eliot's *Daniel Deronda*', in *Victorian Science and Victorian Values: Literary Perspectives,* ed. James Paradis and Thomas Postlewait (New Jersey: Rutgers University Press, 1985), p. 272.

10. *Ibid.*, p. 273.

11. Catherine Belsey, 'Re-reading the Great Tradition', in *Re-Reading English*, ed. Peter Widdowson (London: Methuen, 1982), pp. 131 and 130.

12. A similar deflection occurs when Amy Meyrick, 'the practical reformer', challenges Mirah on the sexist ritual of the synagogue. The initial, relevant, and notionally feminist inquiry, '*does* it seem quite right to you that the women should sit behind rails in a gallery apart?', is not addressed. Instead, it is sidestepped through an emphasis on Mirah's naïveté and goodness, then diverted and trivialised into an issue of curiosity and good manners:

> 'Yes, I never thought of anything else,' said Mirah, with mild surprise.
> 'And you like better to see the men with their hats on?' said Mab, cautiously proposing the smallest item of difference.
> 'Oh yes. I like what I have always seen there, because it brings back to me the same feelings – the feelings I would not part with for anything else in the world.'
> After this, any criticism, whether of doctrine or practice, would have seemed to these generous little people an inhospitable cruelty.

(305)

CHAPTER 11: CONCLUSION

1. Leslie Stephen, in *A Century of George Eliot Criticism*, ed. Gordon Haight (Boston, MA: Houghton Mifflin, 1965), p. 136.

2. *Ibid.*, p. 136.

3. Anthony Trollope, in *A Century of George Eliot Criticism*, p. 150.

4. Henry James, in *ibid.*, pp. 46, 87 and 81.

5. The view of Eliot as unduly earnest was not helped by the appearance in 1885 of John Cross's biography of Eliot, which sanitised and sanctified his wife of seven months, and was described by Gladstone as 'not a Life at all. It is a Reticence in 3 volumes' (quoted in Gordon Haight, Preface to *The George Eliot Letters*, I, p. xiv).

6. George Saintsbury, in *A Century of George Eliot Criticism*, p. 166.

7. *Ibid.*

8. *Ibid.*, p. 168.

9. Lord David Cecil, in *A Century of George Eliot Criticisim*, pp. 205, 209, 210.

10. Virginia Woolf, 'George Eliot', repr. in *Collected Essays*, vol. I, ed. Leonard Woolf (London: Hogarth Press, 1968), p. 196.

11. *Ibid.*, p. 197.

12. *Ibid.*, p. 201.

13. F. R. Leavis, *The Great Tradition: George Eliot, Henry James and Joseph Conrad* (London: George Stewart, 1948) p. 30.

14. Joan Bennett, *George Eliot: Her Mind and Her Art* (Cambridge: Cambridge University Press, 1948), p. 12.

15. See, for example, Basil Willey, *Nineteenth-Century Studies* (London: Chatto and Windus, 1949); George Levine, 'Determinism and Responsibility in the Works of George Eliot', *PMLA*, 77 (1962), 268–79: U. C. Knoepflmacher, *Religious Humanism and the Victorian Novel: George Eliot, Walter Pater, and Samuel Butler* (Princeton: Princeton University Press, 1965).

16. See, for example, Stephen Heath, *The Nouveau Roman: A Study in the Practice of Writing* (London: Elek, 1972) and Colin MacCabe, *James Joyce and the Revolution of the Word* (Basingstoke: Macmillan – now Palgrave, 1978).

17. See Carol Christ, 'Aggression and Providential Death in George Eliot's Fiction', *Novel*, 9 (1976), 130–40, and Leo Bersani, *A Future for Asyntax: Character and Desire in Literature* (London: Marion Boyars, 1978).

18. Bersani, *A Future for Asyntax*, p. 55.

19. *Ibid.*, p. 63.

20. See Terry Eagleton, *Criticism and Ideology* (London: Verso, 1978).

21. David Lodge, '*Middlemarch* and the Idea of the Classic Realist Text', in *The Nineteenth-Century Novel: Critical Essays and Documents*, ed. Arnold Kettle (London: Heinemann, 1981), pp. 218–38.

22. Penny Boumelha, 'George Eliot and the End of Realism', in *Women Reading Women's Writing*, ed. Sue Roe (Brighton: Harvester, 1987), p. 20.

23. George Levine, 'George Eliot's Hypothesis of Reality', *Nineteenth-Century Fiction*, 35 (1980), 6.

24. Felicia Bonaparte, *Will and Destiny: Morality and Tragedy in George Eliot's Novels* (New York: New York University Press, 1975), p. 11.

25. Levine, 'George Eliot's Hypothesis of Reality', p. 5.

26. K. M. Newton, Introduction, *George Eliot (Longman Critical Readers)* (London: Longman, 1991), p. 16.

27. See J. Hillis Miller, *The Ethics of Reading* (New York: Columbia University Press, 1987); 'Narrative and History', *English Literary History*, 41 (1974), 455–73; 'Optic and Semiotic in *Middlemarch*' in *The Worlds of Victorian Fiction*, ed. J. H. Buckley (Cambridge, MA: Harvard University Press, 1975), pp. 125–45; Cynthia Chase, 'The Decomposition of Elephants: Double-Reading *Daniel Deronda*', *MLA*, 93 (1978), 215–27; Levine, 'George Eliot's Hypothesis of Reality', p. 5.

28. Deirdre David, *Intellectual Women and Victorian Patriarchy: Harriet Martineau, Elizabeth Barrett Browning, George Eliot* (Basingstoke: Macmillan – now Palgrave, 1987), p. 229.

29. Elaine Showalter, 'The Greening of Sister George', *Nineteenth-Century Fiction*, 35 (1980), 292–311.

30. Zelda Austen, 'Why Feminist Critics are Angry with George Eliot', *College English*, 37 (1976), 549–61.

31. See, for example, Françoise Basch, *Relative Creatures: Victorian Women in Society and the Novel, 1837–67*, trans. Anthony Rudolf (New York: Schocken Books, 1974); Patricia Beer, *'Reader I Married Him': A Study of the Women Characters of Jane Austen, Charlotte Brontë, Elizabeth Gaskell and George Eliot* (Basingstoke: Macmillan – now Palgrave, 1974); Jenni Calder, *Women and Marriage in Victorian Fiction* (London: Thames and Hudson, 1976); Elaine Showalter, *A Literature of Their Own: British Women Novelists from Brontë to Lessing* (Princeton: Princeton University Press, 1977).

32. Boumelha, 'George Eliot and the End of Realism', p. 25.

33. Gillian Beer, *George Eliot*, (Brighton: Harvester, 1986) p. 180.

34. See, for example, Mary Jacobus, 'The Question of Language: Men of Maxims and *The Mill on the Floss*', *Critical Inquiry*, 8 (1981), 207–22; Catherine Belsey, 'Re-Reading the Great Tradition' in *Re-Reading English*, ed. Peter Widdowson (London: Methnen, 1982); Margaret Homans, *Bearing the Word: Language and Female Experience in*

Nineteenth-Century Women's Writing (Chicago: University of Chicago, 1986).

35. See, for example, Gillian Beer, *Darwin's Plots: Evolutionary Narrative in Darwin, George Eliot and Nineteenth-Century Fiction* (Cambridge: Cambridge University Press, 2000); Susan Graver, *George Eliot and Community: A Study in Social Theory and Fictional Form* (Berkeley: University of California Press, 1984); Sally Shuttleworth, *George Eliot and Nineteenth-Century Science* (Cambridge: Cambridge University Press, 1984); Nancy L. Paxton, *George Eliot and Herbert Spencer: Feminism, Evolutionism and the Reconstruction of Gender* (Princeton: Princeton University Press, 1991).

Index

LIBRARY, UNIVERSITY OF CHESTER